SERIOUS FRAUD OFFICE

SERIOUS FRAUD OFFICE

Brian Widlake

LITTLE, BROWN AND COMPANY

A *Little, Brown* Book

First published in Great Britain in 1995
by Little, Brown and Company

Copyright © 1995 by Brian Widlake

The moral right of the author has been asserted.

A CIP catalogue record for this book
is available from the British Library.

ISBN 0 316 91139 9

Typeset by Hewer Text Composition Services, Edinburgh
Printed and bound in Great Britain by Clays Ltd, St Ives plc

Little, Brown and Company (UK)
Brettenham House
Lancaster Place
London WC2E 7EN

CONTENTS

ACKNOWLEDGEMENTS

I have interviewed a good many people for this book: police-men, senior counsel, MPs, the Director of Public Prosecutions, Mrs Barbara Mills, and the Director of the Serious Fraud Office, George Staple. I have also talked to those who have found themselves on the wrong end of the law or too close to it for comfort. They have all been most helpful. My thanks, too, to Lord Roskill, who was also generous with his time and his valuable opinions.

For my chapter on Barlow Clowes, I drew liberally on Lawrence Lever's *The Barlow Clowes Affair*, quite the best account of a classic scam which showed that civil servants have little place in the management of financial regulation; a fact, I regret to say, which has been all too prevalent in the direction of the Serious Fraud Office.

INTRODUCTION

Fraud is the least satisfactory of crimes; it does not respond to categorisation. Unlike rape, arson or murder it cannot be put into a convenient pigeonhole. It comes in too many shapes and sizes. It includes theft, market manipulation, insider dealing, cheque and mortgage fraud, long firm fraud, advance fee fraud, misrepresentation, obtaining property by deception, conspiracy to defraud and a host of other scams which sections of the white collar community (loosely, the middle classes) have seen fit to inflict on their fellow men. The best known fraud in this country was the South Sea Bubble of 1720, a piece of market manipulation which was enormous, extraordinarily bold and which dragged down some of the richest people in Britain. Intelligent, educated men can rarely resist a well-presented, rational scheme for personal enrichment, nor are they ever likely to.

Yet the largest fraud ever perpetrated occurred within the last five years when BCCI, the Bank of Credit and Commerce International, collapsed owing something like $10 billion. It was a worldwide fraud and most of its perpetrators have fled to Pakistan. This, though, was a fraud that did not depend on other people's greed for its success. BCCI was a bank; banks are to be trusted, therefore it is safe to put your money with a bank. Thousands of perfectly innocent Asian businessmen, in this country and elsewhere, simply had their bank deposits removed by unscrupulous operators. It was the size of the fraud that was breathtaking and it was only possible because BCCI was a properly constituted bank. Translated into Western European terms, it was the equivalent of the directors of Barclays Bank running off with their customers' money. But nobody can say that BCCI's depositors were greedy; they simply used a banking service which was run by crooks whose avarice set new standards of magnitude.

Most fraudsters, though, are not unlike the architects of BCCI; they just work within parameters which are much less ambitious. The solicitor who steals his clients' deposits, or the broker who uses his clients' money as his own, or the insurance salesman who sells policies with no intention of passing the money to the life companies − they are all fraudsters. The difference is that they don't work on the same awesome scale as the men from BCCI.

The best way to think of fraud is that it is stealing. And theft, even when it is quite small, can cause untold misery and hardship to those who lose their money. The high street insurance broker who promotes a bogus scheme which entices people to part with their hard-earned savings can cause, in his own small way, just as much unhappiness and depression as Asian businessmen went through when they lost their money with BCCI. Fraud does not have to be huge to take its psychological toll.

As it is technically and legally defined, fraud does not have to be theft. It is subject to numerous variations of type, style and technique. In some cases of market manipulation in the City, for example, it was legitimately argued that there were no victims. The offences were technical, yet they still broke the law. Cases like these haven't helped the prosecutors, but they have been of enormous benefit to defendants. Juries and judges alike have had to struggle with their complexity. The result is that some cases have taken years to conclude, often unsuccessfully, and have consumed millions of pounds of taxpayers' money.

It is an immense business. At the end of 1992, the Serious Fraud Office estimated that the total value of the fifty-seven frauds it was investigating at that time amounted to £6,252 million. That takes no account of the nine hundred cases which were being investigated by the Fraud Squad over the same period. And there is evidence to show that fraud is growing in size and complexity every year. It is not a crime that can be shrugged aside. Investors and savers have lost billions. No one thought when they joined Robert Maxwell's pension schemes that they would probably lose most of their money through an alleged fraud. *Caveat emptor* has a particularly hollow ring when many fraudsters are fully paid-up members of regulated financial institutions. Investors have a right to feel they are being protected when they see initials showing that the people they are dealing with are self-regulatory organizations, headed by the Securities and Investments Board. But these regulatory bodies referred forty-nine cases for criminal investigation in the year ended March 1993 – an increase of 50 per cent over the previous year. That takes no account of member firms who were found to be in default or were disciplined in some other way over the same period.

It is not a sunlit scene and it has not been for many years now. The government appointed the Roskill Committee to look into the problem in 1983. One of its recommendations was for a new, unified organisation which was to be responsible for all the functions of detection, investigation and prosecution of serious fraud. The result was the Serious Fraud Office, set up by the Criminal Justice Act of 1987. But detection was dropped from its remit.

This was just as well. Since the SFO opened for business in April 1988, it has had its hands full. It has committed some dreadful howlers. It has lost some very important, headline cases. It has been accused of gross impropriety. One of its accountants went to prison. It has let Asil Nadir slip through its fingers. It has played practical jokes in court. It has suggested that a judge could be party to a conspiracy to pervert the course of justice. It has indirectly caused the resignation of a Tory minister. One of its directors has been accused of being a gunslinger, figuratively of course, while another has been named in a civil action involving a £50 million will. It has managed all that in just six years. People who supported it are now against it. And the police, an important part of the SFO, have become increasingly disenchanted with the way it works.

As this book goes to press, two matters have arisen which are likely to affect the way the authorities view the prosecution of serious fraud in this country.

The Brent Walker case, in which George Walker was cleared

of orchestrating a £19m fraud at his company, may well see the end of the SFO in its present, specialised form. The case took three years to bring to court, lasted four and a half months and probably cost the taxpayer £40 million. The man the SFO were determined to get was finally acquitted by a jury which spent seven days of deliberation before finding in Walker's favour. Instead, the people on Elm Street had to be content with the conviction of Brent Walker's former finance director, Wilfred Aquilina, who was found guilty by a 10–1 majority on one charge of false accounting involving £2.5 million. But he was cleared of four other charges involving £9.5 million and conspiracy to falsify accounts. The SFO's pickings at the end of the day were pathetically thin and a waste of precious and expensive resources. It was far from being the first of the SFO's headline failures in dealing with major fraud.

Well before that case was concluded at the end of October 1994, an inquiry had been set up by the Attorney General, Sir Nicholas Lyell, to see how the new, high-profile SFO was tackling its remit and whether it needed to be restructured. That inquiry was expected to report at the end of 1994, but there can be little doubt that the SFO has not come up to the mark and that there is a need for radical change.

The outlook for the SFO in 1995 looks even bleaker than its colourful, embarrassing past. The Guinness case – the most high-profile and 'political' of its prosecutions – returned to haunt Elm House when the Home Secretary, Michael Howard, referred the cases of four defendants to the Court of Appeal. (Three of the defendants – Ernest Saunders, Gerald Ronson and Tony Parnes – had been sent to prison, and Sir Jack Lyons stripped of his knighthood.) The argument is that the SFO failed to disclose the findings of a City tribunal which found no fault with the share-dealing techniques used. It is alleged that Mrs Barbara Mills, now Director of Public Prosecutions, was one of the SFO's prosecution team who decided to withhold the evidence. If the Appeal Court finds against the SFO, the damages for the defendants will inevitably run into millions of pounds.

This book is about the Serious Fraud Office. It is also about fraud, a growing cancer in society.

1

EARLY BIRDS

There has never been much to say for the month of March in Britain. It is the end of winter, but falls short of spring – a grey, intermediate month of overcast skies, wind and squalls of cutting rain.

The village of Frittenden in Kent was no different from the rest of the country on 10 March 1988. It is a pretty, well-heeled, sprawling village with more than its fair share of fine old houses, beamed and well gardened, outwardly contented and secure against recession. The kind of place it would take an economic earthquake to shake to its roots.

At seven o'clock that morning the 3rd Baron Spens was up and about, getting ready for the day. It was a perfectly normal morning in a sprawling, fourteenth-century manor house, comfortable but not grand, and home to one of Spens's great hobbies, stamp collecting. Within months, his treasured collection was to be sold along with the rest of Spens's assets. The instruments of that downfall weren't far to seek.

Sitting in Spens's circular drive were two unmarked police cars, four policemen and two dogs. Spens had never at any time been noted for violence, but clearly they were not taking any chances. They knocked on the door, and announced that the Baron was under arrest. Spens's wife, Barbara, asked them in for tea and coffee while Spens got ready.

He asked them why they hadn't arrested him in London and they replied: 'We always do things this way. Anyway, there's a lot of money involved and these are very serious charges.' Spens recalls, 'They were really quite sweet.'

Spens at that time cut a pretty substantial figure in the City. He was not only physically well-padded, but he gave a passable imitation of Toad in Kenneth Grahame's immortal book. He beamed amiably from the social pages and generally sported a very large cigar. The word the journalists used was flamboyant. He had been managing director of Henry Ansbacher, a second-tier merchant bank, and had earlier been a director of Morgan Grenfell. He was forty-six and had been doing well until the Guinness scandal blew up in his face.

Spens was taken first to his private office in London where he handed over a number of personal documents, including bank statements and diaries. There were more police already waiting for him there. He was then driven to Holborn police station, where the press had turned out in force to record his arrival. By this time Spens's solicitor, Andrew Moore, had arrived and there was a brief interview with a detective sergeant which proved abortive because Spens refused to answer questions. After that Spens made the acquaintance of Detective Superintendent Richard Botright, who was a member of the Serious Fraud Office's Guinness team, and who became a part of all the Guinness suspects' lives.

'Botright came in looking very serious,' Spens says. 'The custody officer asked me to empty my pockets, took a note of their contents, and Botright allowed me to keep my cigars. When I went to pick up my lighter, he told me I couldn't have it so I asked him how I was to light them. He said, "That's your problem, son." It was like a little light bullying at public school.'

Spens was then shown to a cell. He remembers it being a 'ladies' cell, about ten by ten, with blood on the ceiling'. He was left there to cool his heels for three hours, on the grounds, Botright said, that the police wanted to look through Spens's address book. On the same day, Spens was charged with theft, conspiracy to defraud and market manipulation. Botright then offered Spens and Moore a covered van in which to leave the building. Spens refused, saying that as he was innocent there was no reason to be furtive. As the two men left, there were cameras and reporters everywhere.

Spens had been released into the custody of his solicitor and the two men stayed at the Berkeley Hotel in Knightsbridge, each in his own suite with an interconnecting door. The following day, at Bow Street magistrates' court, bail for Spens was set at £500,000 and there was no trouble in finding two people to stand surety for him.

Three days later, on 13 March, the *News of the World* printed a piece about Spens having an illegitimate baby by his secretary. When he asked the reporter who his contact for the story had been, the reporter said he couldn't remember.

Spens was now firmly established not merely as an important player in the Guinness scandal but as a man whose private life was reprehensible. He fitted the image of the wicked, autocratic banker perfectly. The media had not only been on the spot when Spens had been charged, but the story had come at a convenient time for shaping public opinion. Spens could have been forgiven for thinking the whole business looked like a calculated smear.

Andrew Kent is a stocky, powerfully-built Australian in his late forties who has an attractive English wife. At some point in his life the equivalent of a heavy truck must have run over his face but he is a man who has been used to taking a few knocks.

One of these occurred on 26 November 1990, when police knocked on his door in Chelsea Square before breakfast and presented him with a search warrant.

'The warrant was faulty,' Kent recalls, 'but I let them in anyway. They said they would get a proper warrant but they never did. They took everything they thought was relevant to my business and I've never had any of it back. That was three years ago.'

At the same time that Kent's house was being ransacked by the police, his partner's house was visited by four members of the SFO. Paddy Mahon, though, was in Geneva.

The SFO's main team was led by Chief Inspector Graham Watson and one of the SFO's lawyers, Helen Garlick, and it had come to inspect the files of the brokers T.C. Coombs in Bonhill Street in the City.

After those raids, Kent and Paddy Mahon found themselves

on an SFO treadmill which continued for three years. On 1 February 1991, Kent was arrested. When he was acquitted after a seven-week trial on 28 August 1993, he had lost his business and his capital and had only his house left. Fortunately Kent is extremely resilient and tough and when the chips are down can still retain his sense of humour. He needed to. Kent believed he was the victim of a City frame-up inspired by jealousy, old rivalries and the bitterness that some people feel towards others who make a lot of money.

Acquitting the Australian, the judge said: 'So much of the real nitty-gritty of what was going on only came out from the witness-box as a result of cross-examination of those witnesses.' Had the SFO known then what they know now, he said, 'it may well be they would not have launched this prosecution in the first place.'

Nazmu Virani is an entrepreneur held in considerable esteem by the Asian community in Britain. His is, or was, the kind of success story which lends lustre to the history of Asian business in a country which is always uncomfortable about success, regardless of colour.

He was a Ugandan Asian who suffered, like so many others, from the tyranny of Idi Amin who believed that Uganda was for the Ugandans, not realising that by expelling the Asian business community he was destroying the lifeblood of his economy. Virani was thrown out in 1972 and came to Britain, where over twenty years he built up a business in property and leisure through his family interests and a company called Control Securities – a 'shell' which he turned into a big and profitable enterprise quoted on the Stock Exchange.

He was a rich man, perhaps worth £60 million, when he woke up at 6.00 am on 17 October 1991 at his large Putney house to find the police at his front door accompanied, as Virani put it, 'by the world's press'. Simultaneously, the SFO raided the homes of Virani's two brothers and also searched the offices of Control Securities. In all the raids the police took away the mandatory loads of documents. Within an hour the shares of Control had been suspended on the Stock Exchange.

There was no secrecy attached to any of these events. The press had been present when the police called on Virani, and at the houses of his two brothers. There was no doubt that the media had been alerted. This was not surprising. One press release had been sent out by the SFO, saying that the office is 'carrying out searches'. Another, issued later, referred to these events in the past tense. It was a silly administrative blunder which didn't fool anyone. The intention all along had been to alert the press. It was no surprise, then, that the shares were suspended as soon as they were.

On 21 June 1992, officers of the City of London Fraud Squad were told to report for work at 5.30 the following morning. Like most people who took an interest in fraud, they knew who they were going to be visiting. After Robert Maxwell's death, and the hundreds of millions of pounds the flamboyant entrepreneur had stolen during his lifetime, it had to be only a matter of months before the SFO focused on others for investigation.

Pandora, Kevin Maxwell's wife, heard a racket outside their front door in Chelsea at 6.30 am. She raised the window and told the people outside to 'piss off, otherwise I'm going to call the police'. Detective Inspector Dick George replied that he *was* the police, and he could have added that he had a large press contingent with him as well.

Elsewhere in London Kevin's brother, Ian, was going through the same experience. So, too, was the American Larry Trachtenburg, a director of Bishopsgate Investment Management which handled all the pension fund assets allegedly stolen by Robert Maxwell.

All three men were arrested, documents were removed from their houses and by mid-morning they had been charged at Snow Hill police station in the City; they appeared in court at lunchtime.

Kevin Maxwell looked gaunt and hollow-cheeked. He had every reason to be: he was facing two charges of conspiracy to defraud and six of theft. His brother Ian had been charged with conspiracy, while Trachtenburg faced two charges of conspiracy and four of theft. At that time their fraud offences totalled £128 million. All but one of the offences were alleged to have taken place *after* Maxwell's death on 5 November 1991. Each of the charges carried a maximum of ten years' imprisonment.

Bail for Kevin was set at £500,000, and for Ian at £250,000. The case promised to be huge. The SFO had been probing five areas of the Maxwell affair: the assets which had been removed from the Maxwell pension funds; money missing from Mirror Group Newspapers; assets taken from Maxwell Communications Corporation; the support operation to prop up the shares of MCC and MGN; and a loan from Swiss Bank Corporation to enable Robert Maxwell to buy First Tokyo Index Trust. Kevin was accused of conspiracy to defraud Swiss Bank Corporation of £55.8 million.

The Maxwell brothers were obvious targets, but the whisper was that many others were going to be investigated by the people from Elm Street. The Maxwells were just the beginning.

The old days seemed to have gone forever for all those people investigated for fraud. Nothing was private any more. Arrests happened in the full glare of publicity. Companies were closed down. And the innocent, curiously, were to suffer almost as much as the guilty, as their reputations were broken publicly on the rack of investigation. A new spirit was abroad: keen, gung-ho, often reckless, indifferent when it frequently got things badly wrong, the Serious Fraud Office made people angry, resentful and often very frightened. The old Fraud Squad was a fading memory. The new people cared nothing for reputation or manners, sensitivities and families. There was very little, apparently, they would stop at to get their man.

2

EARLY DAYS

So far as the police were concerned, it was the Fraud Squad which marked their first official involvement in the investigation and prosecution of the crime. The squad was formed in 1946 but there is no meaningful documentation about the way it was then run or its staffing – in other words, its *modus operandi*. Records of cases exist, but there is nothing from those early days to suggest what the command structure was or how the squad went about its business. The police in those days weren't much concerned about staffing or their role in social and criminal terms. They saw their job as catching criminals and prosecuting them successfully.

There were no royal commissions or independent inquiries, such as Sheehy in 1993, reporting on pay and performance. There was little agonising in the media about corruption, perversion of the course of justice or negligence and incompetence. There were jokes, of course, which there aren't these days – unless they concern 'fitting up', corruption, brutality and racism. A policeman's life was remarkably and refreshingly simple. He filled out a report with a blunt pencil and the aid of his tongue and plenty of carbon paper. TV's PC Dixon, with his blue lamp and 'Good evening, all,' wasn't that far from the truth. The life of the local police station reflected the criminality of a village. The heavy stuff was left to the Murder Squad, the Flying Squad and the Vice Squad: in other words, the CID. In hierarchical terms, these boys ruled the roost. The police were then lucky enough not to be overwhelmed by bureaucracy. Everything was filled out in quintuplicate in the old Fraud Squad and that was the end of the matter.

These days, information technology and its attendant computers and word processing have enabled mountains of paper to be produced and circulated. Between the wars, not only was there no technology, there were very few police officers who dealt with fraud – three in the City of London and six in the Metropolitan Police. They worked directly under someone in the office of the Director of Public Prosecutions, but the 'system' was not a success. In fact anyone working on fraud then was hampered by a lack of legislation and almost total ignorance of what was happening in the market place.

In the twenty years up to the beginning of the Second World War, anyone could carry on the business of dealing in securities and they did so with abandon. Roughly five million pounds a year, or thirty million over the whole period (£846 million at today's prices), was lost to the bucket shops whose operators tended to come from the United States or Canada. Luxurious offices and glossy prospectuses were generally enough to pull in the punters. When sufficient people had been conned, the share-pushers decamped with their money back to North America and hapless investors were left without any remedy.

Share-pushing, though, wasn't exclusively the prerogative of Americans. The best-known of our home-grown fraudsters was probably Horatio Bottomley, the journalist and financier, and probably the outstanding fraudster of this century, Robert Maxwell notwithstanding. Bottomley, who was born in 1860, lost both his parents when he was five and was put into an orphanage from which he ran away when he was fourteen. After a couple of years as an errand boy, he worked in a solicitor's office for five years and spent the next three as a shorthand writer in the supreme court of judicature; invaluable experience for someone who was to spend the rest of his life in and out of court on charges of fraud.

He started the first of his ventures when he was twenty-four – a small suburban weekly called the *Hackney Hansard*. The paper did well enough for him to found the Hansard Publishing Union five years later with capital of half a million pounds. Two years later, in 1891, the business went belly up and Bottomley was left bankrupt. He was charged with conspiracy to defraud and decided to defend himself, which he did with such brilliance that he was not only acquitted but Mr Justice Hawkins, who tried the case, urged Bottomley to study law. Bottomley, though, couldn't get admission to any inn of court and decided instead to make finance his career. He promoted a number of businesses with staggering speed, beginning with the Joint Stock Trust and Institute, followed by Associated Gold Mines of West Australia, Great Boulders Proprietary Gold Mines, West Australian Loan and Finance Corporation and Nil Desperandum Mines. None of them paid any dividends to speak of. In ten years Bottomley started fifty companies with capital totalling well over £20 million and spent much of that time in court. Between 1901–05, sixty-seven bankruptcy petitions and writs were filed against him. When he was thirty-seven the *Financial Times* bestowed a rare accolade on him when it published his photograph in its series 'Men of Millions'. At that time it was thought that Bottomley had probably made £8 million out of promoting companies.

But then success and money went to his head. He began to spend wildly. First there were horses (he won the Cesarewitch and the Stewards' Cup). He also squandered huge sums on theatrical and publishing adventures, a large house in Sussex, a luxurious flat in Pall Mall and a villa in France; added to which there was a great deal of entertaining and travelling, which his substantial income could barely keep up with.

Bottomley, though, was a man of many parts. He was an outstanding speaker and a brilliant journalist. At one time he could get £100 for an article (almost £5,000 a piece at today's prices) and could have earned a very large income from his speaking and writing alone. But Bottomley was made of much more entrepreneurial stuff than that. In 1898 he bought the *Sun* and in the same year founded the magazine *John Bull* with just under £100,000 (most of which was provided by someone else). He became Liberal MP for South Hackney in 1906 and a year later the shareholders of the Joint Stock Trust petitioned to have the business wound up. The liquidators spent eighteen months looking at the books but most of them were missing. In 1909 he was charged with fraud at the Guildhall but with his usual verbal dexterity talked his way out of it. It was a tribute to his speaking skills that he invariably drew large crowds when he spoke in court and leading counsel found him almost impossible to handle.

But Bottomley by now was beset by debt and most of his business ventures had failed. In 1911, when he was fifty-one, he petitioned for bankruptcy, disclosing debts of well over £9 million (1994 prices) and assets of £2 million. Prudently, he had put his country house and French villa in his wife's name, so they couldn't be touched, and three years later applied for the Chiltern Hundreds.

Anyone with less resilience would have called it a day. Not Bottomley. He advised his friends that he had put his 'sordid past' behind him. Nevertheless, he continued to make pots of money by organising sweepstakes and lotteries on sporting events. With the outbreak of war in 1914, his communication skills had a field day. He gave patriotic speeches at £50 (£2,000) a time all round the country and wrote articles for the *Sunday Pictorial*, all of which revived his national reputation. Bottomley was on his way back, his entrepreneurial fire rekindled. In 1915 he launched a series of new financial enterprises which the public backed to the tune of £36 million at today's values. He paid off his creditors, discharged his bankruptcy and won back his seat at South Hackney, standing as an independent, with a huge majority. The old magic, it seemed, never failed.

His last enterprise, however, did for him. It was ingenious, because it appealed to patriotic fervour. The scheme was a version of the government's victory bonds, which had been designed to raise money from the public to put the country back on its feet (in fact, they were the forerunner of today's premium bonds). The government, though, had designated the bonds in units of £5, which were too expensive for the average citizen. Bottomley was quick to spot the scheme's flaws. He formed a company which issued what he called 'unit premium bonds'. The idea was to make the victory bonds affordable. His units would be bought for £1 each and when a saver had accumulated five units Bottomley guaranteed to

buy a victory bond on the saver's behalf. It was an early form
of hire purchase. He also added an important attraction for
those whose only chance of becoming rich was to gamble.
The interest earned on the victory bonds (about 3 per cent)
would be pooled and then raffled. The lucky numbers would
get prizes. Queues of people, apparently, lined up outside his
office to buy Bottomley's bonds. He gave out some prizes,
but only a few. The rest of the money he pocketed. Every
fraudulent scheme needs a veneer of validity to pull in the
punters. Bottomley understood the psychology of the people
he dealt with. He knew they were greedy and naive. They were
easy money. He took them for the best part of £5 million.

For this fraud Bottomley was sentenced to seven years'
penal servitude in 1922. Five years later he was released
and in 1928 tried to rehabilitate himself by founding a new
magazine, *John Blunt*, but it failed. Five years later he died
in obscurity and poverty. He was seventy-three.

It has been said to the point of tedium that if fraudsters
put their considerable talents to earning money honestly,
there are no mountains they could not climb, no goals they
could not achieve. That is manifest nonsense. Bottomley, in
spite of his enormous gifts, was hopelessly flawed. Fraudsters
generally are. They cannot resist an easy buck, a fast deal, or
the self-delusion that goes with both. Many are no more than
common thieves. Robert Maxwell built an empire based on
greed – the greed of the people who worked for him. Later,
he added another compelling ingredient – fear; the fear of
greedy people employed by him who didn't want to lose
their jobs and all the perks that went with them. He could
manipulate and order around these people as he wanted.
They enabled him to steal on a grandiose scale. His gifts
as a conman lay in an unfaltering understanding of human
weakness. That was the one thing that he and Bottomley
shared. Had Bottomley ever managed to get a pension fund
or two under his control, though, one dreads to think what
heights he might have scaled.

Given the limitations of the law and policing in Bottomley's
day it is not surprising that he got away with so much for
so long. The law about false pretences, for example, did

not cover schemes which made promises about payment, profits or interest in the future and there were many promotions around which did exactly that. Police had to rely on Conspiracy to Defraud, a clumsy catch-all provision that lacked precision. Only in 1939 did the Prevention of Fraud (Investments) Act come into being which killed share-pushing overnight (not much happened during the war except the black market, where anything scarce became a source of enormous profit to intelligent and diligent opportunists).

In 1946 things changed, although it isn't clear why. Fraud was given a higher profile by the authorities. The Director of Public Prosecutions (DPP) chaired a committee consisting of the Solicitor to the Board of Trade (now the DTI), the Official Receiver in Bankruptcy and the commissioners of the two London police forces – the Metropolitan and the City police (the latter, apart from traffic control and some major terrorist acts in the last two years, have always been heavily involved with fraud because so much of it occurs on their 'patch').

By that time, there were six policemen in the City who dealt with fraud and about twenty in the Met – scarcely enough to deal with the petty fraud committed by the secretaries of sports clubs in the whole of the London area. The committee, however, managed to give the Fraud Squad (official title: The Metropolitan and City Police Company Fraud Department) a remit to investigate substantial fraud in companies, their shares and debentures, together with investments in those companies and any such allied matters; as well as what it called 'difficult cases of substantial fraud involving expert investigation of the accounts of any company or business'.

This was a huge remit for a squad of such slender resources, especially for men who had only the vaguest notion of what a balance sheet was, let alone a profit and loss account. Almost twenty years later, the Fraud Squad's terms of reference were widened to include expert investigation of cases of 'substantial fraud involving large sums of money committed by individuals or partners in any business'. Many City firms in those days – particularly stockbrokers and jobbers – were partnerships and not companies and some of the most common cases involved theft of clients' money, the use of client money to purchase shares for the benefit of a partner, and so on.

When James Crane (later commander of the Fraud Squad 1971–76, and after that Chief Inspector of Constabulary) joined the squad as a detective constable in 1949, police investigators used to work in pairs. 'A senior, more experienced man with a rookie, that was the system. And it never really changed, unless it was for a really big fraud when you might have as many as eight men working on a case with substantial input from outside – whether it was accountants, bankers or whatever.'

Sir James, now seventy three, a man of considerable charm and intelligence, stressed to me the importance of targeting a fraudster properly. 'You have to know who you're after and why. It's no good saying you *think* someone might be guilty. Your preliminary investigations should take you much further than that.

'I'm not much of a believer either in announcing to the world that you're undertaking a major investigation into a suspected case of fraud. If you're talking about a public company and you announce that you've raided it, then you could be in danger of causing a major collapse in its shares. That does no one any good, least of all the investors. You can achieve far more if you use discretion, talk to people in the City and get their co-operation. I think that's the advantage of the soft, quiet approach as against the highly publicised, macho affairs we see these days. You often achieve much more by quietly chatting to people.'

Crane led the Fraud Squad in the most highly publicised case of public corruption of the day – the Poulson scandal. But he remembers some of the smaller cases with ironic affection, particularly a man called Hymie, a stylish conman who had worked four or five countries, always using the same technique. Hymie, a Canadian, had operated very successfully in Canada, where he was wanted by the Royal Canadian Mounted Police. He had an unusual line of salesmanship.

Hymie would go along to a supplier and introduce himself as the chairman of a large retail store group in North

America, saying that he bought from suppliers from all over the world and, provided the products were what he was looking for, always purchased in very large volumes. This would, of course, whet the appetite of the supplier who would begin to fantasise about the size of potential orders. Hymie, however, was subtle. Once he had dangled the carrot, he would put it away, saying he would very much like to see the supplier's production processes. Quite often he would suggest improvements to both the products and the processes. Hymie didn't rush anything; he always took his time. Then he would take his victim as easily as a great white shark polishes off a victim. He would explain that it was a very expensive business, travelling the world seeing prospective suppliers. There were air fares, hotels, other travel, all the usual expenses. By that time the supplier was so desperate to have his custom that he would offer to pick up the bill for all expenses.

Hymie was making £100,000 a year in the early seventies working this scam – close on a million a year in today's terms. It was hard work, but evidently he enjoyed it. He went down for four years.

Crane's biggest case, though, was Poulson. It was to lead to the creation of a special squad within the Fraud Squad to deal with nothing but public corruption. The scandal was regarded with such seriousness by the Heath government that the Attorney General, Peter Rawlinson, asked to see Crane. Crane then had to make an oral presentation to Rawlinson, saying how far he had got in his investigations, the prospects for convictions and how long it would all take. At the end of Crane's presentation, Rawlinson told him he could have anything he wanted and appointed two counsel to conduct the crown's case, Sir John Cobb and Peter Taylor. Taylor was then a Queen's Counsel and went on to be Lord Chief Justice. 'By the time he'd finished his cross-examination of Poulson, the man was destroyed,' Crane says.

Poulson was jailed for seven years in 1974. From the time he had been first questioned by Crane's men, it had taken just nine months from investigation to conviction, which makes today's drawn-out fraud investigations and trials look absurdly laborious. Poulson had spent more than half a million pounds on suits, presents and holidays to win public contracts. William Pottinger, a civil servant who was also involved with Poulson's corrupt deals, went to prison for five years. Another public figure, T.Dan Smith, Newcastle's former Labour leader and the architect of the new Tyneside, was imprisoned too.

It was a painful affair for the Heath government. In 1973, Ted Heath had publicly criticised Tiny Rowland, of the public company Lonrho, as the 'unacceptable face of Capitalism', yet one of his own ministers – Reginald Maudling, the Home Secretary – had been obliged to resign from government because he was chairman of one of Poulson's companies. Maudling kept extraordinarily bad company when it came to money. He had also been involved with the Real Estate Fund of America as president, which he later described as a job which would give him a little pot of gold for his retirement. It never did. Jerry Hoffman, the Fund's founder, went to prison a year or so after Maudling's appointment.

It was certainly Crane's most important case at the Fraud Squad. He actually spent half his career in fraud, and showed that he was a policeman head and shoulders above many of his generation. Most of the values he instilled in the five years he was commander hold good today. He was succeeded by another Fraud Squad man, Tom Edwards, whose roots and heart – by his own admission – were with the Flying Squad. Edwards is a tough, ruddy-faced Welshman, stockily built, who used to sit up in bed at nights boning up on the rudiments of accounting so he could gain some understanding about the numbers which made fraud tick. A chat with Edwards, who has the physical presence of a Welsh international second row forward, could not have been unimpressive. I had the feeling, talking to him last year, that no one would have found an investigation led by him an agreeable experience. He has no-nonsense eyes and a firm manner. He spent seven years in the Fraud Squad and lives in retirement very close to Jim Crane in Wales.

I think, though, I would have preferred to face Edwards than Crane. Crane didn't get to be Chief Inspector of

Constabulary by mistake. That's a job which involves look-ing into the interstices of a force, assessing its leadership, management, effectiveness and cost controls. Crane is subtle, patient and never misses a point. A dangerous opponent, with an easy smile and impeccable manners.

When Crane went on to higher things in 1976 and Tom Edwards took over, things at Richbell Place in Holborn didn't really change at all. The Fraud Squad was still undermanned and badly resourced in terms of access to forensic accountants and other expertise it needed for complex cases. The Squad draws on a panel of accountants operating under the umbrella of the Institute of Chartered Accountants, and officers have to make a strong, convincing argument for their use. Requests for specialist help are controlled by budgets and necessity, not by hunches. The ultimate test is whether the specialists will produce worthwhile evidence in court.

When the Serious Fraud Office came into being in April 1988, every fraud squad in the country, however big or small, became part of what is now known as the Fraud Investigation Group (FIG) working under the Crown Prosecution Service which is run by the DPP. The Fraud Squad (the City and Met) still retains its rather superior identity to fraud groups in the rest of the country because of the large caseload of fraud London generates. In terms of fraud in general in Britain, by far the bulk of it is handled by the Fraud Squad, the West Yorkshire Fraud Squad, Strathclyde and the West Midlands. Large conurbations, of course, produce much more fraud. By contrast, the Sussex Fraud Squad comprises two men, and Surrey three. This is not as absurd as it looks. A Sussex fraudster, for example, is quite likely to commit fraud in the City of London – for example, if he works for an investment bank in the Square Mile – or in the West End of London. In each case, he would be investigated by the City of London or the Metropolitan branch of the Fraud Squad.

However, the Sussex and Surrey figures paint a bleak picture of police manpower and priorities. In the big urban conurbations of Britain, the maintenance of large, permanent fraud squads simply can't be avoided. In other county constabularies, where fraud is not a major problem, chief officers are reluctant to commit manpower which could, in their view, be better used policing the streets or dealing with violence on council estates. Police authorities, too, are not likely to be sympathetic towards a chief constable who has an interest in fraud while mayhem is occurring in the towns for which he's responsible. It means, though, that when a large fraud occurs in, say, Brighton, the chief officer will have to lay off men on an *ad hoc* basis to deal with it. They won't be experienced and they certainly won't have the expertise for the job.

This highlights another problem the police have in dealing with fraud: the majority of policemen regard it as being outside the mainstream of career policing. Until recently, police used to be seconded to the Fraud Squad whether they liked it or not, generally for two- or three-year periods. That has now stopped, and the Squad is policed by men who have volunteered for the job. There's a realisation that fraud is now a big business and not merely a marginal crime. There's also an awareness that it's possible to do a great deal of fraud work and still be promoted to the highest echelons of the police.

Sir James Crane was one case in point, Tom Edwards another. Commander George Churchill-Coleman, head of the Fraud Squad in 1993, spent eight years as commander of the Anti-Terrorist Squad before moving to fraud. But earlier in his career he had worked for almost nine years one way or another in fraud or as a senior investigator at the Department of Trade and Industry.

Churchill-Coleman was involved in the Iranian embassy siege as a superintendent, and also worked in the Murder Squad. In spite of this tough, violent background he could be mistaken for a senior industrialist with his well-cut suits and neatly barbered silver hair. He spits out words at the rate of a machine-gun and Sir James Crane recalls that when Churchill-Coleman charged the corrupt architect, John Poulson, he had to read out the charges three times before Poulson got their drift.

Churchill-Coleman believes that the Fraud Squad is much more pro-active than it used to be. It is three times the size it was when he joined it as a detective constable in

1965, then about fifty strong. It also has a surveillance squad numbering some twelve men, a six-man intelligence unit and a section dealing with computer crime, headed by Inspector John Austin who is also a very big number in Interpol's computer section. Austin and his wife reputedly sleep surrounded by computer screens which are set to alert him when money over certain amounts starts to move through the British banking system. Austin is a star at computer crime conferences, a dedicated original, who should make a fortune when he retires.

Much of the fraud in Churchill-Coleman's area is reported by the public. 'But the complaints have to have some substance,' he says. 'There has to be some evidence for us to go on. For example, a huge parcel about six inches thick was left at our Richbell Place reception marked for my attention. As I'd only been gone from the Anti-Terrorist Squad for about ten months, I immediately had it checked out for explosives in case it had been left by some old friends. In fact it contained a very substantial dossier from directors of a company who suspected that one of their number was acting fraudulently.'

He says that there are many more early warnings these days for the Fraud Squad to act upon. The most important of these is big movements of money through banks. The banks are now required by law to report unusually large transfers of money abroad. These can be traced to fraudsters shipping money out to buy assets overseas (villas, property, restaurants and so on), which effectively buries the cash and makes it very difficult to track down; drug money being laundered; or the dispersal of money into securities and overseas bank accounts where it can be lost from sight, often permanently.

Churchill-Coleman, one of the four Fraud Squad heads I interviewed for this book, is a man of very strong views and powerful convictions. He may have delivered these at a startling rate, but the messages were quite plain. He is not convinced, for one thing, that enough is being done to take the profit out of fraud.

'There are far too many people coming out of jail and then going on to enjoy the assets they've salted away. As long as that continues to happen in major frauds, it will be very

hard to convince anyone that committing fraud isn't worth
it. If you can get the profit out of it, there will be very little
incentive for people to commit it. It's terribly important for
us to concentrate on the recovery of all the assets – not just
money, but villas, yachts and other investments – so that a
fraudster is stripped of everything. Prison of itself is not
enough.

'There's also a naive belief that fraudsters are in some way
different from the common run of criminals. The only thing
that makes them different is the type of crime they commit.
The common assumption seems to be that these people are
gentlemen. In many cases, of course, they have a different
social and educational background from the ordinary run of
criminals. They talk better and dress better and are used to a
quite different lifestyle. But they are still criminals. They don't
mind who they do down or the financial suffering they are
capable of causing. They also deal, many of them, in very large
numbers – numbers which can cause incalculable harm not
just to individuals, but to companies and their shareholders.
These are not one-off burglaries, where some of the family
silver is stolen. They are major crimes where a lot of people
get hurt and they are committed by people with criminal
minds, whatever school they went to or whatever family they
come from.'

Churchill-Coleman is also concerned by the huge cost
incurred when liquidators try to recover assets. 'This more
often than not runs into millions of pounds. We've seen
the enormous costs incurred by liquidators trying to track
down where all the Maxwell assets are. These run into many
millions already. It cuts down enormously on the amount that
might be recovered in the end and on the amount the Maxwell
pensioners are likely to get.

'If they can do it properly, then liquidators should be
employed in-house by people like the Serious Fraud Office.
It means that more will be left in the pot at the end of the
day for the people who really need it.'

The Fraud Squad Churchill-Coleman runs comprises around
150 people. Its headquarters in Richbell Place, at the back of
Holborn police station, are badly lit and look as if they have

been furnished with chairs, tables and carpets from a bankrupt furniture emporium. Churchill-Coleman's office would
drive the average sales manager to resignation. He doesn't
even run to a conference table, just three very uncomfortable
armchairs well below the height of his desk. While he talks,
a squawk box is constantly crackling in the background, a
reminder that even in the politer world of fraud policemen
are busy at all hours of the day.

From this dismal, depressing building Churchill-Coleman
directs a force of eight separate squads. His second-in-
command is a detective chief superintendent. Beneath him are
four detective superintendents, then a group of chief inspectors, inspectors and detective constables running squads
which cover fraud in such areas as mortgages, advance
fees, public corruption and general fraud. What squads deal
with, though, is not immutable; fashion in fraud changes
and when one type of fraud becomes immensely popular,
a squad is likely to be set up to deal with it. In the last
couple of years advance fee frauds have come into fashion
in a big way, largely because so many people need loans to
keep them going. They pay money upfront in order to get a
loan that's been promised, but never see it.

It clearly pays policemen to have specialist knowledge of
certain kinds of fraud because it can cut out the problem
of the learning curve. The danger is that a policeman can
become too sophisticated and assume too much knowledge in
his witnesses and a jury. The police are fond of saying that if a
policeman can understand a complex fraud, then anyone can.
There is a lot to that argument. Fraud has become Byzantine
in its complexity and any evidence, to be worthwhile, has
to be reduced to simple concepts and facts that a jury can
grasp. Churchill-Coleman is not against policemen having a
long spell in fraud because it can improve their tradecraft
enormously – as long as there is no danger of 'blunting a
man's edge'.

The Fraud Squad's budget in 1992/93 was £10 million,
roughly half of the SFO's. The squad has worked remarkably
well over the years, bearing in mind its budgetary and manpower restrictions. But the growth of serious and complex

fraud made it inevitable that another organisation should take on the heavyweight cases. These, in the past ten years, have grown to awesome proportions, both in terms of money and complexity. The father of this new élite organisation – the Serious Fraud Office – was a man called Lord Roskill.

3

ROSKILL AND THE CRIMINAL JUSTICE ACT 1987

The Serious Fraud Office did not come into being by accident or through government whim. The government decided that fraud had become such a serious problem that it needed to be looked at by a committee capable of making sensible recommendations. It fell to the lot of Lord Hailsham, then Lord Chancellor, to appoint a law lord to take charge of it. Hailsham, a clever if eccentric legalist, irascible and difficult, thought that a committee of lawyers would be quite the best people to produce the answers. The man he appointed, Lord Roskill, had a mind of his own and thought it would be better to appoint a committee with a much broader base of experience and whose whole life had not been spent at the bar.

Roskill is one of those men the British legal sytem is particularly good at producing: a Rolls Royce mind capable of grasping complex detail quickly, then shaping the right conclusions. He has considerable charm and excellent manners. He was a Winchester ('Manners makyth Man') exhibitioner, took a first in Modern History at Oxford and in the same year became Harmsworth Law Scholar in the Middle Temple. For some years, when he was a practising barrister, he had a flat in Shepherd Market, the centre of Mayfair prostitution, because it was cheap. When he became a high court judge at the age of fifty-one, it was suggested that his London address did not accord with his status. 'We judges are always being accused of being out of touch with life, I told them, but acceded to their request.' He and his wife spend the middle of the week these days in an airy flat at the top of New Court Temple with distant views over the Thames. He was appointed a Lord Justice of Appeal when he was sixty and at the age of eighty-three his intellectual vigour seems undiminished. He still has a dauntingly good memory.

His fraud trials committee had to have members whose experience was relevant to its terms of reference: 'to consider in what ways the conduct of criminal proceedings in England and Wales arising from fraud can be improved and to consider what changes in law and procedure would be desirable to secure the just, expeditious and economical disposal of such proceedings.'

So there was Lord Benson, one of those accountants who, apart from making money, made it his business to be in or a part of the interstices of public life, but one of whose most important jobs was chairman of the Royal Commission on Legal Services; he had more than a passing acquaintance with the English legal system. There was David Butler, a tall millionaire with a passion for cricket, who was chairman of Butler Cox, the information technology consultants; he was there to advise on the presentation of complex information in court. Sir James Crane was another member. It seemed wise to have a practising judge. Judge John Hazan had been assigned to the Central Criminal Court (Old Bailey), but as prosecuting counsel to the Inland Revenue and a recorder of the crown court he would have had a good deal of experience of fraud. There was Sir Arthur Knight, a former chairman of Courtaulds. Knight had sat on the commission of inquiry into the siting of the third London airport and Roskill, who had been chairman, had been impressed by him. Dr Barbara Marsh was a JP and vice-chairman of Shropshire County Council. And Walter Merricks was a solicitor representing the Law Society.

The committee was appointed at the end of 1983 and reported in 1986: good going, bearing in mind that it took evidence, either oral or written, from almost two hundred people and organisations, and produced a closely researched and argued report of 250 pages. It did not take long for them to find that the system, such as it was, for bringing serious fraudsters to book was in a dreadful state of dereliction.

The opening of the report laid out the scale of the problem. This summary was written by David Butler; Roskill had wanted a lay view, and it was delivered with punchy clarity.

The public no longer believes that the legal system in England and Wales is capable of bringing the perpetrators of serious frauds expeditiously and effectively to book. The overwhelming weight of the evidence laid before us suggests that the public is right. In relation to such crimes, and to the skilful and determined criminals who commit them, the *present legal system is archaic, cumbersome and unreliable* (my italics). At every stage, during investigation preparation, committal, pre-trial review and trial, the present arrangements offer an open invitation to blatant delay and abuse. While petty frauds, clumsily committed, are likely to be detected and punished, it is all too likely that the largest and most cleverly executed crimes escape unpunished. The Government has encouraged and continues to encourage ordinary families to invest their savings in the equity markets, particularly in the equities of formerly state-owned enterprises. If the Government cherishes the vision of an 'equity-owning democracy', then it also faces an inescapable duty to ensure that financial markets are honestly managed, and that transgressors in these markets are swiftly and effectively discovered, convicted and punished. Self-regulatory mechanisms designed to encourage honest practices are now coming into force. Where those mechanisms are abused, the law must deliver retribution, swift and sure.

It has a fine, judicial ring about it, and there is no mistaking its message. Roskill went on to warn the government that substantial alteration to any of his committee's proposals might do damage to the structure of the whole. There were more than a hundred recommendations, only one of which was not implemented – the proposal for a fraud trials tribunal, a replacement for trial by jury in cases of complex fraud, only to be used when it fell within certain guidelines. This was politically unacceptable. Its critics felt that a tribunal composed of a high court or a circuit judge, together with two lay members who were skilled in business practices, smacked of élitism. While it seemed obvious that comprehension of complex evidence would be at a much higher level if the tribunal procedure were adopted, it was equally obvious that members of the general public would think the system was a fix, based on class, education and experience.

This proposal will probably come up again. Roskill was trying to address the problem of complexity, which becomes a huge difficulty for ordinary jurors who are asked to wrap their minds around intricate financial transactions which have been put together with the object of being undetected. It is one thing being asked to give a verdict on someone charged with murder, quite another to do so on a person who has moved millions of pounds through dozens of accounts in different banks in foreign jurisdictions in a case where the charges are false accounting and theft. The scale of the problem is often complicated by a skilled defence which will do its best to cloud already muddy waters even further.

Complexity, as Roskill realised, was probably the most important aspect of serious fraud cases, but by no means the only one. Complex fraud usually takes much longer to investigate than other forms of crime and consequently it is much more expensive to prosecute. It used to take much longer than usual, for example, to get such a case into the crown court because of the lengthy committal proceedings in the magistrates' court and, once in the upper court, prosecution, defence and witnesses were condemned very often to trials of interminable length. It could take two to three years from the time a fraud first came to the notice of the authorities until the verdict was delivered in court (it still does, in spite of Roskill, and it sometimes takes longer). The whole process was, and still is, a massive drain on resources.

Roskill said the intentions of his committee were to 'tip the balance in favour of justice, economy and expedition and against injustice, waste and delay': a statement of intent that no one could argue with. The committee went on to identify the fault lines in the existing system and how they could be straightened out. The most serious areas that needed drastic improvement were the prosecution and defence, the competence of judges and counsel, and the preparatory hearings leading to the main trial. These were all a mess which no one, before Roskill was appointed, had bothered to consider in a structured way.

The prosecution was a serious stumbling block to an expeditious trial. Roskill said that prosecuting counsel should prepare a 'case statement' which included the primary facts; the sources, witnesses and exhibits on which those facts depended; the law the case relied upon; and how all these related to each count in the indictment, with references and cross-references. However, the case statement was not to end there. Allied to that, the prosecution would have to serve on the defence the appropriate schedules and charts which it proposed to use and should also prepare a glossary of technical terms for the jury's use, together with any visual aids it may need in the presentation of its case. Furthermore, the judge would be empowered to order the production of all relevant visual material and numerical information.

The case statement was to be made available before the first preparatory hearing, Roskill said, so that the defence would have the opportunity to make any submissions on it to the judge at that time. The judge would then rule on admissibility, and the case statement would be amended accordingly. In effect, then, the case statement would be a substantially expanded version of the indictment and in its revised form, after submissions had been made, copies should be made available to the jury. The Roskill proposal was a much more elaborate and clearly defined alternative to the previous sketchy arrangements, whereby the case statement or summary was often little more than a note of the prosecution's opening speech, accompanied by copies of witness statements. Consequently, judge and defendants were bogged down with mounds of paperwork without any clear indication of the prosecution case and how the evidence would be pieced together.

The Roskill proposals for the prosecution make the task of assimilation at an early stage much easier for the judge and the defendants' counsel than the old haphazard arrangements.

But Roskill also thought that what was sauce for the goose should be sauce for the gander, and that a substantial onus should be placed on the defence as far as disclosure was concerned. Before Roskill, the defence were not obliged to indicate what their case would be. The burden of proof lay entirely with the prosecution. The court may never have heard the defendant's version of events other than his plea of not guilty. If the defence did decide to give evidence and call witnesses, this occurred at the end of the prosecution case.

One of the main arguments against this system was that it made fraud trials longer, less efficient, more obscure and ultimately less just. There were two important points here. First, lack of disclosure by the defence meant that once defence counsel were on their feet and rambling through their case, the jury would have forgotten the prosecution's main arguments or would only have had a chance to discover what the real issues were after days or weeks had elapsed. Defence disclosure would help to shorten that time-gap and keep the jury's noses closer to the case. The defence would be able to indicate much earlier what parts of the prosecution's case they were going to challenge, thereby eliminating much evidence which was never in dispute between the parties.

The second point was that there would be less scope for fabricated defences. Defence disclosure before the preparatory stages of the trial would give the prosecution time to investigate claims it thought were dubious.

There can be little doubt – though Roskill said there was no research available to support the claim – that defence disclosure was bound to shorten trials, simply because much that was irrelevant would have been eliminated from the proceedings before a jury got its teeth into a case. On the question of a jury losing its way under the old system, there can be little doubt about that either. Juries find it hard enough to keep track of proceedings in the general run of cases, let alone complex fraud.

If shorter trials mean more efficient trials, then the case for early defence disclosure was proven. The committee further argued that any failure by the defence to make disclosure at the preparatory stage of a trial 'may be a matter which is relevant to the credibility of the defence advanced at the trial'. Two inferences, according to the report, could be drawn from such a circumstance: that defence counsel may not have done their job properly, and also 'the stronger the prosecution's case the more significant would be the defendant's failure to disclose the general line of his defence'. Roskill argued that judge and prosecution should be free to comment if the defence lead evidence which could have been mentioned at an earlier stage. This proposal went into the Criminal Justice Act of 1987 virtually unchanged.

The Roskill Committee went much further than simply tackling changes in the law. It didn't shirk the controversial question of competence, whether the competence of judges to try serious fraud cases or of counsel to appear in them. Roskill found that the overwhelming majority of fraud cases in the crown court were tried by circuit judges, i.e. judges ranking below those who sit in the high court. This is because of the peculiar pecking order by which the severity of crimes is rated. There are four classes of crime: class 1 covers murder and a small number of very serious offences, class 2 manslaughter, rape and other serious offences, while classes 3 and 4 deal with the remaining offences and can be tried by any judge.

Murder is the prerogative of high court judges and class 2 is normally tried by the high court. Roskill found that between 1979 and 1983 only three fraud cases out of 129, each lasting for more than twenty working days, were tried by a high court judge. An obvious reason for this is that there are not enough high court judges because the government won't make the money available; another is the very heavy workload that high court judges have to deal with anyway. Roskill wanted the Lord Chief Justice, who is responsible for deploying judges in the Queen's Bench Division, to allocate more senior judges to cases of complex fraud even if it meant re-classifying some offences. But he also recognised that it wouldn't always be possible to get high court judges to try serious and complex fraud cases and that circuit judges would have to be selected on the basis of an informal rating of aptitude for trying these cases.

However, the right judges are not much use if prosecuting

counsel are not up to the mark. Bad counsel can not only lose cases, they can also waste time and thus add to the costs of a trial. Roskill argued that a number of important prosecutions in fraud cases have been handled by counsel without the experience or the ability to do the job properly. The law, like most other professions, has its good and bad practitioners. Roskill did not think that because counsel were competent at prosecuting crimes such as murder and rape they necessarily had the skills for prosecuting serious fraud. Competence, he said, was the only criterion that mattered. To that end, he thought that a list of the right counsel should be compiled and kept under review by judges experienced in trying fraud cases. He also thought that senior prosecuting counsel should be given able junior counsel whenever possible so that the latter could gain the relevant experience.

Roskill went a bit further; he saw compelling arguments for judges and counsel to have some training in accountancy and information technology, and thought accountancy should be a compulsory subject in training for the bar, either at the bar examinations stage or during pupillage.

What Roskill did not manage to address, in his advocacy of using the best and most suitable counsel for the prosecution of fraud, was the question of cost. Government departments, and especially the Serious Fraud Office, are not made of money. Roskill wanted not simply the best counsel, but he wanted them involved in cases virtually from the beginning so that they could control the direction of investigation and prosecution. 'Unless advice of high quality is available from the outset of investigations of this type, the inquiries will be slowed up and valuable time may be wasted pursuing the wrong lines of inquiry. It is undesirable that the investigation should take one course and for that course to be found not to be the right one by counsel who is brought in to prosecute at a much later stage, perhaps after the case has been committed.'

Roskill went on to argue eloquently for counsel staying with the case throughout so that the 'same person who has given the inquiry direction will be involved in the presentation of the prosecution. A considerable advantage of involving counsel from the beginning is that he will have had the opportunity of becoming familiar with the case and less of his time will be taken up at the stage when the case is being prepared for trial.'

Although Roskill was not to know at that time that a Serious Fraud Office was to come into being with government lawyers at the helm, he considered that the extra expense of employing counsel at an early stage was justified by 'a speedier and better targeted investigation . . . For these reasons, we attach considerable importance to the appointment of a competent counsel on the initiative of the Case Controller soon after the suspected fraud comes to light.'

In the Barlow Clowes case, the SFO had two full-time QCs and one part-time, and two junior counsel, as well as an assistant director of the SFO as case controller. What Roskill did not take account of is that the best counsel are very expensive (they can earn up to £500,000 a year, or £10,000 a week), and that was to have some bearing on the way the SFO was to work. It has meant that the SFO has not always been able to employ the counsel of its choice, but has had to opt for second best.

The most important recommendation Roskill had to make was the 'formation of a single, unified organisation responsible for all the functions of detection, investigation and prosecution of serious fraud'. The advantages of such an organisation, Roskill thought, would be that fewer serious frauds would be allowed to escape prosecution by slipping through the net of a series of independent organisations working in this field (the Fraud Investigation Group, the DTI, the Inland Revenue, the Customs and Excise and so on); that overlapping of resources would be avoided; that it would help investigations to lead to more effective prosecutions; there would be room for greater efficiency and the reduction of delays; it would remove unhelpful restrictions on the disclosure of information from one organisation to another, and a unified organisation would have full powers of investigation.

The organisation Roskill described was his ideal. What came after his report, however, was the Criminal Justice Act of 1987 which created the Serious Fraud Office. The CJA was 'an Act to make further provisions for the investigation of and trials for fraud; and for connected purposes'. There were three significant bits of Roskill in it. The first was the procedure for transferring a fraud case from the magistrates' court to the crown court. Under the old arrangement, there had to be a hearing in the magistrates' court before the case could be committed to the crown court. Some of these committal hearings could be immensely long and protracted, especially in cases of complex fraud, and a heavy additional cost (not that counsel would have objected), quite apart from the wear and tear on a defendant. Roskill said they should be abolished and the prosecution be entitled to give the court a notice of transfer to the crown court. However, under the Act, the notice has to be issued before the magistrates' hearing starts. If not, the committal procedure has to go ahead in the normal way.

The second piece of Roskill was also designed to make fraud trials less time-consuming and more efficient. Once the case has been transferred to the crown court, the judge can order a preparatory hearing because he considers that the case is so serious and complex. This is designed to familiarise the judge with the issues, and to help the jury understand them. Roskill was very strong on the importance of these preparatory hearings. He was also emphatic that the judge should get all the papers relating to the trial well in advance so that he could familiarise himself with them before the hearings began.

The committee quoted from the findings of the court of appeal looking into a complicated commercial fraud case, which found that the judge allocated to the trial could not cope with the work on hand:

Before the trial started there was a pre-trial review (now known as a preparatory hearing). A full scale review was certainly needed. However it was only a day or two before the review that the judge was provided with the papers, which were massive, and a copy of the opening speech of leading counsel before the committing justices. The review produced no worthwhile result. This was not the fault of the judge. He could not be expected to master this complicated case in the time available to him. Had he been able to do so we have no doubt that he would have done some extensive pruning. That would be an important object of a pre-trial review in cases of this kind. Prosecuting counsel who have been immersed in the details of a case for months sometimes do not appreciate the difficulty which a judge and a jury may have in assimilating the evidence. At the pre-trial review the judge (and he should normally be the one who is going to try the case) should be ready and willing to take the initiative to ensure that all unnecessary detail is omitted. This he cannot do unless he is given the papers well before the review hearing and has time to read and analyse them. If he is not he may think it is right to postpone the review. We are sure that a robust pre-trial review in this case would have resulted in a shorter and more satisfactory trial.

In other words, the judge was in a mess, but his dilemma encapsulated the importance of properly conducted preparatory hearings. What the court of appeal did not tackle in their comments, but Roskill addressed, was that counsel did not always take these hearings seriously, or as someone said, 'a general sense of the uselessness of the occasion generally prevails.'

One of the reasons for that, Roskill maintained, was that pre-trial reviews were not regarded as part of the main trial – i.e. after a jury had been sworn in – but merely as a preliminary. The committee said that they should be seen as part of the trial and to that effect a change of name to 'preparatory hearing' ought to be made. This was also written into the Criminal Justice Act of 1987.

The committee also made the point that as the preparatory hearing would be formal, any proceedings at the hearing could be referred to in the trial, so that if a defendant decided to retract admissions made at the hearing this could be put to him in cross-examination. They also made the recommendation that counsel who appeared at the preparatory hearing should be counsel who are briefed to conduct the case at trial.

The powers, then, that a judge has been given under the Criminal Justice Act for the conduct of preparatory hearings are very wide. He can decide, for example, whether a case should be discharged. He can make orders for the production of a case statement from the prosecution and, similarly, order defendants to produce statements setting out in broad terms the nature of their defence and where they take issue with the prosecution. He can decide the admissibility of evidence and questions of law relating to the case. He can adjourn a preparatory hearing from time to time, order the production of charts and visual aids to help the jury in their comprehension of the case later on, and also has the power at trial to refer back to the cases disclosed at the preparatory hearing if those cases are suddenly altered (this was also a Roskill recommendation). The point was to alert the jury that one or both of the sides had decided to take a different tack. Counsel were also entitled to comment on any change.

While Roskill enhanced the importance of the preparatory hearing for all the right reasons, the reality has turned out to be rather different through no fault of his. The appointment of one judge for an important trial does not happen enough, so some counsel claim, and if a judge is appointed to conduct the whole of a trial he doesn't get the time to read himself in. Consequently, the judge doesn't know enough about the case to start with, so he errs on the side of the prosecution because he thinks it is probably safer to preserve the *status quo*.

Another complaint, which Roskill tried to address, but apparently without much success, was the quality of the judges picked for important trials. Criminal law, unlike, for example, commercial law, is not a specialty. Any judge can be appointed to a criminal case even if he has never heard one before in his life. Allied to this paradox there is another which some counsel claim makes the administration of criminal justice even more difficult; namely the fact that not one of the judges who sit in the House of Lords at the present time has ever practised at the criminal bar. The result, their critics say, is that they are continually 'cocking up' the criminal law. It is also said that the court of appeal does not like sending cases to the Lords for that very reason.

If that is the prevalent system, or lack of one, it is hardly surprising that some judges without any criminal experience end up trying extremely important cases. Mr Justice Laws, who presided over the Levitt case, had never heard a criminal case before. Mr Justice McKinnon, who tried the immensely complex and costly Blue Arrow case, had no experience of criminal cases either.

If that can happen with high court judges, it is not difficult to see what occurs when circuit judges tackle fraud cases. With a few exceptions, circuit judges do not have the calibre of their high court colleagues. High court judges are elected to their jobs, but lawyers can apply to be circuit judges; their quality is variable and some circuit judges try cases for which they are quite unsuited. The result is that their decisions are often reversed on appeal – another time-consuming and expensive process.

When Roskill recommended that a new, unified organisation for tackling serious fraud should be considered, he also suggested that police should be given powers of investigation comparable to those of the DTI under section 447 of the Companies Act, 1985. Section 447 is pretty draconian. It requires a company to produce its books or papers for examination by the DTI's officers. Present and past employees and directors of a company can be compelled to explain entries in these documents, and failure to do so is a criminal offence. These explanations are admissible in evidence against the person concerned and if DTI officials believe there are reasonable grounds for suspecting that any requirement under section 447 hasn't been complied with, they can apply to a magistrate for a search warrant. Section 447 has to be used in the strictest confidence because if the news got out that a company or its directors were being investigated the effect on market confidence would be disastrous. Broadly, information can only be disclosed when criminal proceedings are brought or when the police and the Department of Public Prosecutions are brought into a case.

In the event, the Criminal Justice Act setting up the SFO brought in a section which had some similarities to 447, but in other respects was quite different. Section 2 confers some very tough investigatory powers on the SFO which have led to widespread concern about its fairness and legitimacy. It requires any person under investigation, or any other person who may have relevant information, to 'furnish information' relevant to the investigation at a time and place specified by the director in writing. But the SFO don't always have to send a letter of request. They can turn up at any time, sometimes at dawn, armed with an arrest warrant, and can then interview the suspect at leisure under Section 2.

'Furnish information' doesn't simply mean give information orally in an interview; it also means the production of specified documents from which the SFO can take copies or extracts. The person producing them can also be asked to provide an explanation of their contents. If the person doesn't produce the documents the SFO asks for, they can ask him where the documents are.

Once the SFO is convinced that a person has failed to comply with an obligation under Section 2, it can go to a justice of the peace and ask for a warrant. The Office must convince the JP that there was a failure to comply, that it wasn't practicable to serve a written notice on the person (thereby warning him they were going to do something about it), that a written notice might seriously prejudice the investigation (the person might shred the documents or get rid of them in some other way) and that the documents were on the premises specified in the information.

Once those conditions have been satisfied, the warrant authorises any constable to enter the premises (using force if necessary), search for the documents, take possession of them and see they are made secure. 'Any constable' means any number of police the SFO think are needed, but they will normally have to be accompanied by an official of the SFO – a lawyer or an accountant, or someone authorised by the SFO. The police do not have Section 2 powers. There are certain exceptions to these provisions: namely, a person cannot be required to produce documents which are legally privileged (e.g. between himself and his solicitor about proceedings in the high court), or documents or information of a banking nature unless permission is obtained from the person to whom the obligation of confidentiality is owed, or unless the director of the SFO, or the deputy director or the chief accountant specifically authorises bankers to provide the information. Banking details are often crucial to an SFO investigation in tracing how money is moved about, frequently from one jurisdiction to another and generally through many accounts and banks.

If someone doesn't comply with these provisions, namely the production of documents and explanation of their contents, they are liable to be imprisoned for six months or fined or both. Moreover, if anyone is convicted in a crown court of knowingly making a false statement he can get two years or a fine or both; alternatively a magistrate can put him away for a maximum of six months, again with the option of a fine.

There are tougher penalties. Anyone guilty of destroying, altering or concealing documents, knowing that they are relevant to a serious fraud investigation, is liable to a maximum sentence of seven years in the crown court, plus a fine, or both; while in a magistrates' court he is liable to six months and/or fines.

Section 2, then, gives very short shrift to people who obstruct an investigation. Where Section 2 has fallen into disrepute, especially among victims of its provisions, and some lawyers, is that it requires suspects to answer questions even if the answers incriminate them, thereby breaking the privilege against self-incrimination. But Section 2 interviews are not admissible as evidence, except where the charged person gives evidence which is not consistent with his Section 2 statement. In those circumstances the Section 2 evidence becomes admissible.

The SFO has long argued that when a Section 2 interviewee discloses information which incriminates him there is a built-in safeguard: the police cannot conduct Section 2 interviews, yet it is they who have to obtain witness statements that can be used in court. The argument goes that when a suspect incriminates himself under Section 2, he is not likely to repeat that admission when interviewed by police for his witness statement. He will be less 'willing' or will say 'no comment'.

Critics of Section 2, though, say there are no proper ground rules for the interviews. The suspect is not given access to the documents about which he is being questioned. He is required to respond from memory and is frequently referred to material which can go back eight or ten years. In the course of a businessman's life he sees thousands of important documents which in later years he can have only a very sketchy recollection of, if any. The SFO investigators sit him down with a pile of documents in front of them, on which they are fully prepared, and proceed to ask detailed questions about their contents; times, dates, the people involved and who said what to whom. The suspect hasn't seen the documents, he has had no opportunity to prepare answers, so he gives answers the SFO know to be wrong. They infer that he is a liar and therefore guilty, and on that basis they decide to prosecute. By the time the trial comes along, though, the suspect is properly prepared and his case changes. He now has a complete defence which, if the prosecution had known about it, might have persuaded them there was no case to answer.

Leading counsel complain that, in the case of an innocent person, the consequences are obvious: he is wrongly brought to trial and time and money are wasted. Most people argue that when a suspect is required to give a Section 2 interview he should have an opportunity to familiarise himself with the documents about which he is to be questioned. Otherwise he cannot be expected to give honest and truthful answers, which is the prime object of the interview.

But Section 2 has another purpose. If investigators are hamstrung by a recalcitrant suspect over his witness statement, they have in their hands his Section 2 interview which could well point them to avenues of fertile investigation where new witnesses can be persuaded to come forward and give evidence. Section 2s, in fact, are not widely used; such interviews probably account for less than 10 per cent of all those conducted by the SFO. Fraud trials do not seem to have been much facilitated – certainly as far as results are concerned – by the use of this draconian power. Its main use is the collection of information.

When I talked to Lord Roskill seven years after the Criminal

Justice Act of 1987 had been introduced, based largely on the recommendations of his committee, he told me he was more impenitent than ever about his recommendation for fraud trials tribunals to replace an ordinary jury. He had been appalled in recent years by the sheer volume of paperwork that judges and juries were supposed to cope with. When the SFO had taken him around their headquarters and shown him rooms full of documents relating to the Maxwell case, he had been astonished.

'If I'd known about the quantity of paper when we were doing our report I would have been even more adamant about the importance of having tribunals. I am horrified by the standards of jurors. They cannot be expected to understand what is going on in complex and serious fraud cases. Two lay assessors, sitting alongside a judge, are far better equipped to get to grips with the issues and to cope with the evidence.'

And once again he returned to the importance of preparatory hearings and the time given to judges to familiarise themselves with cases. 'We placed a great deal of emphasis on the prosecution producing a proper case statement early on. There is no reason why they cannot do so. They have dealt with the case for months on end, they have read all the documents closely. Even if a judge can assimilate thousands of pages of documentary evidence, he will be no wiser unless he has the case statement to guide him. Once he has that in his hands, he can then decide which of the thousands of documents are relevant and take steps in the preparatory hearing to prune down the case into manageable and comprehensible proportions.

'Things aren't made any easier these days when you have counsel perhaps labouring a point to death and thereby wasting a great deal of time. Sometimes counsel appear to think the judge is as stupid as the jury. A judge can generally get a point the second time around, if not the first. But three or four times is not unusual. The difficulty here is that a judge these days cannot be rude to counsel who hasn't mastered his brief or who is wasting time. He'll be seen to be favouring one side or another and the jury will take the wrong inference. Rudeness has disappeared. It's a reaction to the days when I was practising at the bar when judges could be particularly brutal and unpleasant to counsel. Old Sir Reginald Croom-Johnson was a terror. I think we all thought that must never be allowed to happen again. But it does mean, of course, that a judge does not have the control over a case he ought to have. Even if a judge is firm, people sometimes think he is rude.'

Nor is Roskill particularly enamoured with some of the judges being appointed to the high court these days. 'You can't get the really good people from the bar because there isn't the money in it. So the Lord Chancellor has to appoint circuit judges to the high court. One must remember that circuit judges apply to become circuit judges. It isn't like the high court. So you get people very often who were not good circuit judges in the first place going into the high court. They're not up to it. That does nothing for the quality of the bench.'

Apart from the quality of judges in general, there is also the quality of the judges deputed to try fraud. Roskill's report made it clear that judges of proven worth should try the big fraud cases, but this depends on such people being available, and on the Lord Chief Justice's department scheduling them for the trials. There is no evidence that that is happening. Judges still get allocated cases on an *ad hoc* basis, depending on who happens to be available. But it doesn't matter how good a judge is, if he doesn't get the time to read himself into a case in the way Roskill wanted it will take him weeks to get on top of a trial, if he ever does. That is wasteful of resources. Worse, it is likely to vitiate the quality of justice.

4

THE PEOPLE ON ELM STREET

The Serious Fraud Office was quite different in concept to anything seen before in tackling fraud. In the first place, it was both its own investigation and prosecution service. It did not refer or defer to the Director of Public Prosecutions, who nowadays conducts all fraud investigations in the first instance through the Fraud Investigation Group (FIG), and then prosecutes cases through the DPP's own agency, the Crown Prosecution Service (CPS). The SFO investigates allegations of serious fraud and then decides whether or not it will prosecute them. It is responsible only to the Attorney General. It is also an organisation based very much on what Roskill wanted, although its remit does not include detection. Roskill wanted that to be part of its work, but in practice it is almost impossible. The role of detection is normally carried out by the public, the media or other interested parties when their suspicions are aroused, while the roles of investigation and prosecution are carried out by the responsible authorities once those suspicions, or relevant evidence, have been reported to them.

The SFO differs in one other important respect from what Roskill envisaged. He saw an umbrella organisation tackling all serious fraud in this country, removing from other government departments the work they already did in that area. Politically that was not practicable: Whitehall departments instinctively oppose any diminution in their powers and fight vigorously to retain them. There was never any likelihood that the SFO would take over the investigation and prosecution roles of the Inland Revenue, Customs and Excise or the Department of Trade and Industry. In the course of time, though, all these departments were to refer cases to the SFO, with the exception of the Inland Revenue, which keeps itself to itself and regards matters of tax evasion, even though they may involve significant sums of money, as strictly its own business.

The SFO's caseload in 1993–94 is a typical illustration of the sources of its work. Among the 79 cases the Office tackled, 21 came from the police, 12 from the Department of Trade and Industry, 18 from liquidators, receivers and members of the public, 5 from the CPS Fraud Investigation Group, 4 from the Bank of England, 1 from Customs and Excise, and 16 were originated by the SFO itself. Very occasionally, other government departments might be involved, such as the Ministry of Defence, where contract fraud may have been discovered.

Given these exceptions, the idea of a Serious Fraud Office was not at all a bad one. It was to tackle serious and complex fraud which, at the time of its inception in April 1988, was deemed to be cases where £1 million or more was at risk. This was quickly outdated by the extremely rapid growth in the size of serious fraud cases; within a few years the figure was revised to £5 million, but that is now beginning to look outdated. The only other criteria needed for the SFO to accept a case are that the facts and/or law are of great complexity, or there is great public interest and concern for some other reason, such as the identity of the suspect (a prominent person, for example) or the use of a novel method of fraud. In broad terms, the SFO has always tried to limit the number of cases it is handling at any time to around sixty; it does not have the resources to deal with more.

Given that the SFO is not messing around with pennies, or with fraudsters who are halfwits (many are extremely intelligent, ingenious and quite often possessed of charismatic personalities), it is an astonishingly dull institution. Outsiders – unless they are part of that select band who investigate fraud in other parts of the world – are not allowed to attend 'case conferences', where the strategy of investigation and prosecution is discussed. My impression, though, is that these are not people in the Raymond Chandler mode; they do not talk out of the sides of their mouths or use streetwise phrases. They are conventional, rather boring and imbued with the culture of the civil service. Yet nearly all of them volunteered to join the SFO. It was new. It was different. It had great potential.

But they are not a new breed at the SFO; they are simply the same breed with different strains mixed together for the first time. There is no doubt that the top dogs are the lawyers, virtually all of them from the government legal service. Some are barristers, some solicitors, but none have the right of audience in court in Britain; that is left to the heavyweight leading counsel from the private sector and their juniors, who can spend years working for the SFO on the most serious cases. Even so, it should not be imagined that the lawyers and accountants who work for the SFO are short of a crust. The gradings these days ensure that staff at assistant director level are paid between £41,000 and £56,000. Accountants whom the SFO bring in from outside – from firms like Coopers & Lybrand or Ernst & Young – are even better rewarded because they are employed to tackle cases, such as Maxwell and BCCI, where the complexity of the financial problems demand the best people money can buy.

But the SFO is undoubtedly lawyer-led. The Office's first three directors, including George Staple, the present incumbent, were lawyers. The first, John Wood, was Deputy DPP before he went to the SFO; a career man from the government legal service. The second came from the private sector, Barbara Mills QC. George Staple is a solicitor from an eminent City firm, Clifford Chance. Accountants hold high positions within the SFO, such as assistant directors and case controllers, and in fact outnumbered the lawyers in 1993. That was symptomatic of the fact that the numbers game in serious fraud is critical to its prosecution and places heavy demands on accountants, who are required to trace huge sums of money through labyrinthine transactions around the world.

In 1993 the SFO employed 136 people full time, not including the police seconded to it. Of that number, there were three assistant directors who had been seconded from accountancy firms. George Staple said it was his intention to increase the ratio of permanent staff to temporary staff and secondments; but that, of course, was dependent on his budget. In 1993, for example, more than half his budget of £21 million was taken up by increased prosecution and investigation costs because of the Maxwell case. And 20 per cent of the total was spent on counsel's fees. One really big case can make mincemeat of an annual budget.

While the SFO can now claim that it employs a dedicated team of professionals, that is not a guarantee of success, any more than appointing SFO directors from the private sector is an assurance that things will work better. Neither Barbara Mills nor George Staple, as it turns out, has shown any appreciable turn of speed over the career civil servant who ran it before; and it can be realistically argued that they have not been up to the job.

The SFO has three cultures co-existing under one roof: the legal culture, the lawyers; the financial culture, the accountants; and the police culture, primarily dealing with investigation. Case controllers are lawyers and are in charge of multi-disciplinary teams, which include accountants and police. The police do the investigatory legwork – or at least that is the theory. SFO lawyers and accountants frequently haul in people for questioning under Section 2, though there is some doubt about the efficiency of the process. It is probably best to see the police role as one in which they take witness statements and raid premises for documents and other evidence. They also make the arrests. They occupy the bottom floors of the SFO's nine-storey building, a sergeants' mess, with the officers – the lawyers and accountants – enjoying the clearer air above.

Some staff complain about a lack of communication between the three disciplines. The police, all of whom have a good deal of experience of fraud, do not regard the lawyers and accountants as hands-on professionals. They also regard their conduct of interviews as exceptionally bad and unstructured. The SFO cannot afford to have weak case controllers where there is more than one discipline involved. They have to be polite but firm. The police do not like taking orders or being patronised. So case controllers not only have to control the direction of a case, they have to show the right kind of leadership, not easily acquired when they have been used to working with their peers.

The SFO first occupied a building in Oxford Street, but quite soon moved to more comfortable quarters in Elm Street, just off Gray's Inn Road and next door to Independent Television News. It is a department of the civil service and the higher the lift rises, the better the quality of furnishings and layout. At the top end of the establishment the predominant colours are royal blue and veneered wood. Otherwise, Elm Street is a boxy glass building of no architectural merit set in an area which has been uniformly drab for many years. The only people who make money round here are the television journalists and the barristers of Gray's Inn, who can earn reasonable money from the SFO should they be lucky enough to secure its patronage. The men at the front desk, who look after security and allocate visitors' passes, are from Burns, the American security agency, although they are English.

The command structure here was originally the handiwork of John Wood, the first director, who came from the job of Deputy DPP and head of legal services at the Crown Prosecution Service. A solicitor by training, he has always worked in the government legal service. He is now DPP in Hong Kong. The first thing Wood established at the SFO was a structure for dealing with cases. He took the idea of a case controller from Roskill and built on it, using the skills that had been allocated to him. Significantly, the police in the equation were not given the same powers as the lawyers and accountants: Section 2 of the Criminal Justice Act removes the right of silence from an interviewee and is the most controversial power ever given to an investigating authority in this country. The police have to make do with the Police and Criminal Evidence Act which stipulates in detail how they should conduct investigations. Ironically, though, their lack of Section 2 powers further distances them from their professional colleagues.

By discipline and background, SFO staff are very different creatures from those in the private sector. They are all

permanent civil servants and with few exceptions are not
accustomed to a competitive environment. Nor do they have
to work under pressure. SFO lawyers set their own pace and
workload and decide in their own time whether they are going
to prosecute or not. This, of course, puts an enormous strain
on those under suspicion of fraud, since they have no idea
how long an investigation is going to last, whether they are
likely to be charged or when the case is going to be heard.
The SFO has only one imperative – getting a conviction.
If that involves thousands of hours of investigation, the
accumulation of tons of documents and the interrogation
of hundreds of witnesses, it will go the full distance. This
culture has been inherited from Wood who, as a diligent
civil servant, did not want to leave any stone unturned.
The consequence is that the SFO never produces a critical
mass, the minimum required to produce convictions. This is
a luxury which cannot be enjoyed by the private sector. It
is prosecution by saturation, a slow, determined erosion of
the defence through time, documentation and psychological
pressure.

This is partly because fraud has become enormously complicated, imposing considerable strains on the expertise of
accountants. At the SFO, some have come from industry, or
the Company Investigation Branch of the DTI. Others will
have worked in the Inland Revenue or Customs and Excise.
Their job is to provide all the financial information necessary
in a fraud case. While all fraud involves money, it comes in
different shapes and guises, from pound notes and coins to
share certificates and bearer bonds. Market manipulation and
share fraud, for example, often take some time to be turned
into cash. The SFO's accountants trace the movements of
money, of share transactions, of anything in or outside the
market place which illuminates the financial progress of a
fraud and brings it home to roost.

Police are seconded to the SFO for two- or three-year
periods. They get their instructions from case controllers and
are drawn from all over the country, depending on where a
fraud has been committed. If in Sussex, for example, officers
from the FIG there will be attached to the case controller

in charge of that fraud at Elm House. If there are not enough officers available, then the Chief Constable will probably allocate more men from other divisions for the investigation. Apart from the City of London and Metropolitan forces (the 'Fraud Squad'), twenty forces worked with the SFO during 1993. By far the majority of the police attached to the SFO come from the Fraud Squad, since most major frauds occur in London.

The relationship between the police and their SFO masters is a delicate one. Very often case controllers and SFO lawyers are dealing with police officers who are very experienced in fraud, so there are bound to be clashes of opinion about the way an investigation is going. Case controllers have no control over police discipline. That is a matter for the police themselves. The liaison between the police and the SFO's officials is handled by two senior policemen at superintendent level.

John Wood set up the SFO with a total staff of just over a hundred people, excluding police. He was given a budget of £8.7 million (£21 million today). At the end of his first year he had 21 lawyers on the staff, 19 accountants/investigators, 9 law clerks and 14 support staff. Two of his assistant directors had been borrowed from the top City chartered accountants Ernst & Whinney and Deloitte Haskins & Sells. He had started what continues to this day – secondments from the private sector. Wood noted in his first report: 'The gravity and complexity of our cases render it essential that we recruit only the most able staff . . . [but] pay restraint in the public sector has resulted in a generally poor response to our efforts to recruit over a wider field.' Wood couldn't hope to match the pay that really good people were getting in the private sector. And that is a problem the SFO is still stuck with.

Opinions vary about Wood, a balding, benign, bespectacled government servant of long standing. Patrick Mayhew, the bluff attorney general at that time, said that he appointed Wood because he was keen to have the benefit of his wide experience as the first controller of the FIG within the old DPP's office. One senior fraud officer from the Met thought he lacked dynamism, though quite a number of counsel speak up for him – subjective judgements, as it turns out, based on dealings with Wood which turned out in their favour.

What is palpably true is that Wood didn't duck the big cases of the day. He took with him from the DPP the most publicised fraud case of the decade, Guinness. He had started proceedings in the County NatWest/Blue Arrow and Barlow Clowes trials by the time he left for Hong Kong. In his farewell second report, Wood did something unusual for a civil servant: he departed from the policy of anonymity normally attached to organisations like the SFO and published not only his own picture, looking very avuncular, but also those of some members of the Barlow Clowes team, the Guinness team, and of some senior SFO officials. They are all neatly dressed, well presented and mostly very cheerful. Detective Chief Superintendent Botright (he dealt with Spens and Seelig) is there too, looking remarkably pleased with life. None of them knew then that the SFO was on the verge of heading into a whirlwind of criticism, during which its competence and operational performance would be questioned by the media time after time; there were to be some absurd embarrassments which would have looked better in a cartoon strip. The second Guinness trial collapsed. The Blue Arrow case found no one guilty after an expenditure of £40 million. Terry Ramsden walked free. Roger Levitt got 180 hours' community service. Andrew Kent walked away from the T.C. Coombs prosecution. And Asil Nadir basked in the sunshine of Northern Cyprus, a constant thorn in the SFO's and government's side as he launched a barrage of complaints about injustice from the far side of the Mediterranean.

On the face of it, John Wood left for Hong Kong at the right time. Yet Wood's record wasn't at all bad. Under him, the SFO was responsible for a total of 26 trials involving 46 defendants, 34 of whom were convicted. Unfortunately for the SFO, it is the high-profile cases that catch the headlines. The Office can always point to a 60–70 per cent success rate in prosecutions but the perception of its success rests on the massive failures, where big City names are found to be innocent, sometimes after years of investigation and lengthy trials.

Wood was pragmatic and knew where his priorities lay when it came to prosecution. His experience at the FIG stood him in good stead. 'We don't want rows and rows of defendants,' as he put it. 'We are looking at major offenders as understood by the media and the City.' This comment came from a note of a meeting between Wood and one of his assistant directors and two solicitors from Slaughter and May who were representing Morgan Grenfell, the merchant bank, in the Guinness case.

Mr Pescod of Slaughter and May told Wood that the bank's instinct was to co-operate at all levels and with everybody. What Mr Pescod had in mind was that the bank was terrified of losing its banking licence. There was the possibility of a criminal prosecution, said Mr Pescod, of a company in the Morgan Grenfell Group itself. One detects a shudder even in the cold print at the possibility. There was another risk, Mr Pescod said, and that was the criminal prosecution of some of Morgan's present employees, 'which would be appalling'. Mr Pescod was also worried that the three executives who left the bank after Roger Seelig (a main player in the Guinness case) might also be prosecuted. In fact, a number of people – probably fifteen – quietly left Morgan after Seelig did; but there was no publicity. Mr Pescod, though, was resigned to Seelig's prosecution.

Wood then enunciated a fear that must never be far from any prosecutor's thoughts. 'The prosecution's concerns,' he said, 'are if Morgan Grenfell involvements in other share ramping operations come to light. The DPP would then be criticised for not having prosecuted the company over that one. There is also the danger of someone taking out a private summons against the company. But we want to target the principal offenders for the principal offences.'

By saying that, he had laid down the operating criterion for the SFO: the SFO's work was about public perception. If the media and the City were satisfied, then the Office had done its job. In a curious way, he was working for two very hard taskmasters: the City would begin to hate the way the

SFO operated and the media would never stop criticising it. Wood had targeted Roger Seelig, a banker with one of the highest profiles in the City – that would satisfy the media. Big, confident names always fell harder. They made news. They were good for the SFO and its image.

Consequently, the impression the SFO has managed to give is that it is always desperate to put away really big fish to justify its existence. It caught a few in the first Guinness trial, lost two in the second Guinness trial (Lord Spens and Roger Seelig) and saw Thomas Ward, the cocky American lawyer hired by Guinness at immense cost as a deals facilitator, fly back to the United States an innocent man.

It seems the SFO cannot abide being beaten. A court finds a man innocent, but the SFO's operators remain convinced that he is guilty; a belief which continues long after the trial is over. The SFO feels affronted, as if someone had deliberately set out to spike the guns of an admirable organisation which seeks only justice. It has lost more cases than an outfit seeking to establish a big reputation ever should and it is always in danger of being embarrassed by its mishandling of cases. Even now, it has a tendency to diminish itself by pretending that nugatory sentences for frauds which deserved much stiffer penalties are in some way victories.

Yet the system Wood put in place seemed eminently sensible and logical. It was Wood who decreed that in order to be considered by the SFO, a case must involve sums over £1 million (since raised to £5 million), that the facts and/or the law must be highly complex, or must arouse great public interest. Once a case is accepted by the director, a case team is appointed and lawyer or accountant nominated as case controller, responsible for the investigation and any subsequent prosecution. The team will then be built up according to the demands of the case, and police appointed by the geographically relevant force. When Robert Wardle, an assistant director, was appointed case controller for the Aveling Barford pension fraud he was given a separate police squad from the Lincoln area. There were three convictions in this case, two acquittals and one heart attack.

The case controller then looks at what accountancy

resources he has available. Wardle, who has been at the SFO from the very beginning, was controller for Nadir, Norton, Deacon and London United Investments when I talked to him, so he has a good deal of experience across a wide range of cases. He said that if a big accountancy input is needed, then outside accountants are called in. They would be needed in very complex cases like Nadir, BCCI and Maxwell.

Then an investigating lawyer is called in. He or she will be in-house and will carry out interviews; these are removed from the case controller for the sake of impartiality. At this point a case secretary is appointed. A good case secretary is very important to the smooth running of an investigation and prosecution. They organise meetings, take minutes, circulate papers among team members and filter out all papers to the relevant investigators. Once a decision has been taken to prosecute, the case secretary will organise statements and exhibits for formal presentation in court. In a large case documents could amount to 100,000 pages. Not all of that is used in court, but it's there if needed. The case secretary will also discuss fees with counsel's clerks and sometimes advise the case controller on which counsel to use. The case secretary is the equivalent of an instructing solicitor and will assist prosecuting counsel at the trial.

Eleanor Phillips is Senior Law Clerk at the SFO – a motherly, middle-aged woman with a strong sense of humour. She points out that some cases can be very idiosyncratic in the problems they present. Towards the end of 1993 she had to arrange a hearing involving British defendants who were alleged to have taken a group of Russians for a bumpy financial ride over car-kits. The Russians paid $5 million upfront without ever receiving the kits – in fact there was evidence to show that there never were any kits. She had to arrange for six Russians to be flown to Britain, put into accommodation in Portsmouth and provided with interpreters and expenses, all at the cost of the British taxpayer. She reduced the costs by buying British Airways excursion tickets. She allowed £68 per head for bed, breakfast, food and pocket money, thinking she had been very prudent. At the last minute, though, she found out that five of the Russians wanted to kill the sixth one. The court appearances had to be re-arranged to protect the endangered man.

Once the case secretary had been appointed, Wardle would bring in the information technology people, if the case merited it. After that, the first case conference is held. The agenda for that covers the identification of the principal offences and the suspected main culprits. This gives the investigation a focus. Then the principal witnesses have to be identified as well as the location of documentary or other evidence and how this may be preserved (preservation is another word for seizure). It's important to get after the documentation quickly so that it isn't shredded or otherwise got rid of. All major fraud is document-based. Fraudsters know that, too. Their first reaction, once the whistle has been blown, is to destroy as much as they can. Peter Clowes's people were even shredding documents in the basement of his offices while inspectors were going through his files upstairs.

Then jobs are allocated to the police and SFO personnel. The conference will also set a target period for the completion of the investigation (in complex cases this can be at least two years). There will then be an assessment of what police and SFO resources will be needed to achieve that target. Counsel are appointed very soon after that to advise and help in the direction of a case. Some counsel involved in very big cases sometimes work in-house at Elm Street.

Case conferences will continue throughout the investigation. These review progress and discuss further action. Everyone who works in Elm House sees each other most of the time, so that informal contacts are made regularly. In time a decision will be made about whether the evidence justifies a prosecution. If it's thought the case should go ahead, case controller and case secretary will prepare the case for transfer to the crown court.

The director not infrequently reviews the progress of a case to see 'it doesn't go off the track', to use the words of George Staple, the present director. He sees his job as instilling a strategic discipline into the way the SFO conducts its business.

Information technology is becoming increasingly important. So much corporate activity is recorded on computer disk, and sometimes on hard copy, that the SFO's IT people generally accompany other staff on a raid. They seize any software they think might be important and put it into sealed bags. They do the same with the contents of in-trays and any other hard copy they think relevant.

According to Keith Robson, head of information systems at the SFO, computer-based evidence is a woolly area and there are arguments about its admissibility in court. Two important criteria, however, are used to establish its evidential credibility: it has to be shown that the computer was functioning correctly at the time – this can generally be established with the help of the computer manager working in the building; and the prosecution has to prove that whatever is on a disk was there at the time it was seized. This is an important point because unscrupulous prosecutors might be tempted to plant information on a disk.

There are two procedures for handling both the integrity of the material on disk and the recovery of material from the disk for use in an investigation. The first concerns the way the software is taken, bagged and sealed. There have to be independent witnesses to see that process through. Bagged disks are sent to a data recovery firm which is independent of SFO staff. These firms copy whole disks and can even retrieve material which has been wiped. Two copies are made onto optical disks which, unlike magnetic disks, cannot be tampered with without trace. One goes into a sealed bag, which can be made available to the defence if they want it, and the SFO keeps a working copy. There have been no serious challenges in court yet to computer evidence.

In spite of these procedures, Robson still thinks that it's better from the SFO's point of view that there should be hard copy inside the raided company of what is already on disk, whether it's to be found in the in- and out-trays or in desk drawers. It helps to add credence to the information on disk.

Once an optical is returned, Robson reports to the case team on the area of information it contains. It can then be evaluated on screen by an expert.

Robson has an internal network in the SFO which supports 250 personal computers. This has a duplication and backup system which means that there is virtually no 'downtime'. The network allows various levels of data to be recorded, sorted, cross-referenced or compared. It also has facilities for graphics, mathematical analysis and projections. Robson's department also simplifies cases for jurors. This is a vital function. Evidence is no good to anyone if it is too complex to be comprehensible. No case can ever stand up without the right evidence being presented as clearly and simply as possible.

There is no special magic, then, about the structure of the SFO. Its organisation looks logical, sensible and undramatic – rather like the people who work for it. Yet on the Richter scale of unpopularity it rates very high. For one thing, it is feared, not in the sense that the Fraud Squad is feared (there is a grudging respect for the boys at Richbell Place, partly because the Squad has been around so long, like an old friend), but because it is new, excessively vigorous, high-profile and at times desperately bad at what it does. It is also invasive and intrusive. When the SFO goes into action on a really big fraud case, the country knows about it within minutes. Cameras pick up bankers and company directors being hauled in for questioning. Stern-faced police look as if they are attending some grim incident from the holocaust. The City of London shudders because it's a club of people who, by social background and education, resent being treated like common criminals. Merchant bankers, particularly, dislike being questioned about the way they conduct their business because most of their business has always been done behind closed doors. Old traditions are suddenly broken and old school ties count for nothing. Everything about the SFO, in other words, is offensive to good taste.

The SFO is also feared because it is equipped by the Criminal Justice Act of 1987 with powers under Section 2 which give people subject to its use very sweaty palms, even when they have nothing to fear. It's an 'or else' section, which has no comparison with any other power used by the police or government departments: 'If you refuse to answer these questions, or produce these documents, without reasonable excuse, then we will put you inside immediately or fine you or both.' The right to silence, which it abolishes, is seen as one of the most precious democratic safeguards in our legal system.

Most people, therefore, regard Section 2 as the equivalent of Gestapo interrogation under bright lights with an inevitable, brutal ending. For example, an executive walks into an SFO interview room at Elm Street to be confronted by the investigating lawyer and accountant assigned to the case. The lawyer has a pile of documents in front of him and picks one up, with the question: 'Do you recognise this and, if you do, then do you remember signing it?' The accountant picks up an invoice and asks: 'Do you recognise this?'

It can be the beginning of a long and harrowing ordeal during which the interviewee may be presented with hundreds of documents and invoices (and he has seen thousands in his time and has probably signed just as many) about which he has only the vaguest recollection.

Put in those terms, a Section 2 interview sounds like a Kafkaesque nightmare with certain incrimination on waking. Some people who have been through the process have found it puzzling, then disorientating because the questions had no set pattern or structure and were randomly asked. The best interviewers in the police have always looked down their noses at SFO officials when they are in this role. The police ask very simple questions which have been carefully structured.

The purpose of these interviews, which the police are not empowered to conduct, is what the SFO calls 'information-gathering'. They claim, with some justification, that information is not likely to be used against potential defendants; under 10 per cent of all Section 2 interviewees end up in the dock.

Chris Dickson is one of the most senior assistant directors at the SFO, a tousle-haired man in his forties with a relaxed, open manner, who would certainly not match up to this Gestapo image. In fact he doesn't conduct Section 2 interviews, because as a case controller his job is to assess evidence impartially. But there is no reason to suppose that his civilised manner is untypical of the organisation. There are some loose cannons in the SFO, but he is not one of them.

'We only use Section 2,' he explained to me, 'when it's clear that the person won't otherwise want to talk to us or be able to talk to us. It's unashamedly a compelling power, so that people have to come to us. And I suppose in most fraud cases there are people whose involvement is greater than those people who are on the edge of things, people who have sailed close to the wind and don't want to talk to us. And we ring them up and say we want to talk to you and they say they don't want to talk and we say we do and that's when we can compel them to come in.'

He is also open-minded about people who say they would like to have copies of documents shown to them at these interviews so that they can take them home and refresh their memories about their content, why they signed them, who was there and so on.

'Unless there's a particular reason why they shouldn't have copies – people, for example, you're suspicious of who might use them to concoct a defence or to tip off others – we would be very keen they should do that because this is an information-gathering exercise. If they can short-circuit your questions by saying, "I can see what you're getting at, I may have something at home that will shed light on these documents," then we would be perfectly happy for them to have copies and come back later with their conclusions.'

It is clear, though, that a few of the SFO's Section 2 customers have no wish to talk about anything. They suffer from instant Alzheimer's, cannot recognise documents, don't recall dates and have no recollection of anything important or relevant to the investigation. These are the people whom the SFO begins to regard as potential suspects or defendants.

There are other people, mostly professional, who are concerned about breaches of confidence or what could be called breaches of privilege in an investigation who are happy to have Section 2 used against them because it relieves them of any obligation of confidentiality they may have to a client or a friend. Once they are compelled to answer, they are let off the hook.

These interviews, as far as one can gather, are run on a reasonably civilised basis at Elm House. Interviewees can turn up with a professional representative, they can take recordings of the interview or buy a copy from the SFO, they are provided with refreshments, lunch breaks and so on, and can take breaks for consultations with their advisers.

There are, of course, occasions when a man incriminates himself out of his own mouth. Exciting as that may be for the interrogators, it is not the end of the line for the suspect, since Section 2 evidence is not admissible in court unless a witness flatly contradicts it on the stand; the only witness statements normally heard in court are those taken by the police, who have no Section 2 powers.

A little acknowledged part of the usefulness of Section 2 interviews is that they can quite often point investigators to new avenues of inquiry which might not otherwise have come up. Section 2, of course, abolishes the right to silence; given this formidable weapon, which many people see as self-incrimination by statute, it might be asked why all defendants charged with fraud do not end up in prison automatically. Section 2, it would seem, is not as fearsome as many suppose, nor is it used as frequently as they think: 10 per cent is a remarkably low strike rate. And it may very well be that its shelf-life will be limited by the European court on the grounds that no man should be required, under any law, to incriminate himself. What is manifestly obvious, though, is that it has precious little to do with the SFO's most important failures. These were failures of judgement, choice and the system.

5

THE SFO DIRECTORS

When John Wood left the SFO to become DPP in Hong Kong, the organisation was almost two-and-a-half years old. Wood had a great capacity for being immensely pleased with life and the progress of the Office. The whole tenor of his conduct at the SFO was one of bullishness. On the whole, his stewardship had gone well. In the first two years of business Wood achieved a conviction rate of almost 74 per cent which, in the world of major fraud, was not to be sneezed at. At the end of the first year, Wood concluded his first report to the Attorney General with the words: 'I am convinced that, in the massive cases to which I have made reference, thorough investigative work has been undertaken – and in appropriate cases prosecutions have been initiated – at a pace which would hitherto have been impossible.'

This was only partially true, as it depended on what yardstick he was using. Wood had brought the Guinness case with him from the CPS, and at the end of his second report Guinness part 1 was still being heard. In other words, it had been well over two years from investigation to trial. Wood was premature in patting himself on the back.

Once Wood had gone, there was some urgency to appointing a new director. Wood had been a civil servant all his working life; it seems no one else from that area was thought suitable for such a high-profile job. Furthermore, by the standards of the private sector at a comparable level, there was no money in it.

Barbara Mills, who took over in September 1990, was a QC and one of the prosecutors in the first of the Guinness cases in which the chairman of Guinness, Ernest Saunders, Gerald

Ronson, head of Britain's largest private company, Sir Jack Lyons and Tony Parnes, a stockbroker, were found guilty. She was by all accounts a highly proficient silk, earning around £200,000 a year.

One's first impression of her is of a short, rather dumpy woman with an energetic,crisp manner. When I went to see her, she was immaculately dressed in a *café au lait* suit with a brown velvet collar, a floral blouse, a small Rolex watch and crimson nail varnish which had been perfectly applied. Her blonde hair is swept back from a pleasant but plain face adorned by a large pair of angular, rimless glasses. As DPP, she occupies a big corner office at the top of 50 Ludgate Hill in the City, from where she directs a staff of 6,000. She succeeded Sir Allan Green who had to resign precipitately after some difficulty with women in the King's Cross area.

Mrs Mills does not look like trouble, but from the moment she arrived at Elm House she was never out of it. Very rapidly she accumulated an impressive file of press cuttings. Many of these suggested that she threw her weight about too much, while others were supportive, saying she was setting the SFO on a serious footing and giving it a higher profile. She was a figure of controversy and rarely out of the news. By the end of her reign at Elm Street she had probably received more flak than she had dished out. And for people charged with fraud who were found innocent she had become a figure of hate.

It was inevitable that someone with her energy and ambition should attract criticism. As a successful, practising barrister she had been around a bit, doing far more interesting and varied work than she was likely to get at the SFO. She had been a DTI inspector, she had sat on the parole board, she had sat as a recorder, she had been legal assessor to the Medical and Dental Council and a member of the Criminal Injuries Compensation Board. She had done a lot, but she didn't consider it was enough.

'There was one area missing,' she told me, 'and that was actually running and managing things. I never envisaged back in 1990 doing anything but being a barrister and maybe becoming a full-time judge. Nor was I at all bored with the work I was doing. I had done rather specialised work over the last few years, getting more and more into dealing with white-collar fraud and in the last two years before becoming director of the SFO doing almost nothing except Guinness. And then this offer came up rather unexpectedly and it suddenly seemed something extremely interesting. A tremendous change of career and a tremendous challenge. Something which I thought was very exciting, that was why I did it.'

And she never regretted it. The only thing she did miss in her new job was the companionship of the bar. Running the SFO was a very lonely job. However nice people were, there was still some work she had to do entirely on her own, decisions to be taken. She missed going back to chambers in the evening and talking about matters in a totally different way. This was the first sign she had given me that she wasn't an automaton piloted by a microprocessor.

One aspect of her work she immediately appreciated was being able to control her diary. As a busy barrister she was controlled by her cases, something all counsel are at the mercy of. However, as a barrister she had no experience of management as such; she had not controlled a large department in the industrial sense. And the SFO was getting on for being quite large; besides which, it was staffed mostly by civil servants who had a different cast of mind to people who work in the private sector. Typically, Mrs Mills was undaunted by these considerations; doubt is wholly alien to her personality and style.

'There is a sort of work at the bar which calls for management qualities. Managing a fraud case in the widest sense is very much a management job. It's managing all the material which comes in in a very jumbly sort of way, because that's the way frauds evolve. So you've got to put it all together. It's also very much about managing big teams. On top of that if you juggle a large family and a large practice, then you're not a bad manager.'

In fact, what she had at the SFO was a very major fraud practice, as it turned out, with civil service support and a secretariat. Instead of the one or two major cases a year she might have been handling in private practice, she was now in charge of sixty or more. It was perfectly evident, though, that she was more than happy with her management style at Elm House. There was a never a flicker of self-doubt because, I suspect, that is one thing Mrs Mills has never suffered from. The outer persona of the neat power dresser is a reflection of the inner person: together, organised and with an uncompromising self-assurance that is disconcerting.

The SFO probably needed a pretty tough personality to manage it. What Mrs Mills found when she got there was an atypical government department, not a bit like the rest of Whitehall. Although she was conscious that she came from the private sector, and there was a danger of a culture clash, she claims that it didn't work out like that.

'In the first place it was very new, so it hadn't had time to develop a culture of its own. Then there were three quite separate groups of people, only a small number of whom fitted the civil service mould. You had high-grade civil service lawyers. Then there were accountants, many of whom were on secondment from the private sector. And finally you had the police. So it wasn't a classic government department at all. But I suppose it was a bit of a culture shock both ways. I hadn't been brought up in the school of writing minutes and putting down everything you've said. That's very much not the tradition of the bar, where you work a lot on the telephone and agree things verbally. You wouldn't bother to note it because you know each other and you're working in a small environment with a few people. And it took me a while to realise that you had to minute everything. But that's one of the things that's impressive about the civil service. It all goes down and then it's filed away. But if you ever want to find out what was said or agreed five years later, there it is and, what's more, they can find it.'

Mrs Mills then exhibited some slight concern – uncharacteristic, I imagine – about her appointment. Her arrival at Elm Street coincided within a few weeks with the departure of one of the deputy directors Michael Chance. It seems clear that she is mildly embarrassed about the coincidence, as if she were responsible for his removal. There was a story put about by the detractors of the SFO that Chance had somehow blotted his copybook, and that Mrs Mills got rid of him.

She is anxious to dispel that impression. 'He left because of a manpower audit which decided the SFO didn't need two deputy directors. And that decision was taken before I arrived. That was an additional hazard of coming into a new organisation where one didn't know much about the structure. And I certainly didn't know much about Whitehall and Westminster and all the things that go with being head of a department.'

But Mrs Mills knew what she wanted. She wanted to become the first lady of fraud, feared by anyone contemplating putting their hand in the till. With demonic energy and impatience to drive her, that's exactly what she did. It is said that she used to go out on dawn raids, on one occasion armed with an axe – stories she dismisses with amused contempt. The truth is much more likely to be that she would have *loved* to go on dawn raids but as director it was out of the question. Instead, she encouraged the SFO to be pro-active. Scarcely a week passed without raids, arrests and charges. Her critics called it a 'scattergun approach': throw everything at the defendants in the hope that something will stick.

Her judgement could be astonishingly poor. If you want to be fair to investors and protect their interests, the last thing you do is raid the headquarters of the companies they've invested in accompanied by the media. It has a dreadful effect on the share price. It happened with Polly Peck and with Control Securities. When the DTI do that sort of thing using their section 447 powers, no one ever hears about the raids because they are conducted in secrecy. The DTI, like the Fraud Squad, understands what damage can be done to a company by such overt investigation, but at Elm Place the suspects came first and investors second. The SFO could have achieved their object without throwing their weight around like televised wrestlers; it is perfectly possible to raid premises without the media knowing.

But the SFO seems to revel in the publicity, actively relishing the razzmatazz. If the raid is on a company, the results are quite predictable: people will immediately think the company is in bad financial trouble. If an arrest is at dawn in the full glare of publicity, the results are also predictable: people will think that the arrested person is probably guilty. There is, after all, no smoke without fire, or so the public believes.

Mrs Mills did nothing to curb this hyperactivity. She says that she would never countenance that kind of thing. Yet it persisted throughout her stewardship of the SFO. Either her writ didn't run throughout Elm Street or, if it did, no one was inclined to take any notice. This is what she is criticised for more than anything else. Counsel see the SFO director as the person who should curb the enthusiasms of the police. At the SFO the enthusiasms of the police *and* the lawyers needed attention.

'I was dead against publicity for arrests,' she insists. 'I was dead against leaks. I put out some very ferocious memos when there were suggestions of leaks. I thoroughly deplore that kind of conduct. But the press have their ways of finding these things out.'

Not only did the SFO get a much higher profile from the moment Mrs Mills arrived, but she became for a considerable time more important than the organisation. She spoke a lot in public and was frequently quoted in the media. The SFO, she points out, never had a press office until she arrived. John Wood never had one, which seems astonishing, nor did Mrs Mills ask for one, but when she arrived there was one in place. That made the organisation more accessible to the media and, by inference, she became quotable because she was a woman with one of the most important jobs in crime. She says she doesn't believe in the cult of the personality, only the organisation, but it took her a long time to persuade the media to get the balance right.

'I was also very inexperienced in dealing with the press in those days. I was amazed at the interest in me and the SFO – it started in that order. By the end I got it round to being the SFO with me behind it. There was another factor that helped to bring the SFO into the limelight. It was just at the end of the Guinness case. Fraud used to be a very boring subject, people didn't really report it, but the Guinness case had a lot of interest in it – interesting personalities, interesting problems and so on. Fraud as a topic moved up the interest agenda. When that happens it gets more publicity and it feeds on itself.'

What also moved up the interest agenda were the cases that were coming into court and the success rate the SFO could claim for its prosecutions. What starts as an investigation under one director, ends up as a trial under another. It is not always easy to separate who was responsible for what. It may fairly be claimed that two major trials were down to Mrs Mills. One was Guinness 2, in which the judge ruled that the burden of defending himself had affected Roger Seelig's health so badly that the trial could not continue. Seelig was linked with Spens and the Crown decided not to proceed against Spens either. It also decided to drop all charges against David Mayhew, a partner in the broking firm Cazenove. But it decided to continue with the prosecution of Thomas Ward, an American lawyer who had been a director of Guinness, and it lost.

There is a cast of mind in the SFO, and Mrs Mills was no doubt partly responsible for it, which cannot bear to lose a case. Innocence is not a possibility they consider. Even when a man is found not guilty, in the eyes of the SFO he is still a fraudster and will probably be so until his dying day. When the SFO lost Seelig and Spens, there was a great tide of resentment against Seelig for not being healthy enough to see his trial through to its conclusion. They felt they had been cheated.

Not Mrs Mills, though. 'I don't think you would call that losing, in the sense that Seelig had a very obvious health problem at that stage. I used to go down to Southwark crown court a certain amount to see what was going on and if you get the sort of reports we were getting, then you've got to take it seriously. I don't take that as a loss. Lord Spens was more or less a consequential decision on Seelig.'

Very well, Mrs Mills was cheated, but it still goes down on the SFO's record. So, too, does County NatWest/Blue Arrow which the SFO comprehensively lost in the most expensive fraud trial in Britain – £40 million of taxpayers' money went up in smoke in a court case which lasted a staggering twelve months (and that does not include the time taken later for appeals). George Staple, who succeeded Mrs Mills, mentioned it in his report for that year, though he was not responsible for Blue Arrow in any shape or form; Mrs Mills was.

Writing of that disaster, Staple said somewhat plaintively that the prosecution called ninety-two witnesses. That was a good start to getting everyone muddled, especially judge and jury. An overall breakdown of the time taken up by the trial indicates that the prosecution took up 25 per cent, compared with 75 per cent taken up by the defence. It can only be said, if Staple was complaining about time-wasting, that the defence used their time to far greater effect than the prosecution, because everyone got off.

The conviction rate for that year was 66 per cent; for the previous year (for which Mrs Mills was responsible for only six months), it was 63 per cent. It does not now look likely that any director will ever again achieve the success rate of John Wood.

In Mrs Mills's view this does not mean that SFO staff weren't up to it in her day. 'People on the outside who say that the in-house government lawyers couldn't survive in the private sector are talking absolute rubbish. I've been on both sides and I think there are a lot of excellent lawyers in the SFO, very good, very keen, doing extremely difficult jobs against the best of civil/criminal solicitors. A lot of the big civil City firms who used to turn up their noses at crime suddenly realised that this was a new world and so they got involved. They're tough litigators and they brought those attitudes to the new world they'd discovered.'

But something went wrong with the prosecution's tactics in her day. Perhaps the up-dated, slicker City solicitors, who have some of the best brains in the business, were too much for her in-house teams and the counsel she hired from outside. When the SFO charged people, they did so with abandon, throwing indictments around like confetti. 'That is something you can never get right,' she complains cheerfully. 'If you go the whole way, you're accused of wasting time and money. If you cut back on the indictments, you're told you're cutting corners.'

Some of the best leading counsel say the SFO can't afford the top QCs any more and argue that is why the people at Elm House are losing more than they're winning, especially in the eye-catching big cases where the critics are always waiting for them to slip up.

Mrs Mills looks a little shifty on the question of money and budgets. 'It's more of a buyer's market now when it comes to counsel,' she says unconvincingly. Then she turns swiftly from the problem to a short homily on the virtues of domestic economy. 'Cases can be a bottomless pit, you can go on throwing resources at them forever. I think it's a very good discipline to work within the budgets you've been allocated.'

In fact, when Mrs Mills prosecuted in the Guinness case she was very well paid for it. When she arrived at Elm Street, however, she decided to cut back on counsel's fees. George Staple has inherited a budgetary system which is little short of absurd: leading counsel prosecuting for the SFO in big cases will be paid less than leading counsel appearing for a defendant on legal aid (see Chapter 10). The SFO cannot hope to win the very big cases, on which its reputation and prestige rest, if it cannot employ the best people. One clerk in chambers told me: 'Sometimes I will be having a drink with my colleagues, when we hear that Mr So-and-so has been appointed to lead an SFO prosecution and all our eyebrows go up. That's what happens when you can't afford to buy the right people.'

When Mrs Mills starts to talk about budgetary disciplines, one knows that she has become a creature of government. It is Whitehall-speak, the kind of thing one would expect to hear from the permanent secretary of the Department of Health. When she talks about her interest in management, she is simply signalling that she has joined the massed ranks of civil servants who talk about management objectives and targets.

That gives a clue to what Mrs Mills is about professionally. From the moment she joined the SFO, she became a career civil servant. She agreed with what she was given, she never complained and she said things the government wanted to hear. She supports the abolition of the right to silence and the right to trial by jury and she has little time for Magna Carta which, one suspects, is not modern enough for someone who likes to think she is a thoroughly modern woman. The financial guideline by which the SFO decides to accept or reject a case was increased during July 1990 from £1 million to £2 million. Mrs Mills went a good deal further: she raised it to £5 million. It gave the SFO star status in the world of fraud and by inference increased her own prestige.

She has a habit of shooting from the hip, and an opinion on some things she has no real knowledge or experience of. For example, not so long ago she opined that the roles of chairman and chief executive in a company should be separated and not combined. She had in mind, of course, the danger of one man who can dominate a board completely (no doubt with Robert Maxwell as her example) and dictate what it should do. Separating the two functions is not really an answer to the problem. A strong chairman will dominate a board, just as a determined chief executive will. Very rarely do they work as equals. Boards of directors don't behave like management textbooks. One has a feeling, though, that Mrs Mills expects them to; it would fit her neat and tidy methodology.

When Sir Allan Green had to step down as DPP, she seemed the obvious choice to replace him. She also became the obvious target for outfits like the Metropolitan Police Federation, the policemen's trade union, which sees her management of the Crown Prosecution Service as disastrous. In 1992, the CPS apparently dropped 190,000 cases the police thought they could win. Mrs Mills suffered from no such inhibitions at the SFO, where money was no object if a case had a high profile. She is beginning to learn that government budgetary constraints can backfire. Cautioning suspects is no substitute for putting them on trial, but the DPP is short of money and the Treasury won't give her any more. But Mrs Mills doesn't complain, she toes the line, an obedient servant of government. She doesn't want to be a high court judge. She is well into her third year of her five-year contract as DPP. The question is, where does she go next? She believes she has been very lucky to move around as quickly as she has.

Her husband, John Mills, whom she met at Oxford, was fired from his job as deputy director of the London Docklands Development Corporation when it was discovered that his import company had sold copper alloy jewellery to Woolworth in the guise of gold plate. 'Law Job for Wife of Gold Con-Man', one tabloid said. On another occasion, he forgot to pay business rates.

But she has been very loyal to him, a good wife, just as it would appear she has always been a good mother, even though her pride in her management skills shines through in this very personal side of her life. 'Nobody has ever been able to say of me,' she once said, 'that I could not do something because of my children.' Or of her husband. It would be unkind to say that she was the woman who was in the right place at the right time. Nevertheless, it is true that there were men who were equally in the right place at the right time, but who didn't want either job.

George Staple, the third and current director of the SFO, does not look as though he were tailor-made for the job. He came from the well-known firm of solicitors, Clifford Chance, where he was the partner in charge of litigation, a very different business from dealing with fraud. He also came to a department which was far removed from the private sector in culture, outlook and operation: the civil service is its own creature and can tame any outsider.

Staple has the manners and deportment of a gentleman. Educated at Haileybury, he walked straight out of school into a solicitor's office and that is the way it has remained. He has, though, considerable experience of the City: legal assessor for the Disciplinary Committee of the Stock Exchange; twice a DTI inspector (Consolidated Gold Fields and the Aldermanbury Trust); a chairman of the Authorisation and Disciplinary Tribunals of the Securities Association; and a member of the Securities and Futures Authority.

All those jobs would have given him insights into how the City conducts its business, as well as how it misbehaves. He has the *gravitas* for the job. He looks responsible, dresses soberly and has a tall, spare frame. Though now fifty-five, he has suffered no loss to a generous thatch of fair hair, in spite of being enmeshed in one row after another at the SFO, though there have been times when he has shown signs of wear and tear. He is attractive to women, smiles easily, but his manner lacks steel.

He came to the SFO in March of 1992 and his reasons for doing so are singularly unconvincing. He was abandoning a salary of around £250,000 for a grade 2 civil service job at £84,000 a year and a five-year contract. He claims that his old job was becoming repetitive after thirty years (most jobs are a little like that). He also thinks (and we have heard this one before) that having taken a good deal out of the private sector, he ought to put something back into the public sector. A noble sentiment, but there is generally more to these things than meets the eye. While it's true that he managed to salt away something while he was a practising solicitor so that he could afford to do his present job, it comes as a surprise to learn that he saw the post advertised in the press and applied for it. It had not been easy to fill. When John Wood left the job was hawked around the Inns of Court for some time before Barbara Mills took the bait.

Barbara Mills, however, is extremely ambitious, while it's said that the driving force in the Staple family is George's wife, Olivia, who would rather enjoy being Lady Staple. In a job like the SFO, Staple is virtually guaranteed a knighthood, provided he doesn't disgrace himself or prove an embarrassment to the government.

His job, as he describes it, is 'part lawyer, part administrator and part Sir Humphrey' – in other words relating in a political sense to the Attorney General. Staple admits that he rather enjoys this aspect of the job. The SFO is approximately the same size as the litigation department in Clifford Chance, but the paperwork is enormous. He works a ten-hour day, does a huge amount of case-related reading and produces a lot of articles and speeches.

He has not had a happy run. Major fraud is no longer something the public and parliament are prepared to keep on the back burner. The heat has been turned up and so has media interest. When the SFO loses a case, the press are snapping at Staple's heels, asking what went wrong, calling for inquiries, questioning the competence of the people at Elm Street.

Unlike Mills, Staple does not want a high profile, but since he has been at the SFO he's had no choice in the matter. Asil Nadir has given him one headache after another, particularly over the matter of 'privileged' documents seized by the SFO, some of which were correspondence between Nadir and his solicitors. Five bags of correspondence were taken by the SFO in two raids in 1990 – one on Polly Peck International, the company controlled by Nadir, and the other on Nadir's Mayfair home.

The bags contained correspondence which Vizards, Nadir's lawyers, complained at the time were covered by privilege. The SFO initially contested the status of the documents but an independent barrister was later called in who supported Nadir's solicitors. Much good it did Nadir. The SFO twice circulated copies of the documents it was entitled neither to look at nor to distribute. They were passed to the SFO's prosecuting lawyers and to the Polly Peck administrators. In September 1993, George Staple told me the bags had not been touched after the barrister had inspected their contents and that was the end of the matter. Three months earlier, the Attorney General had told the House of Commons the same thing. But as Sir Nicholas Lyell was obliged to tell the Commons early in December, he had misled the House. To be exact, he said his statement that the documents were not circulated was 'incomplete' and 'misleading' – two words calculated to give the impression that nothing much had gone awry. But it had. The SFO cannot exist without documents, they are its bread and butter. But they are also vital to the defence.

Peter Knight, a partner at Vizards, wrote to Staple in July

1993 – a month after Sir Nicholas had 'misled' the Commons – suggesting that 'no workable system existed' in the SFO for handling privileged documents. This, apparently, activated Staple to institute a 'detailed enquiry' within the SFO to find out what had happened to the papers.

Almost six months later (they pace themselves well at Elm Street), Staple was able to report to Peter Knight that 'copies of certain privileged documents were in error circulated to the prosecution on two occasions. The SFO very much regrets this incident and the fact that earlier enquiries failed to establish the true position. The reason is being pursued further. Appropriate steps have been taken to ensure there is no repetition.'

Stung by Knight's comment that 'no workable system existed' in the SFO for handling privileged documents, Staple said 'no further evidence has come to light to substantiate any of the other allegations which have been made about the SFO's handling of Mr Nadir's case.'

Things, though, were rather worse than they appeared. It's the timing that's important. The cover-up had been going on for two-and-a-half years. Sir Nicholas told the House: 'I regret that the fact that copies of privileged documents had been circulated was not acknowledged by the then case controller [the Nadir case controller at that time was Lorna Harris, who moved to the private sector in 1993] to Mr Nadir's solicitor, and that no attempt was made to retrieve them until December 1991, despite Vizards' frequently expressed concern about the matter and the fact that the then case controller appears to have recognised *at least by January 1991* [my italics] that copies of potentially privileged documents had been circulated.'

Did Lorna Harris reveal these facts to Staple when questions were being asked about the bags of correspondence early in 1993? Did she cover them up? Did Staple know what had happened, but resolutely refuse to reveal them in order to protect an employee? It scarcely matters, though in the interests of fact (I would not be as bold as to say truth) it would be interesting to know, because any light shed on the operation and management of a department such as the SFO might help others to arrange matters better in the future.

The harsh fact is that Staple was responsible for the management, direction and policy of the SFO when this astonishing blunder took place. He knew how sensitive the Nadir business was; indeed he was at the helm of the SFO when Nadir fled the country and made a public laughing stock out of the fraudbusters. Anything touching on Nadir was as sensitive as 100 lbs of Semtex attached to a seven-second fuse, but with remarkable insensitivity for an important manager in charge of an increasingly accident-prone organisation, he took no steps to defuse the time-bomb.

By that time, though, Staple was probably well under the thumb of his civil servants; not just that, he had become one of them. Civil servants work under the umbrella of the Official Secrets Act, which can be as large and as impermeable as anyone wants it to be. Answers are obfuscated, ministers are protective, parliament and the public are kept in the dark. For several years, for example, there were dark mutterings about the behaviour and ethics of Mrs Harris, who has been described by different counsel as 'hysterical and incompetent'. It was Mrs Harris who was involved in the circulation of Nadir's privileged documents. Staple, who must have been well aware of the general dissatisfaction with Mrs Harris, said that her departure from the SFO in the autumn of 1993 was at 'her request'. She departed for the private sector, to APACS (the Association of Payment Clearing Services), jointly owned by banks and building societies, where she is head of the fraud prevention unit (plastic card fraud mainly). Staple dressed up the move as a secondment. Since then, he has become noticeably protective of the SFO.

The embarrassment over these revelations of incompetence in the Nadir case followed only a few days after the fiasco over the Roger Levitt trial, an episode not as lingering as Nadir for persistent pain but one which, in many ways, was even more damaging. While people are slowly becoming anaesthetised to the Nadir circus, the media and everyone who followed the affair could not have been blamed for expecting a heavy sentence on Levitt. The case had a high profile. Freddie Forsyth, the thriller writer, had lost a packet at Levitt's hands and complained publicly about it; and the film director, Michael Winner, had written with asperity about the 'financial adviser'. The charges against Levitt were extremely serious, but Staple somehow managed to turn an open-and-shut case into a triumph for the self-styled financier. Minutes after his sentence of 180 hours' community service, Levitt's moustachioed face could be seen beaming triumphantly and insolently from every front page. And the champagne he was drinking was not supermaket bubbly, but Dom Perignon.

Levitt had managed to pile up debts of £34 million. When his group collapsed four years ago it left some fifty investors with losses of between £2 to £3 million and it owed other creditors, mainly banks and insurance companies, more than £30 million. The SFO investigation lasted nearly three years before it came to court.

In the preparatory hearings in February 1993, the judge had ruled that the twenty-one counts the SFO wanted to bring against Levitt would have to be split up, otherwise the trial would become unmanageable. Staple then decided to go for a charge of fraudulent trading, which carried a maximum potential sentence of seven years in prison. The charge included the misappropriation of clients' funds which had been used to prop up a group that was hopelessly in debt for millions; and the deceptions Levitt had used to squeeze money out of the banks for the same purpose. These were covered by the Companies Act charge of fraudulent trading.

But as too often in the SFO's short and flawed life, there had been a grave miscalculation. In May 1993, in another preparatory hearing before Mr Justice Laws, the defence argued that other allegations against Levitt, such as lying to institutions to raise money, were not part of the fraudulent trading charge. If that were the case, they could not be raised by the prosecution at the trial.

The judge accepted the argument. So did the SFO, otherwise it would have gone to appeal, as it was entitled to do. That was a major strategic blunder because an enormous chunk of very damaging evidence simply dropped out of the trial. It could not be used.

What happened during the actual trial in November is shrouded in secrecy. David Cocks QC, prosecuting for the SFO, was not prepared to acknowledge my fax asking for a briefing as to what had happened – a polite way of asking how the prosecution had managed to cock up the case. And Jonathan Goldberg, Levitt's QC, was equally uncommunicative. Cocks was so furious about Mr Justice Laws's decision that he wrote an article in *The Times* saying that many judges were not up to trying serious fraud, an obvious swipe at Judge Laws. Cocks was badly piqued. Yet he must have had some idea what to expect from Laws and Goldberg.

At a hearing in judge's chambers on 22 November 1993, which was six days before Judge Laws handed out his extraordinary sentence on Levitt, Cocks and Goldberg appeared before him. By way of preamble, Goldberg explained to the Judge that he was appearing for a very strong-willed and determined individual and that he (Goldberg) had less influence than was perhaps normally the case.

'All efforts hitherto,' Mr Goldberg continued, 'to find a way of shortening this case have foundered, as you know, mainly on the rock of Mr Levitt refusing to acknowledge any wrong doing. However, the events of the last weekend may mark a turning point which, if not seized, we fear will not come again.'

Mr Goldberg then referred the judge to the Terry Ramsden case which had been reported in Saturday's papers. The Judge was not sure that he had seen the report. Mr Goldberg helpfully refreshed his memory. 'In that case,' counsel went on, 'a very experienced Old Bailey judge, Judge Pownall QC, felt able to pass a suspended prison sentence in a major Serious Fraud Office prosecution arising out of the solicitation of some £90 million in investments by false representation.

'Having read that in the papers, Mr Levitt telephoned my instructing solicitors and in due course myself. As a result of the instructions he gave Miss Wass (Goldberg's junior) and I over the weekend, I had a discussion with Mr Cocks this morning which was confirmed in writing. What I said to him was this and I would like to tell you if I may, and tell you his response.'

Goldberg asked Cocks whether he would accept a guilty plea from Levitt to Count 1 on the basis of an admission to Fimbra solely. Fimbra was the regulatory body responsible for companies like Levitt's and Count 1 referred to deceiving it about the company's financial solvency. He also proposed to Cocks and Staple that all other outstanding charges and indictments whatsoever be not proceeded with thereafter.

And then we come to the crux of the matter. Goldberg then put it to Cocks in the letter that if Cocks was instructed (i.e. by the SFO) to accept such a plea, that he was then instructed to seek an indication from the learned judge *on sentence* (my italics) and Mr Levitt would then decide what do do.

Nothing could have been plainer than that. Goldberg then went on: 'Mr Cocks, as I understand it, took all the necessary instructions at the appropriately high level [it was in fact Staple, because Cocks said so in chambers], and he has been kind enough to come back to me in writing, in fact.'

What Cocks said was that the prosecution accepted the guilty plea to the Fimbra charge and was prepared to drop all the other charges. Goldberg then went on to elaborate for the judge the basis of Levitt's plea. It was based, he said, on section 200 of the Financial Services Act, 1986.

> *Mr Justice Laws*: It is misleading a regulatory authority.

> *Mr Goldberg*: Yes. 'False and misleading statements of or in connection with any application under this Act', which means when an inspector comes in, in this context, 'or the purported compliance with any requirement imposed on him under this Act', which means your duty as a Fimbra registered person to tell the truth to the inspector.

> *Mr Justice Laws*: What is the maximum penalty on trial on indictment?

> *Mr Goldberg*: 205, to imprisonment for a term not

exceeding two years or to a fine or both. So in short, two years.

Cocks and Staple thought it was seven years.

Goldberg then went on to outline what the shape of his plea in mitigation would be. It would, of course, be much longer in court and Goldberg could be guaranteed to make the most of every favourable fact. There was, for example, Levitt's young daughter who had a severe psychiatric problem connected with her father's arrest. Consequently, there were problems for her at school. There was the hounding by the press. The family had suffered a lot and the case had been hanging over their heads for three years, since December 1990. Levitt was an undischarged bankrupt who had been unable to obtain any work for a long time. It was a dress rehearsal for what would need a full orchestra and a very strong violin section.

Mr Justice Laws then called a short adjournment while he considered what kind of sentence he would hand out to Levitt if he pleaded guilty to the single charge of deceiving Fimbra. On his return this is what he said:

I have considered with care what Mr Goldberg has said to me and I am able to indicate, subject to what I will say in a minute, that on the specific basis of the prospective plea outlined to me – namely that there will be an admission of the deceptions of Fimbra, but no admission of any other part of the case – *I would not pass an immediate sentence* (my italics).

I should make it clear that in saying that, as I suppose is obvious, I am saying nothing whatever about other penalties which I might think appropriate to pass [such as disqualifying Levitt from holding directorships]. Also, it is subject to me being persuaded in open court that the plea, if offered, is a proper one on the facts of the case. Also, I hope it goes without saying that I am giving no indication of any kind as to what would be a possible sentencing outcome on any other basis, such as if the case continued. Nor, obviously, am I saying anything about the position in due course of any of the other defendants.

That could have left no one present in chambers – Cocks, Goldberg and several other barristers who had clients involved in the case – in any doubt about the judge's intentions as far as Levitt was concerned. Of course, Levitt seized the offer with both hands.

The SFO had been painted into a corner entirely through their own fault. They should not have accepted the Fimbra plea, because that was conditional on all other charges being dropped. They had nothing to fall back on. The man whom the public had every right to assume was about to spend several years in prison was going to walk free with a nugatory sentence.

What happened next, though, was a furious row about the way Goldberg went about the plea of mitigation in court. Goldberg painted a picture of Levitt the businessman which no one recognised. Levitt, he told the court, had put £22.5 million of his own money into the company in a last-ditch effort to prop it up. A dishonest man, Goldberg argued, would have been doing the reverse: he would have been taking money out. What Goldberg did not say was that virtually all this money was borrowed or obtained by deception. It certainly wasn't Levitt's own.

The prosecution was placed in the absurd position of not being able to use any of that evidence because they had agreed to drop it during an earlier, preparatory hearing. That didn't worry Goldberg. He described a man who was prepared to bankrupt himself in order to save his firm and 450 jobs.

Mr Justice Laws was very angry. He criticised Goldberg's professional conduct and accused him of 'gravely mis-representing the true facts about the way Levitt came by his funds' and of 'openly subverting' an earlier ruling the judge had made.

'The impression was that they [the funds] were raised honestly, that was precisely the impression given. He [Goldberg] says again and again it was Levitt's own money. It amounts to forensic myopia of the highest terms,' the judge said in what was an extraordinary rebuke by a judge to leading counsel during the course of a trial.

After Goldberg's speech, which followed a three-day address to the jury by the Crown, David Cocks asked the judge to abort the trial. He argued that defence counsel's remarks had 'wholly subverted' the hearing. But the judge rejected the application for a new trial. The Attorney General said the case could not be referred to the court of appeal as there were no grounds for referral. Jonathan Goldberg was reported to the Bar Council by Cocks for his conduct, but at the time of writing the case is still under consideration.

Twelve days later Cocks had his say in *The Times*. If the intention was to vindicate himself and George Staple, then he failed. Much of his criticism was aimed quite correctly at those judges who were not up to handling major fraud trials. But he carefully avoided any discussion of where the prosecution had gone wrong in the Levitt case. It was a shocking cock-up right at the top of the SFO. If George Staple and the people at Elm Street couldn't put Levitt away with the mass of evidence at their disposal, then it raises very large question marks over the competence of the organisation. The SFO tried to pass off as a good result the 180 hours' community service that Levitt was 'sentenced' to. The real result, though, was for Levitt. While he walked out of court virtually a free man on 10 January 1994, it was also convenient for Cocks as well because it enabled him to appear for the defence, later that month, in a grain fraud case on which it was rumoured that his brief fee was around £75,000.

The difficulty about life in the fast lane is that if you make a mistake, people will notice. If you make a lot of mistakes, they may well want you taken off the road. George Staple's stewardship of the SFO is suspect, because in very important cases the people on Elm Street have a dreadful capacity for getting it wrong. From the start of the Levitt investigation, to bringing the case to trial, took three years at a cost of £1.4 million. That was 5.5 per cent of the SFO's annual budget, an exorbitant charge for a failure.

Not only is George Staple in the fast lane, he also has a

habit of running into cones. Ten days after the Levitt fiasco, a writ was issued in the Chancery division of the high court which named Staple in his former job at Clifford Chance. It was the last thing a man in his position needed. And now that the case is in the open there is no question of hushing it up, nothing the establishment can do to sweep it under the carpet.

The writ alleges that Staple and another solicitor were negligent in the way they handled the will of the London property man, Eric Hopton, who died in 1991, aged seventy-two, after a heart attack. Negligence is something no solicitor wants to be confronted with, because it challenges his professional competence, and raises the question of whether he can have had a motive for acting negligently.

While Staple is not named as a defendant, his name appears sufficiently frequently in the Statement of Claim to bring his integrity into doubt if the case is proved. The plaintiff is Rona, Lady Delves Broughton, whose father-in-law, Sir Jock Delves Broughton, was acquitted of murdering the Earl of Erroll in Kenya fifty-three years ago. Erroll was a professional adulterer of charm and good looks who had hopped one bed too far. So much for background notoriety.

There are two aspects to Lady Delves Broughton's case. The first thing that has to be established is that Staple was the solicitor for Hopton *in all matters* except the dead man's will. Staple knew Hopton well and was a friend. He was also an executor of the Hopton estate and a trustee. The other Clifford Chance solicitor involved in the writ, and who is a defendant, is David Bowyer. It was Bowyer who was charged with drawing up Hopton's will and carrying out the dead man's wishes.

That was where the two solicitors stood in relation to each other professionally. Hopton was a close friend of the Broughtons; he had been at Eton with Sir Evelyn Delves Broughton, Rona's husband, who died early in 1993. Hopton's assets were all tied up in the Belgravia Property Company which owned much of Chesham Place, an 'exclusive' address off Sloane Street in Knightsbridge. The investment, as it turned out, was extraordinarily shrewd.

When Hopton died it was worth around £50 million. Staple had executed a declaration of trust in Hopton's shares, identifying Hopton as the beneficial owner. The two men clearly had a close relationship and, according to Lady Delves Broughton, Staple was one of the few people Hopton trusted.

In 1984, David Bowyer prepared the 'first will' for Hopton. Rona Delves Broughton did not receive a mention. Then, on March 1st, 1990, things allegedly began to go badly wrong between Hopton and his lawyers. Hopton indicated to Bowyer that it might be necessary to reconsider much of the first will. He invited Bowyer to discuss matters but Bowyer didn't bother to seek his client's instructions. Later that month, Clifford Chance accepted Hopton's instructions on the new will and the settlements it contained. Towards the end of March, though, Hopton had a major heart attack and the prognosis for his recovery was poor. Around the end of the month, so the writ alleges, both Bowyer and Staple knew about the heart attack, and that the outlook wasn't good. From these facts, so the allegations go, George Staple could have deduced that Hopton's health was such that Bowyer should have acted rapidly in relation to the new will.

Almost four months later, in the first week of July, Hopton's nephew, Christopher, told Bowyer that his uncle wanted to review his first will, but Bowyer said he would be away on a three-month sabbatical from the beginning of August. Later that day, Christopher repeated his uncle's message to Bowyer who, so the writ says, responded the next day by sending his client copies of the first will.

If people wonder at this stage of the saga whether anyone knew or cared about what they were doing, they may be forgiven for doing so. Here was a man who had been struck down by a major heart attack and who had been seriously ill for four months and the most his lawyer could do – after repeated requests – was to dust off some copies of the first will and send them round. Four days after this startling burst of activity – it was by now 9 July – Christopher Hopton told Bowyer that his uncle wanted to make a number of changes in relation to the legacies in the first will. Nine days were allowed to elapse at the slumbering offices of Clifford Chance before Bowyer saw fit to see Hopton in the presence of his nephew.

The most important change Hopton wanted to make to the will was to leave Rona Delves Broughton £1 million or 500 shares in the Belgravia Property Company. By 22 July, the writ alleges, Hopton's health was so bad that Bowyer should have taken Hopton's instructions and carried them out. But that was asking too much. George Staple had begun a sabbatical in July and Bowyer was about to go on one for three months. The result was that the two men did not get together until 3 or 4 November, when they discussed Hopton's wishes.

Somehow, by December 5th, Bowyer had managed to draft a new will. Five days later, so it is alleged, Hopton told Bowyer that he wanted to leave his goods and chattels to Rona Broughton as well as the £1 million. Bowyer assured Hopton, according to the statement of claim, that if Hopton died before the new will had been executed, then effect would be given to Hopton's instructions through his nephews, Christopher and Nicholas.

Hopton died exactly a month later on January 10th, 1991. No new will or trusts had been executed. Around that date, according to the writ, Bowyer told Christopher Hopton that he was under no legal obligation to effect Hopton's wishes. This was quite contrary to what had been said to Hopton by Bowyer a month earlier. Suddenly the goal posts had been moved.

Then, on March 1st, Rona Delves Broughton telephoned Bowyer after she had received a call from Nigel Dempster of the *Daily Mail* asking her about the provisions Hopton had made for her in his will. Bowyer said that George Staple was expert at dealing with the press. On the same day Staple phoned Rona Delves Broughton, which gave her an opportunity to ask whether she had been left anything. Staple avoided the question.

It may be argued that whatever Staple did in an earlier part of his career – a year earlier, in fact – has nothing to do with his competence as director of the SFO. That, of course, is very much in doubt. What Staple did at Clifford Chance was, allegedly, to exhibit negligence of the gravest kind towards his friend and client, whose interests ought to have come first. As far as conduct goes, it is far from unique in the legal profession but it can only bring a good deal of discredit on Staple who does, after all, occupy a position of considerable public importance.

He should have stood down immediately because there was more embarrassment to come and he was well aware of it. The second writ came only a fortnight after the one from Rona Delves Broughton. It was the same complaint, but from a different source, the plaintiff this time being a great-nephew of Hopton, who also alleged negligence. He was to have been a beneficiary under the Hopton will, but because Staple and Bowyer allegedly dragged their feet he didn't get a penny.

Much of this may seem academic. Neither case has yet to come to court and Clifford Chance is contesting the allegations. But when the professional conduct of a public figure responsible for the prosecution of serious fraud is called into question it can legitimately be asked if his credibility and image are not at risk. The Serious Fraud Office is held in low public and professional esteem as it is; the last thing it needs is a director whose integrity is in question. It does need a director who can impose on his staff proper standards of operational conduct and ensure that there is no deviation from those standards. George Staple's shortcomings in this regard are demonstrated in his handling of the case of Michael Ward.

Ward, the former chairman of European Leisure, stands charged with share ramping. He is a tall, affable man, aged forty-six, from a privileged background. Educated at Charterhouse and Queens' College, Cambridge, he is an accountant by training who went on to be a director of the merchant bank, Samuel Montagu and S.G. Warburg. When Ward decided to branch out for himself, he had no difficulty in doing so, making a series of rapid acquisitions which turned his company into one of the largest entertainment groups in Britain. It owned the Hippodrome, which Ward bought from Peter Stringfellow for £7 million, the Camden Palace and a string of bars, clubs and discos in Paris and Majorca. He lives in one of those enormously expensive houses in Belgravia which can't make up its mind whether it's an hotel or a home.

When I met Michael Ward late in 1993 he was being treated for depression at the Charter Clinic in Chelsea and was perfectly open about his problem, as he was about his failed marriage to Leonorra, from whom he had obtained a divorce. Leonorra, an Australian model, ended up in the Charter Nightingale, the sister clinic of the Chelsea establishment. Ward is charming, well-mannered and courteous, but during his period as boss of European Leisure he began to attract a hostile press from one Sunday newspaper which accused him of numerous things which went well beyond anything the SFO charged him with or even interviewed him about.

There developed a relationship between the Sunday newspaper and the SFO. Several weeks after the announcement of the SFO investigation in March 1992, Ward claims that his ex-wife, who was then under treatment, together with a conman she met and had an affair with in the Charter Nightingale, went into his house and took personal documents belonging to Ward, some of which were privileged as far as his case was concerned, and some of which contained financial information which he needed for his defence. The documents were taken to the nearest branch of Prontaprint and photocopied.

Leonorra returned the next day on her own to complete her packing and meet the removal men. She opened the door to them with a buzzer from an upstairs room. By coincidence, her male accomplice was driving past, saw the open door and entered the house. They went into Ward's study and returned to Prontaprint for yet another photocopying session. When Ward returned from holiday he noticed that his documents had been tampered with and a great number were missing.

Ward simply could not believe such behaviour, and later set up a tape-recorded conversation between Leonorra and the journalist to whom the copy documents had been given, some of which is reproduced here.

> *Leonorra*: [Michael] came back from holiday and found all these documents had been stapled together really badly. He said it was obvious they had been copied and he said there were a whole lot of documents missing.
>
> *Journalist*: Yes.
>
> *L*: I mean, when you were in Chester Square, did you take any documents away?
>
> *J*: Well, when we were at Chester Square we photocopied a load of documents, yes.
>
> *L*: Was everything – was everything – I mean on the Friday I remember, but on the Saturday when X [the conman] was hovering around the filing cabinet a bit did he take anything else out?
>
> *J*: Yes, he took a whole load of stuff to be photocopied and then he took it back.
>
> *L*: He put it back?
>
> *J*: Oh, yes, all the documents were there.
>
> *L*: Well, there's a whole load of stuff that's not.
>
> *J*: Well no, that's not right. That isn't right because I mean I assume X took it back. What happened was he took it to the photocopying shop, photocopied it and I just went off with the photocopies and that was it. What happened was he went back and as I understand it he put them back . . . I give you my word of honour that I don't have any documents which are other than copies.

There was then some discussion about the conman, who had given the journalist the impression that he was a rich man. It appeared that the journalist gave X £2500 which he was to pass on to Leonorra for her story. Leonorra never saw the money. The journalist said he had thought that X and she were an item and that if he gave the money to X he would automatically give it to her. It was all meant for Leonorra. This is followed by discussion about what a phoney X was, and how the journalist was going to sort out the money business with X once he could get hold of him.

Eventually, they got around to talking about what the journalist had done with the photocopies.

J: In the end I decided that most of the documents I had, which were copies, were of no great interest and I put them in the bin to be quite honest. *There were one or two of them which were very incriminating to be quite honest with you, and I thought, well, what I am going to do is I am going to give them to the SFO as they are carrying out an investigation* (my emphasis).

L: It's the SFO's business to do whatever they want to do with them.

J: Correct. So I gave them to the SFO. They called me up and said this is very interesting, and in the course of the conversation they said they would quite like to speak to you. Now I said I wasn't prepared to give them your number but I would make a few enquiries and I would see what the position was. But there is no heaviness about it, they weren't saying 'She must speak to us or else' or anything like that, if anything it's quite the opposite. They weren't sure whether they should approach you or not . . . It's not a heavy number with them.

He went on to tell Leonorra that there was no hurry. They had evidence that Ward had been paying money to a woman called Y.

L: Do you think he'll go to jail for 25,000 years?

J: No, but I think he'll – you know, he may go to prison for a couple of years.

It was during these exchanges with Leonorra that J showed his relationship with the SFO. Referring to the charge of share ramping, he told Leonorra 'the bit they have the strongest evidence for . . .', indicating that he had discussed with the SFO the progress of the case.

This is followed by some speculation about what Ward might be charged with. Then a note of apprehension creeps into the conversation. It comes from the journalist, who is now worried about Leonorra as a trustworthy source.

J: . . . All I want to know is whether – regardless of what his motives for doing it were – were the facts correct? I mean he deposited an account with £50,000 in cash and you made a deposit for him of £50,000.

She agrees, which must have been a relief.
He asks another question about information she had given him and her reply must have been less reassuring:

L: To be honest with you a lot of those three months that I was in a clinic is very fuzzy . . . I was seriously, heavily drugged up. I mean I was in there for a nervous breakdown . . . my memory of that period is very fuzzy because I was getting a pill at 8.00 am, midday, 4.00 pm, 8.00 pm and midnight. I was on six pills a day.

J: Even when I – even when I met you?

L: Yes, I was sedated the whole time because I had had a nervous breakdown. A serious one. I think X did do a bit of brain fucking on me.

J: Well, my concern – well, I've got two concerns. First of all, that X has ripped you off and he's deceived me. He's taken money which was meant for you. But my second concern is that the information we used and put in the newspaper is accurate, otherwise you know, we lay ourselves open to a massive libel suit.

And that – apart from a few pleasantries and some more comments about X – was the end of the taped conversation.

This revealed two things of significance, both of which reflected on the way in which Staple ran the SFO. First, that the journalist gave to the SFO copy documents the originals of which might have belonged to Ward, and which could have been either privileged or, according to the journalist, incriminating. The journalist told Leonorra that the SFO 'called me up and said this is very interesting'.

The second point was that the SFO had passed on information that a woman called Y had been paid money by Ward to buy shares in European Leisure.

To take the matter, first, of the papers removed by X from Ward's house, some of which were passed to the SFO. On 8 April 1993, Ward's lawyers, Peter Carter-Ruck, wrote to Peter Kiernan, the SFO's investigating lawyer on the Ward case in these terms: 'During the last interview my client asked you to return to him all documents that have come into your possession through Mr J [the journalist] or Mr X which derive from a visit those gentlemen made to his home in March 1992. While some of the documentation was returned having been copied, many documents were not returned.'

Kiernan replied six days later: 'Miss Palubicki [an SFO officer] has reviewed our documents and has discovered a small number of documents which may have originated from your client. Copies will be available at the next interview when Mr Ward can confirm if they were in fact part of those taken from his home, whereupon copies will be provided.'

Kiernan, however, was not anxious to discuss the matter of the taped conversation, with its revelation that the SFO had discussed with the journalist aspects of the SFO's investigation.

Eventually, both matters ended up with George Staple. But before that, Peter Carter-Ruck had written to Staple himself, first about the documents passed to the SFO by the journalist, which X had taken from 'Ward's filing cabinet in his study, without his knowledge or consent, some of which have not been returned and are, therefore, stolen'. The firm also raised once again the taped conversation with its record of discussions between the SFO and the journalist. It also mentioned another piece of published information in a paper which, it said, could only have come from the SFO.

Four weeks later, Staple replied. 'In relation to documents handed to this Office by journalists,' he wrote, 'I believe you have been supplied with copies of them. It does not appear from the papers, and especially not from J's conversation with Mrs Ward, that they were obtained unlawfully.'

It is quite true that J did not discuss with Leonorra Ward in the taped conversation the details of how the front-door lock to Ward's house had been changed by a locksmith, so that she could get in; she wanted, apparently, to remove some of her clothes and belongings. But what was obvious from the taped conversation was that Leonorra had no intention that anyone should return to Ward's house.

L: . . . I met with you on the Friday and everything, but on the Saturday, I even said to you on the Friday night, please, look, leave me alone, I've had enough . . . I can't, my brain's exploding, I'm on overload, I wasn't expecting to see you on Saturday.

J: Leonorra no, I agreed with him by that time, we'd already agreed that I was going to pay a sum of money to you for the documents and I thought that you were aware of that.

Did it occur to Staple, one wonders, to inquire how the documents which came into the SFO's possession were acquired in the first place? Did he ever ask anyone whether they had been obtained with Ward's consent and, if so, how? Did it occur to the director to ask about the state of Mr and Mrs Ward's marriage, whether the taking of documents was authorised by Mr Ward, or what inducements had been offered to her? If he had listened to the tape with any care, he would have heard the journalist saying to Leonorra that she should have received £2,500. But did Staple ask himself why a payment was needed? 'It does not appear,' the director said blandly, 'that [the documents] were obtained unlawfully.' This was not the response of a man who had done his homework; it was the reply of a man who knew perfectly well that the matter could be left to atrophy and who relied on what he was told (just as he had relied on Mrs Lorna Harris).

Let us suppose, though, that Staple had been diligent enough to find out just how the documents had been acquired. Would he have done anything about it or would he have kept mum? Civil servants never admit anything, so why should he have admitted to that?

Staple makes no reference in his letter to the section on tape where J tells Leonorra that the SFO has evidence on the woman Y being given money by Ward to buy shares in European Leisure. One is not surprised. Indeed, much of the investigation into Ward and European Leisure was media-led. They initiated the story and hung on to it like a bulldog with his jaws clamped on to another dog's jugular.

Staple partly admits it in his letter to Carter-Ruck. 'In particular,' he says, 'the article which you claim contains "fresh libellous allegations" was something wholly new to this office, and as you know *sparked an investigation into the facts it alleged* (my italics). It appears to me that that is not wholly unobjectionable, but a proper reaction to what you must agree to be a most serious allegation. I am satisfied that that matter has been properly dealt with, and I reject the suggestion that any part of the investigation is being influenced in its direction by the interests of [J's newspaper].'

No influence on the investigation? So what about the papers sent to the SFO by J? What about the SFO telling J about the woman Y? And what about the SFO investigation into the paper's allegations? And what about Staple's comment that as a result of those allegations the journalist was contacted for the purpose of gathering evidence?

Staple ends his letter, as he generally does with complaints, to the effect that if it's a formal complaint about the conduct of police officers, then he will arrange for the appropriate steps to be taken. But he warns: 'However, you should be aware, as I am informed, that any internal complaint inquiry by police will not proceed during the currency of criminal proceedings to which they relate. In any event, you are free to draw the position to the attention of the trial judge if you so wish in the course of the proceedings that have now begun.'

It was curious he should have said that because there seems to be one rule for people like Ward and another for Mr Justice Tucker who, during one memorable period of the temporarily aborted Nadir case, stood to be accused of attempting to pervert the course of justice. The police are now investigating those allegations, even though criminal proceedings at that time were continuing.

Staple is now too bogged down in the organisation he is attempting to run to give it the forceful leadership it needs if it is to avoid any more painful, unnecessary mistakes. He has not got those qualities. He is essentially reactive by temperament, not proactive. Nor is he tough enough. The irony is that Barbara Mills was tough all right, but even she did not have the right combination of skills to stop the train from bucketing off the rails. Nor has Staple any experience of crime. His professional life was in litigation. He has little knowledge of how the police operate. And before he came to the SFO, he knew next to nothing about fraud. The Fraud Squad, which can have as much as a fifth of its manpower attached to the SFO for some cases, does know what fraud is all about. Many of its officers have been in the business for twice as long as the lawyers and accountants on Elm Street. They do not work with the benefit of Section 2. Yet Staple and his civil servants rarely listen to police advice or learn from the voice of experience. George Churchill-Coleman, head of the Fraud Squad, advised Staple not to accept only the Fimbra charge for deception for Levitt; Frederick Forsyth, the thriller writer, made the same case against a single charge. But Staple and his civil service acolytes chose not to heed those warnings. They knew better and apparently always have. The sergeants' mess at Elm Street is very largely ignored by the officers on the upper floors. One very senior Fraud Squad member told me: 'I was totally in favour of the SFO when it came into being. Now I am totally against it. It is hopelessly unprofessional.'

Like Barbara Mills, Staple quickly became a creature of Whitehall. It will not be the first time that the government has made an important appointment without reference to the background, relevant skills and competence of the man to whom they are offering the job. The job was vacant, that was the point. And Staple was available.

6

BARLOW CLOWES

The Barlow Clowes scandal was at least something the SFO could get its teeth into, knowing that it had a good chance of success. The charges weren't technical and hard to comprehend, as they were in County NatWest/Blue Arrow, or riddled with City politics and old enmities, as they were with T.C. Coombs. In those two cases there were no victims to latch on to, no hapless innocents who had been taken to the cleaners by ruthless financial manipulators. That was what made Barlow Clowes so refreshing. The sum of money that had gone missing, around £140 million, was outrageous. Many innocent investors had been hit. And the man who had done the damage, Peter Clowes, fitted the bill perfectly.

Clowes was no City slicker, with a public school background and respectable parents in the Home Counties, but an out-and-out crook, fat, short and unattractive, who ate, dreamed and slept other people's money and spent it like water. Clowes was one of those operators who didn't need to be charged with anything: he looked like a walking indictment for fraud and should have been locked up on sight. That was the picture.

The scenario, then, was perfect for the SFO. But it had taken nine years to get Clowes into court. Since 1982 he had been quietly pillaging other people's money, then he gradually became more sure of himself until he reached the stage where he was recklessly taking it and spending it wildly on himself and his family. This had nothing to do with the SFO, but everything to with the Department of Trade and Industry, whose job it was to license and keep an eye on people like Clowes.

Many of the biggest British crooks have sprung from nothing and, after blameless but threadbare beginnings, have been infected by the virus of greed. In nearly every case, the condition is untreatable and can only be halted by a spell in prison. It also seems that the people most vulnerable to the virus are those who crave the material trappings of wealth – houses, planes, yachts, champagne and so on – and not the possession of money itself. There have been many financiers who have not been particularly interested in Old Masters or châteaux. Their motivation has been the creation of wealth and the deal-making that goes with the process. Material acquisitions have been a secondary consideration.

Most people from Clowes's background are content with one TV set, one car and one annual holiday. By British standards this is called lack of ambition. It is, happily for the middle classes, a syndrome which mainly affects the working class. But middle-class parents invest many thousands of pounds on their children so they can discreetly acquire the material things of life roughly in proportion to their acquisition of directorships. The comment that you can only wear one suit, drive one car and live in one house is the grossest piece of hypocrisy. The crucial phrase is *at any one time*. Sequentially, the enjoyment of many assets is not a problem.

For Clowes, the desire for accretion was never discreet or easy paced. His descent on the path to hell began with early employment with the great master of wealth-acquisition, deceit and psychological manipulation – Bernie Cornfeld ('Do you sincerely want to be rich?'), founder member of Investors Overseas Services, who was to die of the deadly virus of greed with which he infected others. It took a little while for the young Clowes to enter Cornfeld's shortlived orbit (by then the great man was burning out), but Clowes had seen a star and never forgot it. He had seen the yachts, the châteaux, the girls, the private jets, and it had burned an image into his mind. Clowes was suddenly head-over-heels in love with greed and the desirable things it could acquire if properly harnessed.

It was not before time. He had done his apprenticeship in

the grim little family business in a Manchester suburb, for which he sold paraffin from a cart. He had learned from his parents, apparently, the price of everything and the value of nothing (Oscar Wilde was sometimes right), and after leaving school with four 'O' levels had a profitable little business trading from market stalls. He changed from that into selling turf, and then into 'landscape gardening'. It was all profitable. He was married. He had his first detached house not, curiously, in some Mancunian suburb but on the edge of a village called Marple. He was to all intents and purposes 'set'. He was in his mid-twenties, employing six people. A success.

Clowes might have had a very successful, established life from then on. He had proved he could be an entrepreneur. He was diligent. He had a head for detail. He was giving Manchester's mercantile classes the lawns and gardens they wanted. Property development was going ahead; that could only be good for business. The future not only looked good, it seemed assured. Clowes had also shown he was flexible. He had moved out of one business into another. He had the entrepreneurial spirit and drive.

And then, as they say, the fickle finger of fate pointed straight at him. The smooth path upwards was suddenly arrested and the course of his life changed dramatically. It was a woman who put Clowes on the road which was to lead to other people's millions. Elizabeth Barlow was the antithesis of Clowes in every respect: tall, confident, socially at ease, where he was squat, unprepossessing, diffident. They might have stepped from the pages of Straparola's *Beauty and the Beast*. And they might never have met had they not had a mutual passion for rally driving.

In 1969 Barlow was sponsored to drive in the Tulip international car rally and invited Clowes to be her navigator and co-driver. They came first in their class. Their mutual passion turned to sex in the car park of a local pub. Another shared addiction was money. Clowes abandoned his businesses and joined Barlow at International Life, a subsidiary of Cornfeld's Investors Overseas Services, where Barlow was selling the Dover Plan, an IOS product. Like all salesmen who fall for another salesman's pitch, Clowes fell for the Cornfeld magic. Later, when Cornfeld went to the wall and Robert Vesco took over and stole £146 million, Clowes transferred his admiration to Vesco. (So did many people. One of Cornfeld's assistants, on meeting Vesco for the first time, said: 'Within a very few minutes of meeting him, I knew I was in the presence of one of the greatest financial geniuses of the twentieth century.')

Almost a year after Clowes arrived at International Life, IOS began to disappear into a black hole. International Life followed it, first into the hands of liquidators, who then sold it on to Keyser Ullman, a merchant bank, who renamed the company Cannon Assurance. Sir Edward du Cann, later to be bankrupted, was chairman of both companies.

A colleague of Clowes at Cannon described him as 'insular, nasty, pompous, shrewd and introverted'. Shrewd he certainly was. He and Barlow were operating their own business, Barlow & Clowes insurance brokers, out of the same premises as their employers, Cannon. But soon, in 1973, they opened their own outfit in Hazel Grove outside Manchester.

Initially, they sold a research service to accountants, solicitors and financial advisers, which was based on a week-by-week analysis of the best rates to be had for guaranteed income bonds, a popular product being sold by insurance companies. The service prospered until Denis Healey, Chancellor of the Exchequer, virtually killed it stone dead when he took away the bonds' tax benefits. Barlow Clowes had been in business just a year.

Conmen are fond of emotive language; it helps to sell products. 'Guaranteed' was a good word, you couldn't go wrong with something that was guaranteed. Similarly with the government's 'gilts', or gilt-edged securities; you couldn't be buying a pig in a poke. In the same way that Cornfeld fell in love with his Dover Plan, Clowes now became obsessed with the idea of selling his own product. That was a long step from being an insurance broker selling other companies' products, which was what Barlow wanted. But it was Clowes who won. He also moved into much larger premises, another unhealthy sign.

The secondary banking crisis had been and gone in 1974,

leaving behind it ruined property companies and fringe banks. But in its wake it left thousands of shattered investors. What they wanted was security. Clowes was going to give them that security, a new gilts service, the safest investment of all. It was a piece of sales psychology hard to fault.

It is unimportant to know what technical view Clowes took of the gilts market and how it should be played. Apparently he was a gilts addict; he thought of nothing else when it came to investment. He talked about gilts with missionary zeal. If belief in a product is nine-tenths of the battle to get it sold, Clowes certainly had it. The trouble was that his gilts service in the early days was not selling as fast as he would have liked. It brought in around £1 million, chickenfeed by comparison with what it was to produce later.

But a million, even in Clowes's language, was a million. With his clients' money he bought two new cars, a small house for his parents, another for his estranged wife, Patricia, and a flat for himself. This was clients' money he was using, something which was to become a habit on an heroic scale. There is never a problem about stealing from clients as long as the money is there when they want it back. The moment it isn't, then questions are asked. This was far from being a problem in 1977, but at that time Clowes's appetite for the good life had been scarcely awakened. Later on, he was to behave with the recklessness of a screaming alcoholic let loose in a liquor store.

Two factors enabled Clowes to indulge himself. First, he was trading illegally, and second, he had teamed up with some stockbrokers – Hedderwick Stirling Grunbar – who had apparently never heard of the Stock Exchange rule book.

That he could trade illegally was entirely the fault of the DTI, whose licensing department left much to be desired in terms of competence. In 1975, when Clowes wanted to leaflet prospective clients with his gilts investment product, he sent the pamphlets to the DTI for approval and to find out whether he needed a DTI licence for what he was doing. The department's view was that he was selling a product, not acting as an adviser. He was therefore managing other people's money and in that capacity he had to be licensed.

That view was confirmed by senior officials at the top of the DTI, but by the time it had been relayed to Clowes in a letter from a junior official the message had become badly scrambled. It said that as Barlow Clowes was distributing circulars the firm had to be licensed. So Clowes simply wrote back saying that he was no longer sending out circulars and the DTI acknowledged that in that case he didn't need to go through the licensing procedure.

Clowes circumvented the problem of distributing circulars by telling all the financial advisers and intermediaries in his area about the service he was offering and they sold it for him on commission. They sent him the cheques and he then invested the money in gilts through the Stock Exchange. Clowes couldn't do the investment directly himself (he was not a member of the Stock Exchange), so he used Hedderwick Stirling Grunbar to do it for him. Hedderwicks at that time were well known gilts dealers and they acted on Clowes's instructions.

Whether Clowes's choice of firm was deliberate or an accident was neither here nor there, but he had stumbled on one man in the gilts department, Agnello de'Souza, who was tailor-made for Clowes's unorthodox approach to dealing. The rule was that gilts had to be paid for in cash the day after they had been bought. That could be tiresome for someone like Clowes if the cash wasn't readily available. The deal he struck up with de'Souza was that the latter could borrow stock belonging to Barlow Clowes clients to settle Hedderwick's deals, in return for which Clowes did not have to stump up cash the next day for his gilts deals. 'Leaving clients' stock on the shelf', as it was called, was strictly against the rules. But then Peter Clowes was never hidebound by the rules, any more than he ever felt a pang of conscience about booking clients' deals when they made a profit to his personal account rather than to the client's account.

This arrangement might have continued until Clowes died, had Hedderwicks not suddenly been hammered in April 1981. Clowes retrieved his clients' stock which was 'on the shelf' just in time. The firm was short of £2 million, owed to them by two former employees of Clowes's, Farrington and Stead, who left him in 1978. Farrington and Stead simply hadn't got the money.

The two men, through no design of their own, could well have brought Peter Clowes to his knees when they applied for a DTI licence in 1979. They were obliged on their application form to give the name and occupation of their previous employer. Down went Barlow Clowes, variously described as being engaged in gilt-edged management or portfolio management. No one at the DTI bothered to check out Barlow Clowes to see if it was licensed.

This time, however, Clowes had his back to the wall. Martin Fidler, who was acting for the Stock Exchange as Hedderwicks's liquidator, discovered that the firm of Farrington Stead and de'Souza had been running a gilts gambling syndicate, using clients' stock 'on the shelf' for capital and replacing it when the client asked for it. Fidler noticed that some of this 'gambling' stock belonged to Barlow Clowes clients and wondered if Barlow Clowes was part of the syndicate. Fidler also noticed that Clowes was trading without a licence. He reported the firm to the DTI's licensing unit.

In a competent, well-run department, the game would have been up for Clowes. But the licensing unit was neither. It had a staff of four civil servants, hopelessly overworked, who regarded the unit as a boring step to better things. When Fidler told them that Clowes needed looking at because of its association with Farrington Stead, they took the easy way out. While the Companies Investigation Branch of the DTI picked their way through the rubble of Farrington Stead, the unit decided to keep a watch on Clowes; no more than that. The CIB, meanwhile, had discovered that not only was Barlow Clowes unlicensed, but it had an offshore business in Jersey. But the CIB never passed this information to the licensing unit. Nor did the licensing unit ever bother to follow up any of the original concerns passed to it by Martin Fidler of the Stock Exchange.

Meanwhile de'Souza, Farrington and Stead had been arrested and their old friend Peter Clowes agreed to act as prosecution witness at the Old Bailey trial. His former partner and mistress, Elizabeth Barlow, had fled the country. She and de'Souza had owned a joint account which owed £100,000 to Hedderwicks. Clowes could breathe freely once more.

A year later Clowes had another stroke of luck. He had discovered a nice pot of gold called 'bondwashing'. He labelled his new product Portfolio 30. Bondwashing was perfectly legal but it only applied to gilts, his favourite investment. Put simply, under the tax laws of the early 1980s he was able to offer investors a deal with guaranteed income and capital *without* any tax to pay. And with it, of course, went total security because gilts were absolutely safe government stock. It was a dream investment vehicle and tailored for pensioners who had savings to invest.

What Clowes needed now was publicity for his new product; out of the blue, it was handed to him on a plate. The BBC's *Money Box* programme phoned him, saying they would like to talk to him about bondwashing. It was a cost-free way to put across his message to hundreds of thousands of hungry investors. Clowes made superb use of it. Portfolio 30 had been given the imprimatur of the BBC. Clowes couldn't have had a better underwriter of the scheme if he had asked for it. *Money Box* had a scoop and Clowes had a ready-made market.

In one year Clowes's gilt funds under management went up almost eight times to £33.1 million. He was now an established gilts specialist. He had arrived. Financial intermediaries sold his product all over the country. And Clowes, thumbing his nose at the DTI, had the cheek to mail Portfolio 30 promotional material to potential clients with his company's name openly flaunted for anyone to see. The civil servants didn't notice. And that was the only thing that mattered.

After that, of course, Clowes changed his lifestyle. The big spender had money to burn and his new wife, a former secretary, was happy to put a match to it. By now he had offices behind the Stock Exchange in London. He bought a new house in the right suburb in Manchester. More important, he started spending wadges of money on advertising Portfolio 30. In less than a year he spent three quarters of a million in the national press. That represented a quarter of a million less than the management fees he was earning. But that wasn't a problem either: he simply took the money from his clients. Clowes, who had never been impressed by the tedium of financial morality, had now committed himself irrevocably to a life of crime. By now, though, he probably thought he could walk on water. He had been overlooked so many times by the DTI, he would have been entitled to think he had their blessing.

If he was walking on water, like all good conmen he had to have stepping stones just below the surface to stop him from drowning. The £750,000 advertising budget had to be explained to the satisfaction of the auditors of his accounts. The UK company couldn't explain that kind of expenditure because there wasn't the cash flow to support it. The money had to have another source. Clowes had already salted away £12 million in his Jersey company, but he couldn't use any of that to explain how he financed the advertising campaign.

But he found an answer: a Gibraltar company with an address in Jersey. Hermes was a shell company (in other words, it existed on paper only), but good enough for Clowes's purposes. Hermes, he said, was in the same business as Barlow Clowes and Clowes had licensed his bondwashing computer programmes to Hermes, for which the fee in 1983–84 had been £750,000. End of problem.

End of that one anyway. The trouble with Clowes's advertising onslaught was that it led many people – City journalists, analysts and fund managers – to look at Portfolio 30 with renewed critical interest and they all came to pretty much the same conclusion: that the bondwashing product did not add up; that Clowes could not get the returns on it he was claiming because that would involve producing a better return than the gilts themselves could produce. Add to that Clowes's guarantee – that investors were guaranteed a return of their capital – and the product was claiming the impossible.

While the City was quietly ganging up on Barlow Clowes, the island of Jersey had decided to take positive action over Clowes's little partnership there. In fact the Clowes operation did no business there at all. It used the local branches of Lloyds and the Midland to hold client money; at that time about £12 million. It was these accounts which concerned the Jersey authorities as much as anything else. They had no control over what Barlow Clowes was doing on mainland Britain and no control over the money being transferred to Jersey. If the business should go bad, then clients might make a claim on Jersey for the money in the local banks if it went missing. Clowes was ordered to be off the island within a couple of weeks and also told that the bank accounts in Jersey had to be closed down. Clowes left, but did not close the accounts and no one in Jersey bothered to check if he had. Like so much in the Clowes scandal, he owed his precarious but continuing existence to the incompetence, omission or inertia of the authorities. These were to stand him in good stead for a number of years yet.

Meanwhile the money came flowing in. At one point it was estimated that Clowes had £300 million under management. It was vital to Clowes, though, that the inflow of money should not stop. He was running at a loss, but as long as new money continued to appear on the scene the loss did not become apparent. And he managed to do this while still unlicensed. More remarkably, he did it against a tidal wave of expert professional criticism which had washed its way through the offices of the DTI regulators, through NASDIM (a fledgling, ineffective self-regulatory organisation), through the Treasury and through the Bank of England.

The truth was that none of these organisations wanted to take the responsibility of closing down Barlow Clowes. In the DTI's licensing unit there was a fear that if they refused Clowes a licence they risked two dangers: first, that Clowes might sue them; second, that he might run off with the money. In the Bank of England and the Treasury, while there was much formal huffing and puffing, there was a feeling that if anyone was going to make a mistake the DTI was the department to pin the blame on (the DTI at that time was going through a particularly lacklustre period). A man called Louth in the licensing unit was mired by indecision, but managed at one stage to get a DTI solicitor to draft a notice of intention to refuse a licence. That was the nearest Louth got to closing down Clowes.

But his next action, some months later, was to put Clowes into the black museum of financial history. Louth had been awaiting an accountancy firm's audit of Barlow Clowes; an audit of Clowes's client accounts on 28 December 1984. All the accountants had to do was ascertain that if investors with Clowes were owed a particular sum of money on that day there was a corresponding amount in money and gilts. The two balanced perfectly. Clowes would have seen to that. He would have made up any shortfall in cash by transferring clients' money held in offshore accounts.

Louth was satisfied and wrote to Michael Howard, the Minister for Corporate Affairs, recommending that Clowes should be licensed without delay.

At around the same time, Clowes decided to enjoy himself at his clients' expense. Instead of putting their money into gilts, he spent it on a château and vineyard in Bordeaux. He had already embarked on theft in a substantial way. He had put clients' money, which should have been in gilts, into two jewellery businesses (later to be called by the SFO 'Mrs Clowes's jewellery box'), a company involving computer products, and an employment agency. He had also diverted more than £500,000 of clients' money from the Lloyds account in Jersey into buying a splendid house in Woking for his assistant and a farm and a mews house for himself near Hyde Park. Throughout these pleasurable episodes Clowes never changed: he remained surly and secretive, driven by a relentless urge for self-aggrandisement. This manifested itself in curious ways. Using a Liechtenstein company, Clowes started buying shares in a publicly-quoted company called C.H. Bailey, a ship repairer. The money for it came via the Midland Bank in Jersey – to be more precise from the Barlow Clowes & Partners Clients' Premium Deposit Account. Clowes could be stupid, careless or arrogant – arrogance he had in plenty – but there was no reason why he should have allowed Barlow Clowes nominees to be named as the purchaser of the shares. As it happened, no one noticed. If the DTI had had its wits about it, it could have pulled the rug from under Clowes then and there.

Clowes also owned a property company called Megerberry

which had bought his company's headquarters, several flats and other properties, all financed indirectly by his clients, but in a deal which he had taken great care to conceal. That was why the C.H. Bailey share dealing looked both clumsy and dangerous.

There comes a time in the careers of most successful crooks when they start to be careless. Clowes became careless to the point of madness, trying anything on sophisticated City advisers and repeatedly getting away with it. The takeover of Barlow Clowes by James Ferguson, in which Clowes had a substantial shareholding, was approved by the Stock Exchange and the Takeover Panel, a masterly piece of deception which depended on everyone not pushing the questions they asked too far. The most important of these was probably the ghost company, Hermes, which Clowes had originally invented to explain where he had got the money for his huge advertising campaign. Hermes, he said, had been licensed by Barlow Clowes to use its software applications. In effect, though, the money Hermes was paying to Barlow Clowes belonged to investors. When the Ferguson accountants looked into the affairs of the Barlow Clowes group, there was an immediate question mark over Hermes. There deserved to be: without Hermes's financial contribution to Barlow Clowes there would have been no profits, only losses. Hermes, then, was crucial to the health of the group and, consequently, to James Ferguson.

After fishing around, Touche Ross, Ferguson's accountants, found that Hermes Management Services had only an accommodation address in Jersey. Nor were there any sales brochures advertising its services as a fund management company, which was what Clowes always maintained it was. As more and more questions were asked about Hermes, it looked as if the Ferguson bid for Barlow Clowes might be in jeopardy.

Clowes, as usual, came up with a bold solution which foxed everyone. He flew to Gibraltar and instructed his lawyers there to draw up a software licensing agreement between Hermes Computer Services and Barlow Clowes which would give the Clowes group an annual income in excess of £500,000. That did the trick. Hermes was given a sufficiently clean bill of health for the takeover to go through.

Luck always marched hand in hand with Peter Clowes. Under the takeover rules, 25 per cent of the shares of the new company had to be held by outside shareholders. Technically, Clowes and his associates held 42 per cent, while the Ferguson associates had another 32 per cent. It was too tight for comfort, so the Stock Exchange asked who the outside shareholders were. Most of them were nominee companies owned by Clowes. But no one found out, so Clowes got away with it.

He was to get away with much more. His bid for Buckley's Brewery was financed entirely by his investors' funds, although at one stage one of Clowes's employees jibbed at transferring £3.5 million from investors' bank accounts to Clowes and tried to indemnify herself with a signed letter, authorised by the company's finance director, saying that she was acting under instructions and took no responsibility for her action.

When a Stock Exchange investigator, looking at Clowes's application for Barlow Clowes and James Ferguson to be members, concluded that the application should be rejected and a full inquiry initiated into both entities, Clowes still had a lot of breathing space. He survived a Takeover Panel inquiry into his exorbitant bid for Buckley's Brewery and how he was to finance it and pressed on with the acquisition of another company. Clowes was by now irrepressible. At one time he actively went about buying a bank, but was warned off by the Bank of England.

Clowes had by now ceased to know the difference between illusion and reality. For years he had been stealing his clients' money. For years he had been lying successfully to the authorities. For years he had been spending lavishly on a glitzy lifestyle designed to impress people and enhance his prestige. It seems clear that by the time the investigators moved in, Clowes was still deceiving himself that he had done nothing wrong. He would say so in court. The government was to blame.

What gave the lie to Clowes's belief in his own honesty were his actions once the DTI investigations began. Clowes knew where all the bodies were buried. He knew what he had to falsify, shred and explain away. But he had, as the phrase goes, so much to do and so little time to do it in. While the DTI inspectors were investigating, Clowes was shredding documents in the offices below them and having the evidence carted over the road to premises the inspectors knew nothing about. He was shredding in Gibraltar. He was inventing deals in gilts to plug embarrassingly large holes, running into millions, in the company's financial records. None of this could remotely be regarded as the behaviour of an honest man.

The fallout from the Barlow Clowes scandal was scattered over a very large area of governmental, institutional and social life. Thousands of investors, many of them retired with nest-eggs to put into some sort of investment which would earn them income, were badly hit – some of them irrevocably. There were stories of heart attacks, nervous breakdowns, misery and depression, conditions commonly associated with financial loss. Clowes had struck where it hurts most, largely at the pockets of people who could least afford it. His later protestations that he would recover all the money for his investors came from one of those fourth-rate scripts which fraudsters keep handy for these occasions.

The government ran into a well-deserved typhoon. The Tories had a notoriously bad record when it came to policing the City and the first thing the government said was that it wasn't their fault. Having appointed Sir Godfray Le Quesne, a former, unimpressive chairman of the Monopolies and Mergers Commission, to report on what went wrong, they had a pretty good idea they had put the inquiry in safe hands. Sir Godfray is a bit like footprints in the sand – easily washed away by an incoming tide, and he duly came up to expectation: he produced a report with no conclusions. There was nothing in it to suggest that the DTI had in any way blundered, or been incompetent, or dragged its feet.

There is nothing more dangerous than a report of that kind: it was a dreary recitation of facts, pretty well all of which pointed to serious errors by the DTI. But if facts are not underlined or commented upon, they lose their force. It was a gift to Lord Young, at that time the DTI's Secretary of State, who blithely told the House of Lords (if he'd tried it in the Commons, his life would have been endangered) that no blame of any kind attached to his department's handling of the whole mess and accordingly there was no justification for using 'taxpayers' money to fund compensation'. Young was always a silky, soothing performer, a former executive of Great Universal Stores and a property developer, who brought to the task of government a highly developed talent for pouring oil on troubled waters. If there were no conclusions, Young believed, there could be no blame.

MPs were not going to swallow that line of patter; most of them had some of the 25,000 affected investors in their constituencies. They were pressing urgently for compensation. Then the Ombudsman, Sir Anthony Barrowclough, decided he would do his own investigation into the DTI's handling of Barlow Clowes. The DTI, he found, had been guilty of maladministration and had not been sufficiently rigorous and enquiring in its approach to Barlow Clowes. He recommended that all investors should be compensated.

It was music to investors' ears, but not to the government's, which disagreed with the Ombudsman's findings. By this time, though, it had a tiger by the tail and had no option but to go along with a compensation package of £155 million, which meant that nearly all investors would get 90 per cent of their money back. After that, the government fired writs in all directions – at financial intermediaries and at the four clearing banks – determined to get back some of the money it had paid out.

The SFO investigation into Barlow Clowes began in the middle of 1988 and took very nearly two years. The case was transferred from the lower court to an annexe of the Old Bailey and the trial lasted 122 working days, or just over six months. The documentation was awesome. There were 7,000 witness statements and 68,000 pages of documentary exhibits, two-thirds of which were bank evidence. This was weeded and pruned and the defence were eventually served with three volumes of case documents and a volume of flow charts. John Tate, the big, fresh-faced case controller, who is also an assistant director of the SFO, becomes very enthusiastic about the arrangements for the trial (it was one of the biggest cases the SFO had tackled).

'The jury were given twelve "rainbow files", each of which contained flow charts and money trails. The purpose of having different coloured files was so the prosecution could ask the jury to turn to the orange file or the red file and so on. There was one file for two jurors. The point of sharing a file is that it's less likely that jurors will fall asleep. We also had overhead projection arrangements for the court so that the press and everyone else could see the flow charts. The case statement, which was drafted in-house by the Barlow Clowes team and junior counsel, ran to four hundred pages. I would write a bit, someone else would do a bit, in fact everybody contributed, depending on what part of the case they were working on. Then it was edited, shown to the police and so on for comment, then written up in the final version.'

Tate's team numbered no more than a dozen; very different from Chris Dickson's BCCI group which at the height of the investigation was fifty strong and had to be housed in another building.

Peter Clowes faced twenty charges, eleven of which were theft. With him in the dock were Peter Naylor, Clowes's most important business associate, who was to get eighteen months; Guy von Cramer, a key figure in the takeover bid for Buckley's Brewery, who was acquitted; and Christopher Newman, the former finance director of Barlow Clowes, who produced the ingenious defence that he was drunk during the three years that he was with the firm and was not really responsible for anything that happened. Ingenious or not, it was good enough to get an acquittal.

Alan Suckling QC led for the prosecution and Anthony Hacking QC had been retained by Clowes (Hacking was later to prosecute for the SFO in the Virani/BCCI case). Suckling had come comparatively late to the case, two other leading counsel having had to drop out, but to compensate he had a stack of juicy evidence to work with.

One of Clowes's many personal extravagances had been his purchase of the motor yacht *Boukephalas* from Christina Onassis. She had bought it for her Russian husband, but he got bored with it. Clowes paid $2.5 million for the 100-footer, which had a top speed of 35 knots and cruised at 32. It was equipped with satellite navigation equipment, a cinema, and had a permanent crew costing £1,000 a week. And it was all paid for with investors' money.

This was just one of the many deals the prosecution explained to the jury, using the flow chart shown on page 108. Clowes used eight bank accounts to pay for the yacht.

Major fraud invariably involves a huge amount of documents – it is a document-based crime. And it is rarely possible for a fraudster to destroy everything that is relevant. He may have a programme of shredding (as Clowes evidently did) which he thinks covers all eventualities, but the advent of the photocopier had done nothing to help him. An incriminating document may be photocopied several times and sent to other offices where it is again copied and distributed. The fraudster is bound to miss something. Panic doesn't help either. Moreover, bank confidentiality is a thing of the past. A Section 2 notice from the SFO will soon uncover the illicit movement of funds from one country to another, from one account to another. Jurisdictions like Switzerland and Liechtenstein, which at one time were secretive and unhelpful, are now prepared to open up the books to investigators and are not the havens for hot money they once were. Tracing it can be a long, intricate and costly business. John Tate says a lot of travel was involved in the Barlow Clowes case for his accountants and investigators because of the various jurisdictions Clowes used in the course of stealing clients' money.

It has to be said, though, that a great deal was running in the SFO's favour in this case. There had been a DTI investigation before they arrived on the scene. The Securities and Investments Board had already closed the firm down. Clients' money had been diverted into all kinds of other investments – jewellery, property companies, the brewery; something Clowes had never been licensed to do. In addition

HOW CLOWES MOVED MONEY AROUND TO PAY FOR THE M.Y. BOUKEPHALAS

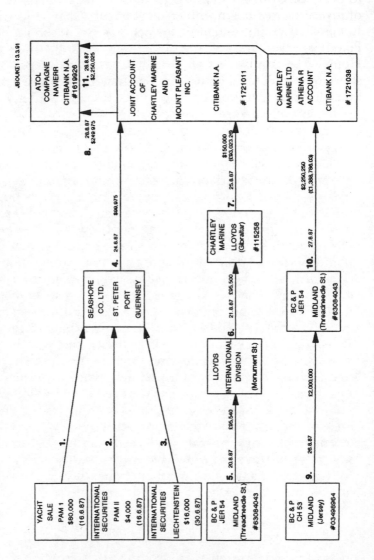

to that, there was the flagrant evidence of his extravagant use of investors' money on a château, houses, yachts and planes. It was theft on a grand scale and obvious for anyone to see. Peter Clowes, then, was a sitting duck for the people at Elm House. The trouble is that the SFO have been desperately short of sitting ducks recently and have managed to miss even the easier targets.

Clowes got ten years for theft and conspiracy.

7

THE ONE THAT GOT AWAY; OR, DECLINE AND FALL OF A MINISTER

Members of Parliament rarely electrify the House of Commons, but on 29 June 1993, it fell to Michael Mates to turn a dull afternoon's business into half an hour of pure theatre. Mates is not a great orator, but he has a fine voice and a workmanlike delivery. Like many a stage performer, he needs a foil to get the best from his performance, and that foil was Mrs Betty Boothroyd, the Speaker, who has built a formidable reputation as someone who knows the rules, idiosyncracies and mood of a unique institution. She is also authoritarian without being oppressive.

Within minutes of Mates getting to his feet to make his resignation speech, the two had locked horns. Five days earlier, Mates had resigned as minister at the Northern Ireland Office, a job he genuinely loved, because of his extraordinary involvement in the legal affairs of the Turkish Cypriot millionaire, Asil Nadir. Nadir was one of those businessmen the British find it hard to understand. His English was imperfect, though he had lived in Britain since he was a boy; he was darkly good-looking, had a reputation for being dangerous with women and had built a business empire which no one fully comprehended. He surrounded himself with fine paintings and good furniture, had a big estate in Leicestershire and kept himself to himself. Worse, he had little time for the City, though the City and many private investors had made substantial fortunes out of Polly Peck shares; the favourite statistic here is that £1,000 invested in Polly Peck International in 1980 would have been worth £1.3 million ten years later. It was also said that he kept going much of the fragile economy of Northern Cyprus, though exactly how was as much of a mystery as the man himself.

Nadir had been in and out of the news for the best part of twenty-five years, often in the guise of the poor little Turkish Cypriot who had risen from rags to riches. The truth was much more prosaic: he had been a hard-working lad in his father's East End rag trade business. When he first came to Mates's attention, the burly MP had difficulty in remembering who exactly he was. That was typical of Nadir: when he wanted to be in the news, he was never far from the front page; when he was out of the public eye, he was less noticeable than a small ad. The British like their big businessmen to be predictable, large and charismatic, not wily, Mediterranean and manipulative.

Nadir was not someone who courted publicity or sympathy. Yet he was to bring down Mates; he was to break a record £3.5 million bail and flee the country; and, while wanted for false accounting and the theft of millions of pounds, he was to maintain a constant campaign from his Cypriot refuge against what he repeatedly claimed was his unfair treatment by British justice. He has constantly embarrassed the government and the SFO with his megaphone allegations from the far side of the Mediterranean. And he has pursued his cause with a relentless determination few businessmen, however wronged, could match.

He certainly got through to Mates – even to the extent of getting a small birthday present from the MP, a cheap watch with the inscription 'Don't let the buggers get you down'. That little gift was to be the cause of Mates's resignation, and the cause of the memorable set-to between Mates and the Speaker as she repeatedly told him to sit down, on the slender grounds that what he was saying was *sub judice*, while Mates stolidly refused to do any such thing. It was a compelling confrontation that held every MP's rapt attention. Even Mates, a former regular battalion commander in the Queen's Dragoon Guards and not someone likely to wilt under fire, admitted to me that the occasion brought him as close to panic as it is possible to be. Yet nothing could persuade him to sit down. Mates was utterly convinced that the Nadir affair stank to high heaven and whether or not the Speaker or the Commons liked it, nothing was going to stop him saying so. At the back of it all was the Serious Fraud Office which Mates has always regarded as an institution that ought to be brought to heel, if not abolished.

Nobody, as Mates now recalls, really remembers what he said in that resignation speech. They remember the row vividly, but few remember the cause of it – namely, the allegation that a prominent high court judge was supposed to be party to a conspiracy to pervert the cause of justice; behind which, so Mates believed, was the dark hand of the SFO.

There had been no need for the MP to get into this situation. The Turkish Cypriot entrepreneur belonged to a long line of alleged fraudsters whom the SFO was anxious to put behind bars, but by no stretch of the imagination was he as important as the men from the Bank of Credit and Commerce International who had swindled its customers out of billions of pounds. In terms of magnitude, they did not inhabit the same planet. Nor was Nadir in charge of a business empire any more. He had fled to Northern Cyprus, leaving behind the bones of a company from which the administrators and creditors were trying to pick the last scraps of flesh. But there was very little remaining of a company which at one time owned hotels, a huge fruit business, a Japanese electronics company and which for many years had been a stock market darling.

Since the end of 1990, Polly Peck had experienced a collapse as dramatic as its rise. There appeared to be a billion-pound hole in its financial structure, representing money owed to creditors. But no one could be sure just how much money had gone missing. Much of it appeared to have taken off for Northern Cyprus, perhaps £500 million, through a network of offshore subsidiaries and banks. And a good deal of that, so it was thought, found its way back to Britain as Nadir illegally bought shares in Polly Peck in a desperate attempt to shore up the company's share price.

Added to that, he was personally indebted to the banks for millions of pounds he had borrowed as part of the same share support operation. That alone was to drive him into bankruptcy, although for people like Nadir bankruptcy is a relative term. The handsome flat in Eaton Square in the heart of Belgravia still afforded him luxurious accommodation. There was enough money around to support a decent lifestyle, even though the horses, the paintings and the country estate were eventually to go. He was very far from being on the breadline.

But he was extremely short of sympathy, an invaluable asset for a man to draw on when he is in trouble. There are plenty of cases where the City rallies around its friends when they get into deep water. As long as the people involved belong to the same club of shared background, education and loyalty, something can generally be done. Nadir had no such privileges. He had Mediterranean good looks and the charm to match them. His unpromising beginnings in his father's East End rag trade business did not impress anyone, in spite of a Queen's Award for Industry in 1973. And he had expanded – into areas which no one really understood. The City had only a tenuous grasp of a business which encompassed cardboard boxes, citrus fruit, fashion and textile outworkers knitting for low wages in Nadir's homeland. The packaging factory he owned in Famagusta became a major stake in a loss-making textile company called Polly Peck. This in turn became the vehicle for Nadir's stock market expansion. But even in those early days, Nadir was becoming a figure of controversy – not in the City but, out of the limelight, in his own country.

He was, of course, well known in Northern Cyprus, his birthplace. He had been spotted by Rauf Denktask, a wily, tough politician, who had been leader of the Turkish Federated State of Cyprus since 1975 and who was to become president of the Turkish Republic of Northern Cyprus in 1983, a republic which has no international status and is recognised only by Turkey.

Denktash wanted to inject some life into the economy of the republic and Nadir was happy to do it. It was his first important break and he made the most of it. Three businesses were established. The first was citrus growing (on land, so the Greeks claimed, expropriated from them). This was allied to the second, a packing factory, giving Nadir a virtual monopoly of the citrus business in Northern Cyprus. The other business was a cottage industry, based on knitting fashion garments for the UK market.

By 1983, these businesses had attracted a good deal of prominence, not all of it welcome. Nadir was making a lot of money, and that was helpful to his share price. On the other hand, the Greeks were kicking up a fuss with the human rights lobbyists, saying that he was exploiting his labour force by paying wages well below subsistence level. When I went to see Denktash in March 1983, nine months before he declared Northern Cyprus a Turkish republic, it was made plain to me that I was not to film any of Nadir's businesses for *The Money Programme*. Denktash, however, was fulsome in his praise of Nadir and scornful of Greek criticism. By this time, Nadir was the largest private contributor to Denktash's party funds.

In this sensitive, highly political context Nadir must have made very little sense to the operators in the City of London. Except for one thing: he was turning in profits which made Polly Peck a go-go stock. Nadir had also added to his Cypriot operations by expanding into electronics in Turkey and the City was happy to go along with his impressive record of growth. The fact that practically no one knew how he was making the money was neither here nor there – it was the figures that counted.

Those figures blipped suddenly in 1985 when the profits fell well below what its own stockbroker had forecast. The City reacted predictably and the shares plummeted. But Nadir was remarkably resilient. In the next five years he became the first European to buy control of a public Japanese company, Sansui, and then he scooped up an internationally famous name, Del Monte, the tinned fruit people. That deal alone pushed up Polly Peck shares by 40 per cent in 1989. By now he had added two more electronics companies to his rapidly growing empire – a joint venture in Turkey with the French electronics giant, Thomson, and a firm called Capetronic. In Turkey there was a Pizza Hut franchise up and running, and Polly Peck was building holiday apartments and hotels in

Northern Cyprus. The shares were now so much back in favour that in 1989 Nadir asked shareholders to invest the best part of £300 million in the business and they readily responded.

Greed is a powerful weapon in the hands of a capable businessman. It is a vice which affects equally the naive and the well-informed. It crosses all social and educational barriers and it generally defies rationality. It also has a lemming-like quality associated with it: once people have identified 'a good thing', they follow the crowd without asking questions.

But it's a rare businessman who doesn't follow the crowd. Having achieved a very large measure of success, Nadir kept to himself. He was not to be seen in all the usual watering holes favoured by businessmen who have 'arrived'. He kept out of nightclubs. He didn't participate in the social scene. And he didn't tell anyone how to run the economy, a common affliction among the newly successful in business. But he was a master of low-key public relations. Here is a man, the message went, who may play his cards close to his chest but who knows what he is doing better than most. He also had the advantage of a fractured English accent which made him hard work over the middle distance. He was not one for the instant, quotable sound-bite, even if he could be persuaded to come to the telephone.

The new, improved Polly Peck, though, proved to be shortlived. Nadir was always a loner, and no man, however talented, can run a large group of disparate businesses singlehanded. He made a nod in the direction of a proper corporate structure by acquiring experienced management from outside, but the relationship didn't work. He even called in the management consultants McKinsey, but no one was impressed. There are some bosses who are psychologically and temperamentally incapable of delegation. Nadir was secretive and sensitive but very hard and resilient with it, not someone to walk away at the first whiff of trouble.

Trouble, though, was only just around the corner a little over a year before Mates started to look into the Nadir affair. There were a number of 'bear' raids on Polly Peck shares in July and August of 1990 orchestrated, so Nadir believed, by the Greeks. The damaging news also slipped out that PPI and Nadir were being investigated by the Inland Revenue. The Turkish government did nothing for Nadir's mounting paranoia when they warned him that a major 'attack' (whatever that meant) would be made against him in October, initiated of course by the Greeks. Byzantine plots and dark intrigues have always been part of the Nadir ethos, even from the early days.

The question of whether that warning motivated Nadir to act as he then did, or whether it was the desire for a change of strategy, baffled even those people who worked closely with him. He decided he must buy back the company (he had only 25 per cent of the equity) and leave the country. Hounded by the twin phantoms of the Inland Revenue and the Greek furies, he may have concluded that it was his only option. If so, he tackled the proposition in a very high-handed way, summoning his board of directors to a Sunday lunchtime meeting on 12th August at which he put forward his proposal.

Nadir had travelled this route a year earlier when he had talked about buying back the company. That was in the middle of 1989 and he had told David Fawcus, his finance director, that the finance was in place to do the deal. Fawcus is a tall beanpole of a man, softly spoken, rational and very conventional for someone working in the environment of Polly Peck where Nadir played his cards so close to his chest. Neither Fawcus nor the rest of the board were a match for a man who was not in the habit of baring his business soul. In mid-1989 Fawcus told him it was a bad time to attempt a buy-out. There was too much happening. The bid for Del Monte was on the go and Sansui was in play. They had their hands full. Nadir accepted the arguments.

Looking back on that 1990 Sunday meeting a year later, Fawcus says that Nadir had flown to Switzerland the previous Thursday, presumably to discuss financing for the buy-out. The following day Fawcus phoned William Grosvenor, the company's public relations consultant, to say there would be some unfavourable publicity in the *Sunday Express* alleging

FO headquarters: Elm House, 10-16 Elm Street, London WC1. *(Press Association)*

Barbara Mills, SFO director, 1990-1992. *(Camera Press)*

George Staple, third and current director of the SFO. *(Topham Picture Point)*

George Churchill-Coleman, head of the Fraud Squad. *(Topham Picture Point)*

Lord Spens. *(Rex Features)*

Patrick ('Paddy') Mahon
and Andrew Kent.
(Press Association/Topham)

Roger Seelig. *(Topham Picture Point)*

Asil Nadir. *(Camera Press)*

Mr Justice Tucker, the judge in the Asil
Nadir case. *(Camera Press)*

Nazmu Virani. *(Topham Picture Point)*

Roger Levitt.
(Press Association/Topham)

Jonathan Goldberg QC,
Levitt's counsel.
(Press Association)

that Nadir was being investigated by the Inland Revenue in relation to offshore dealings in Polly Peck shares. On Saturday Fawcus got a telephone call from Peter Compson, a PPI director, saying that Nadir had landed at Luton in his private jet and wanted a board meeting on Sunday.

Fawcus managed to get through to Nadir later that Friday and learned that Nadir had not only resuscitated the buy-out idea but was now so far along the road that he thought an announcement should be made the following week. Fawcus told him it was inappropriate, it was much too rushed. He again told him it was inappropriate half an hour before the board meeting began. Polly Peck shares were standing then at around £4.50 and Fawcus thought that a fair price to offer the remaining 75 per cent of shareholders would be around £6 a share. That would cost £1.75 billion to fund. Where, Fawcus asked, was the money coming from? Nadir indicated that a lot of it would be coming from Turkey, but was no more specific. This time Fawcus couldn't talk Nadir out of the deal. Nadir went on to convince his board that he had the finance available and wanted to go ahead with the buy-out. He then withdrew from the meeting while his directors discussed the proposal.

They decided to get independent advice, and after a good deal of ringing around managed to get in a partner from Clifford Chance, the City solicitors, and an adviser from Standard Chartered Bank. Their advice was to go ahead and disclose the buy-out proposal to the market as soon as possible. That meant the next day, Monday 13 August. At this stage there had been no indication, from Nadir or anyone else, how the institutions would react to the offer, always an important constituent – sometimes crucial – when it comes to getting an offer accepted. Nor had any price been mentioned. Nor was it mentioned on Monday, when the bid became public.

The following day, Tuesday, Friends' Provident, quite the biggest institutional shareholder with 4.5 per cent of the equity, rang Fawcus to say they weren't happy with it but would be prepared to remain minority shareholders in a private company. That was not the plan at all; Nadir was looking for a buy-out, not a new form of partnership. The smaller institutions, amounting to 0.25 per cent, said much the same thing. Under the terms of the offer, Nadir had to get 92.5 per cent acceptance from the outstanding shareholders if he was to succeed.

'At that stage,' Fawcus said, 'it was pretty obvious that the buy-out wasn't on. The institutions, representing 4.75 per cent, were against it. A lot of other shareholders wouldn't bother to respond, probably from inertia. The arithmetic was against the buy-out succeeding and I told Nadir so.

'On Wednesday, Nadir said he was going to call it off. I said that would seriously damage his credibility and harm the company. It was much better to bid and fail rather than walk away from it. But Nadir was insistent and on Friday the whole thing was scrapped.'

The moment that happened, Fawcus recalls, the shares plummeted. Early the following week, the Stock Exchange called in Nadir and Fawcus and said they were going to conduct an inquiry into what had happened. The Exchange said they would allow the Polly Peck board to see a draft of their conclusions so that they could comment on them. The PPI board would get the document at 2.00 pm, giving the board just an hour to respond before the report was published at 3.00 pm. In the event, Polly Peck got the draft only twenty minutes before publication was due and telephoned the Exchange at 3.15 pm on Friday 24 August, wanting to make six points. But they could find no one in authority there. Monday was a Bank Holiday and Friday afternoon was evidently being treated as part of the long weekend.

When the report was published, the Polly Peck directors realised the Exchange had given them only a small part of the document for comment. It criticised Nadir for his timing and lack of preparation, and there were veiled criticisms of the board for allowing the buy-out disclosure to go ahead so soon – in spite of the fact that the directors had been urged to do so by their advisers. Nadir was also criticised for convening a board meeting at only twenty-four hours' notice. But, astonishingly, there was no mention of how Nadir was going to finance the buy-out. The Stock Exchange said it was passing the report to the DTI and the SFO. A month after this, the board of Polly Peck wrote to John Redwood, at that time corporate affairs minister at the DTI, to ask if he would appoint inspectors to look into what was happening at Polly Peck.

The letter was signed by Asil Nadir, and it was obvious that he was a badly shaken man. 'The situation', he wrote, 'has deteriorated most seriously with damaging media reports of alleged actions of various governmental bodies . . . So intense and severe is the attack on the company and on myself that we, on our own, are unlikely to be able to find a fair hearing. Therefore the board of Polly Peck International plc formally requests that the Secretary of State appoint independent inspectors to investigate and report under the appropriate section of the Companies Act.'

It looked a highly responsible plea to the minister. Here was a chairman who took seriously his stewardship of a large public company. But it was a cry in the wilderness. Redwood, every bit as tough and ambitious as Nadir, probably realised the difficulties. He noted that the Secretary of State was at present 'satisfied that the SFO have the necessary powers to investigate all the allegations of which we are aware'. That was the last thing Nadir wanted to hear. Redwood then went on to offer the company an investigation under Section 431 of the Companies Act; 'but I must warn you that asking for an enquiry under that section would mean that your company could be required to meet the costs of the investigation. These could exceed £1 million.'

It was a kind but expensive offer, and not one which Polly Peck could possibly take up. Such an investigation would have taken months anyway, far too long to be any use, and it was clear that Redwood was happy to leave the whole business to the SFO. That was the sting in the tail. The people at Elm Street had got there first.

Shortly before this, Fawcus attended the opening of a Polly Peck hotel in Northern Cyprus, where he began to learn things about Nadir he had never suspected. His informant was Dennis Robertson, the senior partner of Stoy Hayward (Polly

Peck's auditors). Back in London, Robertson told Fawcus that stockbrokers' records showed there had been dealings in Polly Peck shares involving eight offshore 'letter-box' companies. Robertson also revealed that the Inland Revenue's Special Office 2 (the commandos of the tax collecting business who specialise in catching rich evaders) had been investigating Nadir for more than a year. They thought that Nadir was using the offshore companies for dealing in Polly Peck shares and probably not declaring his taxable profits to the Revenue. They were apparently interested only in his tax liabilities which, as a UK resident, he was obliged to pay. However, the Inland Revenue were also convinced that funds from Polly Peck subsidiaries had been used to pay for the share deals.

All this was news to Fawcus, particularly the intelligence that the Stock Exchange surveillance department had known what had been going on for some time and had not chosen to tell the Polly Peck board (nor, for that matter, had Stoy Hayward). So the board, the company's shareholders and the public were in total ignorance of the real situation. Fawcus was so shocked by this state of affairs that he traipsed off to report the matter to the SFO in Elm Street, only to find that a Polly Peck manager had already talked to them.

As Nadir had said to Redwood, the company was by now in desperate trouble. There were whispers of insider dealing and the shares started to slip. Nadir himself began to buy Polly Peck stock by the thousand, saying they were cheap. But the rot had started. The SFO added to the prevailing nervousness about Polly Peck when they raided Nadir's private company, South Audley Management, in the full glare of publicity on 19 September. At that point Polly Peck shares 'fell out of bed'. There has been much speculation about what happened next, especially about the share suspension, but Fawcus knows what happened because he was closely involved.

At 8.30 am on 20 September, the day after the SFO raid on South Audley Management, Fawcus met Nadir and told him there were rumours in the papers that Polly Peck was losing a lot of money. The shares were in free fall. Nadir then told Fawcus at 11.30 am that he was in serious financial trouble. Merrill Lynch were trying to sell 5.5 million of his Polly Peck shares because they had made margin calls on them (in other words, they were trying to recover some of the money Nadir owed them). Fawcus asked Nadir what the total extent of his borrowings was against PPI shares and Nadir replied they were in the region of £70 to £80 million.

Fawcus then came up with a number of suggestions, three of which concerned rearrangements of Nadir's personal finances. The other was to ask the Stock Exchange for a suspension of the shares. Nadir said he had no time to put any of the first three suggestions in place and Fawcus should ask BZW, one of Polly Peck's brokers, to arrange for a suspension.

Astonishingly, Nadir then revealed to Fawcus that earlier in the morning he had been in touch with Lehman Brothers (another of Polly Peck's brokers) asking for a suspension but this had not been forthcoming.

It was by now almost lunchtime. Fawcus rang BZW with no luck, but he left urgent messages. BZW phoned back later that afternoon, by which time the suspension was in place. He then tried to get hold of Peter Barton at Lehman Brothers, but he was not around. His office eventually found him and Barton returned the call half an hour later. Fawcus told him that if Nadir was forced into a major sale of Polly Peck shares the market in them would collapse and all shareholders would be hurt. Barton agreed and said he would try to get a suspension. But he had difficulty in getting hold of the right people at the Stock Exchange. Eventually, someone was pulled out of a lunch and the suspension went ahead at about 2.15 that afternoon. The whole process had taken about an hour and a half, in which time the shares had fallen by around 50p to their suspension price of 108p. As Fawcus put it, someone had managed to 'make a packet'.

Of course, much earlier that day Nadir had been in touch with Lehman Brothers, according to Nadir, about suspension. Who it was who made 'a packet' and if it was ever investigated, if true, we are never likely to know. I wrote to the Stock Exchange asking about timings of the suspension, share trades at that particular time, and for any information which might have indicated unusual dealings. I received a dismissive note from a man called Peter Gerrard, the Exchange's 'General Council', who said he could give me no information because of the confidentiality restrictions imposed by the Financial Services Act.

On the afternoon of the suspension, Nadir went voluntarily to see the SFO at Elm Street and was interviewed under Section 2. When he emerged three hours later, the press and cameras were waiting for him. After that, the pressures on Nadir began to mount very quickly. The banks had already started to call in their loans. Consequently, the company began to raid its subsidiaries for funds to meet the banks' demands. The end of the game was in sight.

A week earlier, Nadir had made one of his last gambits: he appealed to the Turkish government for help. President Ozal approached Mrs Thatcher on 12 September. Pragmatic as ever, she replied that it was a matter for the SFO. The next man to try was the Turkish Minister for Economic Affairs, who contacted Whitehall on 28 September, a week after the suspension of Polly Peck shares. Then something quite bizarre happened. An official from the Foreign Office replied on the same day that nothing short of £100 million would have to be injected into the company by 10 am the following Monday. Even that, he said, would not necessarily save the company. The Foreign Office is not noted for its financial expertise, let alone for replying to a request in a matter of hours. Where they had conjured the figure from, whose advice they had taken, how they arrived at the response, can only be a matter for the wildest conjecture.

Whoever was responsible, whatever tortuous routes the reasoning followed, is neither here nor there: Turkey did not put up the money and if it had it would not have been enough. It might, however, have injected some confidence into the market to give Polly Peck some badly needed breathing space. Investors might have thought that with the Turkish government in support the company was viable. But the dream was illusory. The money did not appear.

All financial crises are full of ifs and buts, but there is a grim truth to the big crises: once they start to roll, it takes massive bank support and very big names behind it to stop the rot. Investor confidence is a fragile thing at the best of times.

Throughout the proceedings leading up to the suspension, the Polly Peck board were mostly in ignorance of what had been going on. Nadir, of course, was the exception: he knew everything but was not known for imparting information. Fawcus believes that had the board been put in the picture by the relevant authorities (particularly the Stock Exchange Surveillance Department), Polly Peck's directors would have been able to do something, even if it was to make the gesture of resigning *en masse* in protest. As it was, by the time they knew anything it was too late. On 24 October 1990, Polly Peck's directors asked for the company to be put into administration. One of the main reasons for the application, Fawcus said, was that the government of the Northern Republic of Cyprus had blocked the repatriation of funds from the island to the company in London, arguing that the money was needed in Northern Cyprus and that if it was returned it would damage the Polly Peck companies out there as well as the economy of the island. The company, then, was insolvent.

Six days after the administrators had been appointed, the SFO made a dawn raid on the company's headquarters in Berkeley Square and took away a substantial number of documents. The SFO's handling of publicity on this occasion was well above their usual standard: the press were actually in position *before* the SFO arrived. Astonished office staff were even told by the press that they were there by invitation of the SFO.

Mates's involvement with Nadir began in the late summer of 1991, after the MP had been approached by a constituent of his, Mark Rogerson, a public relations adviser to Nadir, who thought his client had been getting a raw deal from the SFO. Mates was then a backbencher, not a minister. Nadir told him the story of how he had been treated and his arrest. 'He fired very wide,' Mates said, 'about everything he thought was wrong. I then spoke to Anthony Scrivener, Nadir's counsel, saying that I was incredulous at what I had heard. Scrivener then confirmed to me that he could smell so many rats he didn't know where to begin. [Scrivener is one of the brightest and most successful counsel at the bar and was at that time chairman of the Bar Council.] I then distilled what I had heard from Nadir and raised those matters in my first letter to the Attorney General, Sir Patrick Mayhew, on 20 September 1991.'

The first concern was about an SFO raid on Polly Peck's headquarters in which they seized privileged papers from Nadir's office (see Chapter 5). This turned out to be a crucial complaint, the truth of which was only admitted by the SFO and the Attorney General who succeeded Mayhew, Nicholas Lyell, more than two years later. Mayhew maintained, in his letter to Mates in October, that the documents which had been copied were not legally privileged. Mayhew was wrong. They were not only privileged but they had been copied and circulated, not only to SFO lawyers but to the Polly Peck administrators as well. The Attorney General could only have got his information from the SFO, where the case controller for Nadir was Mrs Lorna Harris, a lawyer who was to gain increasing notoriety among counsel and solicitors for not being up to the job.

Some months earlier, Mrs Harris had made her presence felt when Nadir applied for a variation of his terms of bail. He wanted to travel abroad, supervised and escorted by the two administrators of PPI who had been given the task of reconstructing the company. The idea was that Nadir would assist them in identifying the company's assets in the Northern Republic of Cyprus, and his application was supported by the administrators. In addition to the two administrators, there was a third – Christopher Morris, of the accountants Touche Ross, whose job was to investigate all claims against the directors and advisers of the company.

Mrs Harris made it plain to Morris and his advisers that if he supported the application, he would be cross-examined. The SFO said they would oppose the application on the grounds of the evidence being offered by the administrators. Subsequently one of the administrators was cross-examined, appearing for himself and his partner. Morris, however, declined to go through the hoops. Mates later complained to the Attorney General that Harris's approach to Morris was 'clearly intimidatory and improper', which Mayhew refuted in his reply. Nadir's solicitor, Peter Knight of Vizards, who was present at the proceedings, confirmed that Harris's behaviour towards Morris was anything but even-handed.

While Mates was not technically right to challenge the SFO's opposition to a variation of bail, although apparently correct about Harris's behaviour, he was right to take up with Mayhew the question of media publicity surrounding the SFO's raids of Polly Peck offices, as well as the media coverage of Nadir being interviewed at Elm Street or being taken into Holborn police station. Mates complained that when South Audley Management was raided by the SFO, there was a press release from Elm Street announcing the raid. The day after, when Nadir turned up at Elm Street to be interviewed, the SFO told the press where they could find him so that when Nadir left the building he did so in a blaze of publicity. He also protested that when the SFO raided the PPI headquarters, the press managed to arrive ten minutes ahead of the people from Elm Street.

Of course, all this was denied vigorously by Mayhew and the SFO. There have been other raids, dealt with elsewhere, where by some process of osmosis the press and TV cameras have had an uncanny prescience about where to be and when. Nobody has ever believed the SFO or the government when it comes to these denials. They are the common currency of Elm Street, under cover of which SFO staff can do pretty much as they like.

There were rebuttals of further claims made by Mates in his letter to Mayhew. (Mayhew, of course, had never met the IRA until he was caught out and had to admit it, so he might be equally economical with the truth when talking about the SFO's actions.) Mates claimed that the SFO interviewed Nadir at Elm Street on 20 September 1990, when he was questioned about Inland Revenue matters by Robert Wardle, a solicitor, who succeeded Lorna Harris as the Nadir case controller and David Morrison, an accountant and an assistant director of the SFO. Mates said that when the SFO were asked about the source of the papers they were using, they mentioned a bank known as KOP, but then went on to say that the SFO actually got the papers two months later, the inference being that the papers had in some way come from the Revenue. Mayhew denied that, saying that they were working off KOP papers at the time. Mayhew only had the SFO's word for that, and as they had already lied about Nadir's privileged documents, there was no reason to suppose that they weren't lying this time. Peter Knight was present at the SFO interview with Nadir. He knew that the Inland Revenue had been investigating his client for the last eighteen months and it was precisely about these matters that the two men questioned Nadir – 'although in a very ham-fisted, amateur way'.

The truth looks a lot more Byzantine. Michael Allcock, of the Inland Revenue's élite Special Office 2, had information from a number of Stock Exchange brokers that there were a lot of overseas companies dealing in shares and probably concealing their profits from the taxman. Allcock identified some of these 'letter-box' outfits as being controlled by Nadir who was using them to deal in Polly Peck stock. Allcock relayed his suspicions to the Stock Exchange Surveillance Department. The question then was, who passed the information to the SFO – the Revenue or the Stock Exchange? The Revenue at that stage appeared to get a bad attack of nerves. That seems to have been borne out by what happened on 21 September, the day after the Elm Street interview with Nadir.

There was a meeting between Knight and two men from the IR in Vizards' boardroom. The Revenue's men were Michael Allcock and R. Cook, both from Special Office 2. They had known about Nadir's interview the previous day because of the press coverage it had generated and the fact that there had been a leak to the media giving the subject matter of the interview. What worried Cook was the allegation that the leak had come from the Revenue. He was also concerned that it might be thought his office had exchanged information with, or passed it to the Stock Exchange.

The Revenue, in fact, has no business passing information about people's private tax affairs to anyone. But Allcock much later admitted passing information to the

Stock Exchange about Nadir companies trading in Polly Peck shares. With his swept-back hair and Clark Gable moustache, Allcock was something of a high roller in the Revenue, rubbing shoulders with millionaire expatriates living in Britain, and clearly enjoying his reputation as a fearless tax investigator. If he wanted to cultivate contacts at the Stock Exchange he was going the right way about it.

Cook also had something else on his mind – namely that the Revenue had passed information to the SFO. Knight took a note of this meeting, which turned out to be a bizarre occasion. He was handed a copy of a note of a conversation which he was allowed to read twice and then hand back. If it were so important, and it evidently was, the Revenue men might have given him more time. It was about five paragraphs long, according to Knight, and referred to a telephone conversation on 21 August 1990, between Michael Chance, deputy director of the SFO, and a Mr Parrott, one of the three undersecretaries at the Revenue.

Chance telephoned Parrott to say that there was to be a meeting on the coming Thursday between the SFO and the DTI and that someone from the Metropolitan Police would also be there. It had been called because of some recent press articles. Chance said he was inviting the Revenue to attend so that they could chair and *exchange information which would assist the SFO in their inquiries* (my emphasis).

Parrott declined the offer, saying he couldn't see any useful purpose for such a meeting. But he did confirm they were investigating Nadir's tax affairs, and this was proceeding satisfactorily towards a monetary settlement. He also said that no offences had been committed of a revenue nature that would result in a prosecution. On those grounds alone there would be little point in the meeting Chance had proposed.

Parrott went on to rub salt into the wound. He told Chance that the SFO was on a fishing expedition, triggered by the press articles, and that they had nothing to go on and were unlikely to find anything. According to Parrott's note of the conversation, Chance agreed that was the case.

This was an astonishing admission, giving every appearance at that stage that the SFO had little idea of where it was going.

That was confirmed by the two men from the Revenue who told Knight that the raid on South Audley Management on 19 September, and the Nadir interview the following day, had been a 'monumental disaster'. They went on to say they couldn't see the point of the raid on South Audley Management, with the disastrous effect it was bound to have, and that nothing of evidential value could be obtained. They also thought the SFO's actions would probably destroy the company; a prescient comment.

This was an alarming meeting by any standards. Whatever may be said about the Inland Revenue, it is not known for its unprofessionalism. The conversation with Knight amounted to a scathing attack on the competence of the SFO. Knight, however, had other things on his mind. He remembered that when Wardle and Morrison interviewed Nadir, they seemed 'singularly unclear what they were interviewing him about'. Whatever the source of their information, they gave the impression they were blundering about and seemed incapable of indicating what the cause of their concern was. Knight and Nadir decided to seek a judicial review of what the then director of the SFO, Barbara Mills, was doing. Mills at that point had been in the director's chair only a few months. The Nadir investigation had been initiated by John Wood, but the case controller, Lorna Harris, was still in charge.

'The nub of our argument,' Knight said, 'was that the director had to have some reasonable grounds for commencing an investigation. It wasn't apparent from the interview what reasonable grounds she could have for suspecting that serious or complex fraud was involved. And that anyone was entitled to know what they were being investigated about in order to rebut the allegations. Otherwise it meant that Nadir was supposed to sit there and watch Polly Peck go into free fall and see all the company's assets destroyed.'

Knight complained formally to Mills about his client's treatment, to which she replied that it was no good writing to her as the matter was being dealt with by the case controller. Knight persisted with Mrs Mills, who eventually said that the reasons she had were her own reasons and she was going no further than that.

Knight then applied to the court for an order to get Mrs Mills to tell them what her concerns were – a process called judicial review. This is a two-stage process, the first of which requires the plaintiff to show that he has an arguable case in law. That was lost before Mr Justice Steyn. However, it went to appeal and it was decided that legally there was a case to argue. They never got any further because Nadir was arrested.

The arrest took place on December 15th, 1990, when Nadir landed at Heathrow from Northern Cyprus. His flight plan had originally been for his private plane to land at Luton airport, but apparently it was diverted at the last moment to Heathrow on police instructions. The SFO, it was said, wanted the publicity and the prestige of the arrest and they had no intention of handing it on a plate to the Bedfordshire constabulary. But the arrangements for the arrest were little short of ludicrous and illustrated the SFO's appetite for high-profile publicity and penchant for drama.

By no stretch of the imagination could Nadir be regarded as a latter-day Al Capone. He is the antithesis of a gun-toting, fast-talking thug. He enjoyed the artefacts of civilisation, such as antiques and good pictures. If he used bodyguards, it was because he was frightened that the Greeks might do something to him.

The SFO viewed him in a different light. When he landed at Heathrow, armed police were waiting on the apron. On board were a handful of people, including the pilot and Nadir; hardly a gang likely to come out fighting. But the SFO had decided to ring the plane with cars and armed police. The police explained their armed presence by saying they were from the Drugs Squad, and had been tipped off that Nadir's plane contained illegal drugs. That gave Nadir an exceptionally poor intelligence rating. Having been told that he was likely to be arrested on his return to Britain, it was beyond belief that he would be minded to stuff his plane with drugs. That, all of it, was down to Barbara Mills, who by that time had her bottom firmly in the chair at Elm Street, with Lorna Harris, the case controller, in charge of operations.

After the arrest, things were never going to be the same for

Nadir. As Michael Mates was to point out much later, Nadir had been arrested 'about eight times without warning. The arrests had been accompanied by great publicity and often coincided with hearings'. Mates was worried about the conduct of the case and felt that Nadir had been unjustly treated. Mistakenly, perhaps, he dragged in a political dimension, saying he thought the intelligence services might be involved and believed there could be strong pressure for the conviction of Nadir in order to provide a solution to the problem of Northern Cyprus; that Nadir dominated the republic's economy, and his conviction would almost certainly lead to its collapse. That is an arguable assertion. No one has ever been quite clear how much of the economy Nadir did control. The larger the slice, of course, the more it enhanced Nadir's importance. It is true, though, that if all Polly Peck's businesses in Cyprus went to the wall the economy would take a very bad knock.

Mates by this time had built up a powerful head of steam against the SFO and was calling repeatedly for an official inquiry into the organisation. But he had one piece of very bad luck. An acquaintance of his, a rich man who had been scammed by a fraudster, claimed that an SFO official had approached him, asking him 'to improve' his statement to the police so that they could get a conviction. When Mates asked him for an affidavit, the man refused.

After the general election in April 1992, Mates became a minister at the Northern Ireland Office. This left him with a dilemma. As a backbencher he had been perfectly in order pursuing Nadir's complaints with the Attorney, but he wasn't so sure he could continue now he was a member of the government. He was kept in touch with what was going on, and Nadir's counsel, Anthony Scrivener, advised him that things were going relatively well. Scrivener had formed the opinion that the SFO didn't have a case and it suited his book for things not to be stirred up.

However, in the autumn of 1992 matters once again took a turn for the worse. This was the dangerous farce surrounding the judge in the case, Mr Justice Tucker, and an allegation that he was involved in a conspiracy to pervert the course of justice. It was not something that Mates could ignore; on the other hand, he had his role as a minister to consider. He took advice 'at the highest level' and was told that as long as his worries accorded with his constituency duties and any 'other proper interests' then it was perfectly all right.

Having had the green light, Mates then went to see the new Attorney General, Nick Lyell, to take up the bizarre case of Mr Justice Tucker.

It was on 2 October 1992, that the SFO set itself new standards of high farce and dubious conduct. It concerned a preparatory hearing before Mr Justice Tucker at the Old Bailey. In court there was a bevy of counsel for the prosecution, led by Robert Owen QC; for Nadir there was the formidable Anthony Scrivener, whose appetite for work is legendary, supported by his junior; two more counsel representing John Turner, another defendant in the case; and one more QC, Mr Alun Jones, who was there on behalf of the Director of Public Prosecutions and whose presence was something of a surprise.

The only person who wasn't there was the judge, Mr Justice Tucker. As 10 am passed without any sign of his lordship, inquiries were made as to his whereabouts. It turned out that he was still in chambers but in good health, a fact which, after what he had just heard, must be put down to the strength of his constitution. The SFO had just put in an urgent submission to the Lord Chief Justice alleging that there was a £3.5 million contract in existence to get Nadir out of the country.

There was nothing very odd about that: the prosecution often grasps at straws which turn out to be chimeras. This allegation, though, was far more serious; it was the sting in the tail that counted, and it was aimed directly at Mr Justice Tucker. The SFO alleged that the £3.5 million 'was to be paid to the judge following the successful application for variation of bail conditions'. In other words, if the judge varied the conditions to allow Nadir to leave the country (and by implication not stand trial) he would be £3.5 million richer. Whether any judge is actually worth three-and-a-half million was no doubt the subject of spirited debate in London's clubland. But the SFO clearly took that view, and by implication thought that the judge could be bribed. It was an astonishing allegation, unprecedented in British legal history.

Mr Justice Tucker could not have been the SFO's favourite man on the bench, since earlier that year Anthony Scrivener had made a successful application to him to have forty-six charges against Nadir dropped. The bribery allegation, following his lordship's favourable decision for Nadir, was just a little too contiguous for comfort. And it so happened that Nadir was about to apply for a variation of bail conditions. If Tucker took it into his head to let him pop off to Northern Cyprus for a pleasant break from British justice, the prosecution would be shattered. One could almost hear the laborious grinding of the SFO's mental machinery and the clucking of tongues at the grim prospect of Nadir slipping through their clutches. A corrupt judge would be an admirable scenario to put the case back on course.

While everyone was scratching their heads, another senior judge, Mr Justice Pill, suddenly emerged, to the surprise of the court. He had been quickly drafted in to replace the hapless Tucker. But applications for variations of bail in a case like Nadir's cannot be disposed of in a matter of minutes by a new judge quite unfamiliar with the case.

'In front of Tucker,' Scrivener said, 'I would have got the application over in forty-five minutes. In front of Pill it would have taken a day and a half while I explained the facts of the case to him. This would have thrown the proceedings into chaos, especially as Tucker was technically in charge of the case and might come back at any time.'

So the hearing was rescheduled for 6 November. This, too, was cancelled, but the judge decided to appear in court to give his reaction to being served an SFO document. Showing a good deal of restraint and composure, Tucker said: 'It is an astonishing document and an astonishing suggestion.'

At that point Robert Owen, counsel for the SFO, decided to twist the knife, when he said: '. . . It is only right that I should mention that those responsible for the investigation instruct those intructing me that there is a probability that officers involved in that investigation would wish to interview your lordship. My lord, I am obliged to mention that because it may be relevant to the question of your lordship's *view of continuing to preside over this matter*' (my emphasis).

Showing admirable restraint, Tucker replied: 'I find it a most unsatisfactory and unsettling situation; I need hardly tell you.' The law is fond of precedents, but his lordship would have been hard put to it to find one on this occasion. He also registered his mounting discomfort: 'What alarms me is the suggestion that someone may come and wish to interview me.'

Anthony Scrivener is a sophisticated, highly intelligent advocate who enjoys one of the most lucrative practices at the bar. His chambers in Gray's Inn wouldn't disgrace a law firm on Wall Street. He is a former chairman of the Bar Council and a formidable adversary in court. He also has the gift of almost total recall to which he allies a good deal of impish charm. But even Scrivener was astounded by what he had heard in court. Dashing back to his chambers he dictated a long letter to the Attorney General, Sir Nicholas Lyell.

The opening paragraph sets the tone: 'I have just returned from court after today's hearing in the proceedings concerning my client Mr Asil Nadir when to my total amazement Prosecuting Counsel announced that the SFO intended to interview Mr Justice Tucker upon the "*allegation*" made. I simply note that I do not believe the *information available* would justify interviewing anyone let alone a High Court judge.'

This was a strong protest from senior counsel, bearing in mind that he didn't represent the judge. Scrivener went on: 'I must confess that it had not occurred to me that the SFO would be considering such a bizarre course of action. It was quite obvious that the judge was visibly shaken by this suggestion.'

Scrivener drove the point home: 'Obviously such a step has grave constitutional implications. It means that a judge who finds against the SFO on some matter (the judge in this case found that over forty counts were bad in law) would be vulnerable to such an allegation and have to withdraw from trying a case. It seemed to us that Mr Justice Tucker was very conscious of this.'

Nadir's counsel went on to complain about the conduct of other issues, all of which concerned his client's problems and many of which were about the SFO. Scrivener could scarcely believe the SFO's handling of the Tucker interview by the police. 'Open letters were faxed to our instructing solicitors,' he wrote, 'and quite deliberately the fax was sent to the Judge around 10.00 am and the one to the defence was delayed to around 5.00 pm! The implication is that either we should be given the shortest possible warning of this or else that, as the Judge remarked, the defence might contact the Judge!

'Before authorising the step of requiring a High Court judge of the highest reputation and integrity to be interviewed by the SFO I would ask you to conduct an inquiry into the way the prosecution in this case has been handled.'

This was a delicate matter Scrivener was referring to. While Lorna Harris was the case controller, Robert Owen QC was directing all aspects of the case for the prosecution. It had taken him and the SFO fourteen months from the date of Nadir's arrest to get the case transferred from the magistrates' court to the crown court. 'At one stage,' Scrivener told the Attorney General, 'when the chief magistrate expressed his annoyance at the time the case was taking and ordered the papers to be ready the SFO did not comply with the date and bluntly told the chief magistrate that it was for the director of the SFO to decide when the transfer should take place, not the chief magistrate. I should say that the chief magistrate did not look kindly upon the suggestion.'

It was a nice form of sarcasm. Scrivener listed a substantial number of complaints, none of which got anywhere with the Attorney General or, indeed, with the director of the SFO, George Staple. In the case of the wretched Mr Justice Tucker and the alleged conspiracy to pervert the course of justice, both had decided to say that it had nothing to do with the SFO but was the province of the Metropolitan Police, who were investigating the matter. In effect, while the SFO were prosecuting Nadir, and while Robert Owen QC thought fit on behalf of the SFO to raise the matter of the judge, the SFO was going to have its cake and eat it by distancing itself from the allegations against the judge, still maintaining that it was of legitimate concern.

The whole business was to backfire embarrassingly in the SFO's face. Robert Owen had told the judge on 6th November that 'there is a probability that officers involved in the investigation would wish to interview your lordship'. A little over a month later Scrivener was on his feet at a different hearing to question Superintendent Thomas Glendenning, the man in charge of the bribery investigation.

Scrivener: Was it ever your intention to interview the person named in the highlighted section of that report [Judge Tucker]?

Glendenning: We have never declared that intention . . . Until we get some confirmation that there is any foundation whatsoever to this dreadful allegation, I cannot say.

Owen and the SFO had got the whole business catastrophically wrong, but that, astonishingly, was not to be the end of the affair. Glendenning had made it plain there was no intention of interviewing the judge, but hinted that he would need some confirmation of the allegation before he went that far.

That did not stop Owen and the SFO from yet again taking the bull by the wrong horns. Three months later, on 8 March 1993, at the beginning of a hearing at Chichester Rents, Owen referred to an application that the judge should discharge himself from the trial. It was a promising start to a hearing where it was alleged not only that Mr Justice Tucker was one of the parties to the charge of corruption, but so too were Mr Scrivener, Asil Nadir and an assistant commissioner of the Metropolitan Police, Wyn Jones.

Proceedings in Beachcomber's Mr Justice Cocklecarrot could not have been more bizarre. Mr Alun Jones, representing the DPP, made the allegations and went on to hint darkly that he knew a good deal more about the details of the allegations than he could disclose in court. But, he emphasised, 'The police have got to the stage from which it is reasonable to conclude that this allegation is not a hoax or a prank.'

One wonders if Mr Jones or Superintendent Glendenning or the Sherlock Holmes at the SFO ever wake up at night sweating with embarrassment at having been taken for a ride. They were all victims of what Mr Jones so emphatically ruled out as a hoax. Oblivious to the absurdity of his situation, Mr Jones continued portentously to delineate that Nadir was either attempting to destabilise the trial, or that someone was doing so on his behalf, or that an attempt was being made to embarrass Nadir by his enemies.

Jones made no mention of the people he had just scooped into the allegations – Mr Justice Tucker, Nadir, Scrivener and Wyn Jones. But that did not escape the notice of the learned judge, who asked, 'Where does that take me, Mr Alun Jones? You have set a scene, you have told me nothing to substantiate any of this, you leave me completely in the dark.'

There is nothing like a barrister who is privy to information he cannot disclose, even to a judge who had allegedly conspired to pervert the course of justice for £3.5 million. No mention was made of whether Judge Tucker was proposing to share the money with Mr Scrivener and Mr Wyn Jones, or in what proportions. Alun Jones was in receipt of vital information and he was deeply conscious of his trust.

It was a moment most people would relish. Solemnly he assured those present, for the second time, that the allegation was not 'being dismissed as a hoax or a prank'. Anxious for elucidation, Mr Justice Tucker asked: 'Would you mind telling me what the alleged connection between Mr Nadir, me, Mr Scrivener and Mr Assistant Commissioner Wyn Jones is?'

Mr Jones might have been forgiven for smirking. Seldom, if ever, do counsel have power over a judge – overt power, that is. Sitting before him was a member of Her Majesty's judiciary who could well have taken, or be on the point of taking, or had in mind to take, several million pounds. This was not an everyday occasion.

'I cannot tell your lordship that,' Mr Jones said portentously.

Their lordships are never told to mind their own business. 'It is,' he went on, 'an operational matter' (a reference to the earnest endeavours of Superintendent Glendenning who, even as Mr Jones spoke, was being busily hoaxed). 'The identity of informants,' Mr Jones continued (by now, no doubt, in a paroxysm of legal contentment), 'is an important consideration I have in mind.'

By this time Mr Justice Tucker was probably wondering if he had walked into a nightmare. Normally, judges control (or like to think they control) events in court. But matters were fast slipping away from him. He was becoming a puppet of 'operational matters', unknown informants, sinister events. He asked again, 'Where do you suggest all this places me?'

At that point Judge Tucker suddenly became an ordinary mortal. It was a cry in the wilderness. Dark forces were at work. This, at last, gave Mr Jones the opportunity to launch into the long circumlocution for which he was being handsomely paid. All that had passed before was of no importance. He was in court to tell the judge that, all things being equal, it would be just as well if Judge Tucker stood down.

Mr Jones put it differently. 'Your lordship,' he pronounced, 'would have to balance the desirability of informing the defence of the material, which is in the possession of the prosecution, if they argue that it is relevant, balance that on the one hand with the importance of preserving the anonymity of defendants upon the other – of course, the doctrine of public interest immunity and the balancing exercise judges are frequently called upon to determine (sic).

'My Lord, it is not difficult to envisage that your lordship could then be in a position of having to look at material to decide whether that material ought to be disclosed to the defence, and your lordship would be looking at material setting out allegations against your lordship, and indeed my learned friend [Mr Scrivener], and deciding in the balancing exercise how that ought to come down, in favour of prosecution or defence.'

In other words (and several hundreds if not thousands of pounds later, as far as the excellent Mr Jones was concerned), the judge might just have a conflict of interest, with the carrot of several million quid dangling before him. He would therefore, in the submission of the DPP, be hard put to it to know what to do.

Judge Tucker is not allowed to disclose his state of mind while this was going on as, technically, he will still try the case if and when Nadir returns from Northern Cyprus. But he must have found the episode deeply disturbing. Having been told that he could, weighing one thing with another, be in pole position to corrupt the trial, he was constrained to ask: 'Supposing I stand down, what becomes of the next judge?'

Mr Jones, who had been hypothesising all along, then said: 'My lord, it is hypothesising.'

Out of the blue, and by this time wondering whether he was in Wonderland, Mr Justice Tucker asked (quite inconsequentially): 'I thought there was the assumption that Her Majesty's judges were incorruptible.'

This was not a notion that had struck Mr Jones before. He hedged; eloquently, but he hedged. He was a paid hedger and he wasn't prepared to let Judge Tucker off the hook. 'Unquestionably the difficulty', he said, 'is it appears to us that if your lordship is put in a position of having to disclose [names of witnesses] or not, my lord, there is that embarrassment of the kind to which we have pointed.'

Namely, that if Judge Tucker were party to a conspiracy, he would be in no mood to play along with the prosecution. Mr Jones then went on to draw a picture in which, hypothetically, something had been alleged against Nadir which involved Anthony Scrivener. Mr Justice Tucker might then be asked to disclose material to the defence and asked to say that the public interest – that is, keeping the informants' names and identities secret – should not come into the reckoning. In that case, his lordship might well be in an invidious position. Mr Jones then submitted that there were serious problems foreseeable and dangers in Judge Tucker presiding over the trial.

A little later Mr Owen, for the prosecution, took up the running where Mr Jones had finished for the DPP. Having painted a black picture of what would happen if the trial were destabilised, he advised the judge to think long and hard before disqualifying himself from the trial. If Mr Owen had been listening he would have been able to infer from what Mr Justice Tucker had said earlier that the judge had no intention of disqualifying himself. After further lengthy comments from Mr Owen it was decided to proceed with the full preparatory hearing.

When everyone reconvened four days later in judge's chambers, things had taken a turn for the worse. Nadir had been arrested by Superintendent Glendenning over the conspiracy matter, though not charged, and Anthony Scrivener decided that he should make an application for Judge Tucker to be discharged from the trial, having supported the judge only four days earlier.

What, precisely, was Mr Scrivener up to? It was counsel's turn to feel that he was in an invidious position 'making an application I do not want to make'. Mr Scrivener felt the situation had changed now that Nadir had been arrested and the police must have had reasonable suspicion for the arrest (Nadir was quickly bailed). He made a number of points, the most important being that if Nadir and Mr Justice Tucker were alleged to be involved in a plot to pervert the course of justice it would be manifestly odd for the judge to try the case.

Earlier the judge, whose patience must have been at breaking point, and who must have been astonished by his own vulnerability, had been forced to say that he had never been aware of any attempt to corrupt, bribe, or influence him in any way at all; indeed, he had never met Nadir. Somewhat plaintively he said: 'It is outrageous that a judge should be required to say such things. You are not, I know, requiring me to say them, but I wish to make my position plain. I have not the slightest idea of what is going on and I am completely unaware of any approach, attempt, anything at all. When I hear Mr Scrivener's name mentioned, a former chairman of the Bar, and an assistant commissioner's name mentioned, you can imagine what I feel about it.'

Apart from the absurdity of a high court judge being accused of corruption without having the remotest idea of what the allegations were, the court faced a very real problem. If the case were destabilised at some point in the future, then Mr Justice Tucker would have to discharge himself. If that happened, a new judge would have to be appointed. Mr Justice Tucker had already made a number of important decisions, some of which might be reversed by a new judge. Months of work had gone into the case, a huge amount of paperwork had been generated and the costs were already substantial. It would mean that everyone would have to go back to the beginning. These were points that the judge did not need reminding of. Yet it was obvious, even with all those attendant risks, that he had to dig in his heels. He couldn't discharge himself without knowing why he was doing so. No one would tell him what the allegations were because they were operationally sensitive and he had no way of finding out. Counsel could warn him time and again what the risks were of continuing as trial judge, but Mr Justice Tucker knew the arguments backwards. Superintendent Glendenning was beavering away on the conspiracy allegations, but showed no eagerness to interview the judge. But theoretically, and at any time now, he could detonate a bomb which could remove Mr Justice Tucker from the case.

Mr Scrivener had at least cleared the air. Against his inclination, he had applied for the judge to be removed from the case and it was up to Mr Justice Tucker to decide what he should do in view of that application. In the event, he ruled that he should continue. Nadir appealed against the judge's ruling to the court of appeal, which upheld Mr Justice Tucker, while the SFO made submissions that the judge should remain with the case.

In a normal world, that should have been the end of the matter. But the SFO, having supported the judge in the appeal court, now asked for leave to appeal to the House of Lords to have the judge removed. There are two possible explanations for this irrational behaviour: either no one at the SFO knew what they were doing any more, or they had just remembered that Mr Justice Tucker had thrown out more than forty counts on the indictment as being bad in law and felt that any replacement would be better than him. They lost.

Anthony Scrivener told me he then thought that the police investigation into the allegations of bribery would never be heard of again. He was wrong. In the latter half of 1993, the whole thing was exposed as a hoax; the police had been duped by a female business acquaintance of Mrs Nadir and a man who was a hardened criminal. The idea was to relieve the Nadir family of £3.5 million on the specious grounds they could get Nadir a variation of bail which would allow him to leave the country. Only one man could have varied his bail and that was Mr Justice Tucker. At one time the police regarded the two conspirators as so important they had actually been put in a safe house.

On Friday 30 April 1993, a small birthday party was held for Nadir in London. Anthony Scrivener was present, so was Michael Mates. Everyone around the table gave Nadir a gift of some sort; they were all small, apparently. Mates's contribution was a cheap watch with the inscription, *Don't let the buggers get you down*. Everyone laughed. As it turned out, that little gift was no laughing matter. In Mates's words, 'That was when the roof began to fall in.' He beamed chubbily when he told me that, but the smile belied the bemusement. Even now, he can scarcely believe that such a small thing could have put the skids under him. But it did. As with the man who wouldn't give him an affidavit about the SFO's alleged corruption, luck had turned against him.

On Monday 3 May, Nadir diligently reported to Savile Row police station, as he was required to do under the terms of his bail. He then spent the evening at his Eaton Square flat, but next morning he was picked up by car and driven to the village of Street in Hampshire. There he met a friend, Peter Dimond, a pilot who had organised Nadir's flight from Britain. They drove to Compton Abbas airfield in Dorset which is well off the beaten track, and not likely to be swarming with curious people at any time. There they boarded a small, twin-engined plane which had none of the trappings of luxury Nadir was used to. They headed for northern France, where they probably re-fuelled, and on to Turkey and Ercan airport in Northern Cyprus. The touchdown would have been around 10.30 pm local time.

There are surprisingly few problems with leaving Britain by private plane. Some businessmen do it quite regularly, preferring the convenience and anonymity to scheduled flights. The paperwork is minimal. There is no requirement to produce a passport, only to have the right documentation on landing. The pilot's flight plan does not necessarily give an indication of destination because flight plans are often changed during flights, one reason being bad weather. There is another way of concealing the destination – by taking on very little fuel at the British airport, then landing, say in northern France, and taking on a full load. It's thought that this was probably what happened. In Nadir's case the risk of detection was tiny. If there is such a thing as a standing ovation at an airport, then Nadir got it when he landed. The hero was home.

He left behind a mixed bag of chaos and embarrassment. He had broken bail, totalling a record £3.5 million. The sureties for that were Mrs Ayesha Nadir, his ex-wife, who was in for £500,000, and Mr Ramadan Guney, a Turkish businessman and a distant relation of Nadir; he had stood surety for £1 million. The rest had been put up by Nadir himself, £2 million lodged up front with the courts. Both sureties stood to lose all their money or risk jail sentences. Nadir, clearly, would have thought £2 million a price worth paying to keep him out of the courts, but it isn't recorded what the other two sureties had to say about their depleted resources; perhaps Nadir had made some arrangement to recompense them. It must not be thought that because Nadir had pleaded poverty he was without funds: the charges against him alleged that he had stolen £34 million from Polly Peck; if true, he must have had access to assets of some kind.

Neil Cooper, Nadir's trustee in bankruptcy, pointed to twenty trusts and companies in offshore centres, such as the Isle of Man and Liechstenstein, in which Nadir had interests. There were also numerous valuable antiques, artefacts, properties and investments, all held overseas by Nadir, which Cooper had been unable to recover. Nadir's explanation that his expenses were paid by friends and associates prepared to support him didn't ring wholly true.

The former Mrs Nadir and Mr Guney were the immediate victims of Nadir's flight. Guney is appealing to the House of Lords over the £650,000 he has been ordered to pay, a galling experience because he claims he told the SFO that Nadir was going to flee the country. But the people who were left with egg all over their faces were the SFO. A huge amount of money and time had been invested in bringing Nadir to trial, the date for which had been set for September 1993. They were now without a trial, without a main defendant and without much of an excuse. No extradition treaty existed between the Republic of Northern Cyprus and the UK, so that avenue was closed to them. There was little prospect of Nadir ever returning to this country because, as he said many times from his bolt-hole in Northern Cyprus, he thought there was no prospect of him getting a fair trial.

While it is true that the SFO had opposed bail virtually from the beginning, on the grounds that Nadir would probably flee, they did not have much of a chance of getting their way. Most serious fraud cases take at least two years to bring to trial (in Nadir's case, three years) and the courts refused to have someone kicking their heels in prison for that length of time. That was why bail was finally set for such a large sum.

When the news came through the following day that Nadir had escaped, I was having a drink with two members of the Fraud Squad. They were not surprised. The opinion was that the SFO had made a mess of things once more. It transpired later that the SFO had received two tip-offs, within forty-eight hours of each other, that Nadir was going to flee the country. These were ignored, so George Staple told me, because Nadir had been reporting as regularly as clockwork to his local police station in London, which his bail required. Once he failed to do so, the police had been told to 'watch all ports'. But Nadir had chosen to leave the country by air.

Staple went on to say something curiously naive about their most high-profile and embarrassing case. 'It costs a great deal of money, you know, to have a man tailed day and night. A great deal of money.' But the SFO had by this time spent hundreds of thousands on the Nadir case, a fact Staple chose to ignore when explaining why the SFO had taken no notice of the tip-offs or bothered to have Nadir tailed. The investment they made in Nadir has been totally wasted.

A few days after Nadir arrived in Northern Cyprus, the pigeons began to come home to roost as far as Michael Mates was concerned. 'The first thing that happened was that I was rung on a Friday evening by Number 10. I was in Belfast, doing a duty weekend. And this was a private secretary on the line. He said: "We've been alerted by the *Mail on Sunday* that you have an improper relationship with Asil Nadir."

'So I said I've had no improper relationship at all. If you like to check around, everybody knows about it. You can ask my boss [Patrick Mayhew], he knows about it. You can ask the Attorney [Sir Nicholas Lyell] because he knows about it. I have been pursuing the case because I think something is quite seriously wrong, but I don't think you'll find that anyone who's involved is surprised. I haven't done anything wrong, in fact I've been taking advice every step of the way.'

That satisfied Number 10 – up to a point. Then the private secretary asked: 'But you haven't received anything from him; there hasn't been any exchange of gifts?' Mates said certainly not, not a penny. He inferred that Number 10 was implying there had been a financial relationship. The private secretary seemed quite satisfied with the answer.

Within the hour, though, Mates received another 'phone call, this time from a journalist on the *Mail on Sunday*, who said he understood Mates had given Nadir a watch with an inscription on it, which the minister confirmed. What did the inscription say, the journalist asked. Mates told him that was his business. And then Mates was asked why he had given Nadir a watch and again the minister said that was his business.

But the verbal sparring turned out to be pointless. Peter Dimond, Nadir's pilot, had been present at Nadir's birthday party and shortly after he landed in Cyprus Dimond gave a press conference during which he mentioned the watch. The

Mail on Sunday was way ahead of Mates. The minister was hooked.

'The inscription said, did it not, "Don't let the buggers get you down"?'

Mates replied that it did.

'Who are the buggers?' the journalist persisted.

Mates told him this was a lighthearted gesture meant to be taken in that spirit. That was the end of the conversation.

And then the penny dropped. Mates now understood what Number 10 had been ringing about. Immediately he rang Downing Street and told the private secretary he had misinterpreted the question.

'I told him that I had given Nadir a gift. It was a token, a watch which had an inscription on the back, that was what the press were on about. I was sorry if it embarrassed anyone. It wasn't particularly ministerial language, but I made a point of telling him that I had never ever received anything from Nadir. And then I told him the circumstances and I said this was because the police came and raided him and took all his defence papers for the second time and as they were leaving ripped his watch off his arm.'

Mates smiled ruefully at the recollection. 'And that was when the roof, as it were, began to fall in. It was the Minister and the Watch on the Sunday. Then it was Prime Minister's question time on Tuesday when Number 10, who were very supportive throughout, said it was a misjudgement but it wasn't a hanging offence.'

The Sunday Times then decided to take the story very seriously. According to Mates, they put their whole Insight team on the story. Their reporters went into shops in Petersfield, where Mates has a house in the constituency, and asked if Mates had come in 'waving bunches of fifty pound notes'.

'They asked if I was a big spender and whether I came in with large amounts of cash. They drew a blank,' Mates said, 'but it was obvious that they wanted to see if I was a crook or not.'

The story of the watch gradually faded, as it was revealed that other Tory MPs, including Michael Heseltine, had made representations on Nadir's behalf. But six weeks after Nadir had fled, Mates had another piece of bad luck. A story came out in the press that Mates had accepted the loan of a car from the PR firm representing Nadir, Morgan and Rogerson; it was Rogerson who had come to see Mates in the first place asking him to look into the unfair treatment of Nadir. Now Rogerson was lending a car to Mates's estranged wife, Rosellen. In the context of gifts, and Mates's denial that he had ever received a penny from Nadir, such a loan from Nadir's PR advisers sat very uncomfortably with the minister's determination to be seen as untainted.

Mates never had a chance to put his side of the story, largely because it didn't fit conveniently into a couple of sentences. He had been looking for a Volvo estate car suitable for pulling his daughter's pony trailer to pony club rallies. He found one at a dealer in Petersfield, but was told by his estranged wife that she'd heard the engine wasn't big enough for the job. Mates then cancelled the deal but was told by someone that a secondhand Volvo with the right engine would be coming on to the market in a month's time. Rogerson, who was a friend, happened to tell Mates that he was looking for an estate for his pregnant wife, Sarah. Mates told him about the one at the garage. Rogerson then asked him what he was going to do. Mates said he was getting the right car in a month and that he would hire one for the half-term holiday. Rogerson said he would buy the car at the garage and lend it to Mates for half-term as the baby wasn't due for a few weeks. So Mates borrowed the car for a total of nine days and paid the insurance.

'And then the press rang up,' Mates said. 'I suppose they got the story while sniffing around Petersfield. Anyway they had a different spin on the whole thing. They put it to me Nadir had bought the car and given it to my wife. I said, "Print that and I'll be a very rich man." They didn't, but they did print one saying I had accepted the loan of a car. I was on to Number 10, of course, saying I'm in trouble again and explained what had actually happened, saying it was just something that happened between friends. I wish I hadn't done it, but at the time you don't think anything sinister.'

It is said by some commentators and MPs that Mates is one of the most unpopular members in the Commons, arrogant and self-regarding and, like Nadir ironically, keen on women. If that is true, then at this stage of the affair he looked ideal cannon fodder for the 1922 backbench committee. They had elbowed David Mellor out of office nine months earlier; Mates would be easy money, another embarrassment out of Major's way.

Mates denies it. 'The 1922 story was completely manufactured by the media. When I read it, I thought, this means trouble, and then I rang up some close friends on the committee and asked if they were going to do something and they said it was probably not even going to be discussed.'

Mates by now was like a cat on hot bricks, especially when a Tory fogey told him that the whole party was against him.

'So it turned out that it was eighty/twenty against me. So I said he would have to tell me who they all were. Oh, we can't do that, old boy, we have our ways. So I told him that the Defence Committee were in Germany and the Foreign Affairs Committee were in Moscow. That meant a dozen or so people I had reason to believe would all be behind me. So within an hour some forty or fifty people – and I say this somewhat immodestly – rang in to give me their support. Then I was told it was all right, things had swung my way.'

What concerned Mates most was that Major and Hurd were in Copenhagen tying up the loose ends of the Maastricht Treaty and whenever they wanted to tell the media how well they had done, they were asked about Mates. Nothing can be much more irritating for a prime minister than when a little local difficulty gets in the way of the big story and the chance to score some brownie points.

But Monday 21 June passed without incident. Then, on Tuesday, the media started on Mates again, saying his fate was going to be decided by the 1922 committee on Thursday. Mates knew that was untrue. The problem was Prime Minister's question time when Major, back from Copenhagen, would certainly be asked whether he was going to come out behind Mates. If he didn't, Mates would have to go.

Mates might just have got away with it, but for two things. The first was when Gordon Greig, the political editor of the *Daily Mail* took him aside in the Commons on Wednesday evening for a quiet drink. As they were discussing Mates's future, Greig produced a fax of a letter Mates had written to the Attorney General complaining about the SFO and the Inland Revenue. It was the first bit of correspondence between the two men to be made public. Mates was shaken. At first he couldn't quite take it in. But Greig warned him that it was going to be on the front page of the *Daily Mail* the next morning. It seemed clear that Greig didn't know who had passed it to the paper; and Mates was desperate to find out.

Just two people, apart from himself, had copies of the letter – Anthony Scrivener, and Christopher Morgan of Morgan and Rogerson.

Mates by now had become paranoid about using the phone, so he rushed round to Scrivener, who confirmed that the letter was safely under lock and key. From Scrivener's office Mates rang Morgan at the Reform Club. Morgan was just settling down to dinner and invited Mates to join him. Over dinner Morgan told him that the letter was safely locked away and could never have come from his office.

Having drawn two blanks, Mates then remembered that when he had been shown the fax, which he hadn't been allowed to keep, the mailing address on the top was the Crest Forte Hotel in Colchester.

'I didn't think anything of it at the time,' Mates said, 'but when I saw a piece about Michael Allcock, the Inland Revenue man, in the *Mail*, it said that he had a house in Colchester. It was then that the penny dropped.'

Allcock, who had been suspended by then on charges of taking bribes when he was head of Special Office 2, must have faxed the letter to the *Mail* from Colchester. Now awaiting trial on corruption charges, Allcock had never seen the correspondence between Mates and the Attorney General but the SFO had. Nicholas Lyell would have passed on copies of Mates's complaints to the SFO for comment and reply. To Mates, reasonably enough, that meant only one thing – that someone in the SFO had given Allcock the letter for onward transmission.

The timing was impeccable. The story would hit the front page of the *Mail* just a few hours before Major was due to get to his feet in the Commons for question time. Publication of the letter would rekindle the row and put Major under enormous pressure.

The letter was not the only thing to be published that day. The story of Mates's dinner with Morgan had been leaked from the Reform Club. That was not suprising in the circumstances – many politicians and civil servants are members, both of them breeds which are notoriously indiscreet.

On Thursday morning Mates thought he might be able to tough it out. He pays attention to the niceties of political protocol in conversation, but at bottom he can be very hard. What he hadn't reckoned on was the Midday News from ITN, which carried the story of his dinner with Morgan. That was just three-and-a-half hours before Major was due to be on his feet.

Politics is a curious business. One indiscreet or silly action does not necessarily sink a man. Two can be understood. Three is very dangerous. It is the cumulative effect that counts. There was no reason why Mates should not have had dinner with Morgan; the two men knew each other very well, and both were clubbable people. But Morgan was an important Nadir adviser. Questions had been raised about a possible financial relationship between Nadir and Mates. There had been the absurdities over the car and the watch. It wasn't the time to be seen with Morgan, it was as simple as that.

Once ITN had put out the story, Mates knew the game was up. 'I think I realised that the *realpolitik* of the thing was that it was asking too much of John Major. Given everything else that was happening, it seemed to me that it was time to go. So I saw him at two-ish and asked him not to say anything, or his people to say anything, until Question Time. He honoured that totally and that was why the world was somewhat gobsmacked when he stood up and answered the question the way he did. So that was that. The end of a very sad story.'

It was and it wasn't. The Nadir affair was to continue haunting Mates, and it is likely to do so for a very long time. He is stuck on a treadmill of righteous indignation, and politics and the media are not likely to lose sight of that whenever the story re-emerges. In all the events that led up to Mates's resignation there was one that never received much publicity. *The Sunday Times* had not given him up as a target for rigorous investigation. While Mates was a minister and still deeply involved with the Nadir affair, the paper went through all his declared business interests for the previous eighteen years. They came to the conclusion that during all the time he had been a minister he had also been a director of a public company. That was a very serious allegation, because under parliamentary rules a newly appointed minister automatically has to give up all company directorships on the obvious grounds of conflict of interest.

When the investigation came to his notice, Mates said that his 'bowels turned to water'. Fortunately for him the story came out a few days after he had resigned. Luckily, too, there was no truth it. Had there been, the last shred of his credibility would have been destroyed. Mates's former researcher was rung up by a *Sunday Times* reporter and questioned closely about any business connections Mates may have had with Nadir. The researcher said he knew for a fact that there were none. The reporter then remarked that he found that interesting because one of his contacts at the SFO had told him that if he looked through the MP's business interests he would find a connection with Nadir.

That, if anything could, made Mates even more determined there should be an inquiry into the SFO. He was convinced that the SFO were feeding the press with any story about him they could think of. It was of course off limits to do that, but then there had been a cosy relationship between one paper and the SFO in the Ward case (see Chapter 5); there was no reason why there should not be the same relationship in this instance. The SFO had lost Nadir to Northern Cyprus, their most embarrassing operational mistake; it seemed logical to pin the campaign against them on the man who had launched it, Michael Mates. If Mates had dirty hands, the SFO could regain a lot of lost ground. Anyway, it seemed quite implausible that any MP should have gone to such lengths without there being a connection, financial or otherwise, with the founder of Polly Peck.

Equally, why should a minister have risked his job? It was naive to suppose that Mates wasn't taking a risk, but Mates finds no difficulty with that contradiction.

'Did I know Nadir was going to scarper? That's what changed everything. If he hadn't scarpered, I guess I wouldn't be talking to you.'

But it clearly did nothing for Mates, supporting a man's case for months on end who then suddenly flees the country. It looked as if his campaign had backfired.

'No, I don't think so. The first thing I knew about his escape was when I was shaving on the Tuesday morning and listening to the Today programme. And I thought, "Oh, Jesus" and I rang Scrivener but he hadn't heard anything, he hadn't switched on his radio. And I said, "Tony, have you heard the news?" And he said, "Have I what?" I said, "He's buggered off. Gone." And he said, "I'm not surprised." And I said, "Well, I'm surprised." Given that we'd seen him on the Friday [the birthday party]. He must have had it all planned.

'But I don't believe it was naive to take up what was a very serious breach of the way we carry out our system of justice. Having started down that particular road and having been given all the concrete evidence of those transcripts alleging that the judge was part of a conspiracy, I hope I'd have the courage to do it again.'

Whether Mates would have the courage to go through the ordeal of his resignation statement in the Commons again is another matter. It was his comments about the judge which made Madam Speaker furious.

'I had to press on,' Mates says, 'I could not have sat down. If I'd sat down without saying a thing about the judge, and because it was in contempt, of course, of the judge's order that it was not to be mentioned outside court, I would have been finished. People would have said, what is he on about? I would have just looked a complete prat.'

Mates could not have chosen a case more full of intrigue or improbability. Nothing about Nadir is simple or straight-forward. In northern Cyprus, Nadir is now surrounded by people who are anxious to avoid prosecution in an English court. There is Mrs Elizabeth Forsythe, from South Audley Management, Nadir's pilot, Peter Dimond, and his co-pilot, Ian Hamilton. There are also three other people who are allegedly involved in something much more serious than helping Nadir to escape – and that is the scam to bribe Judge Tucker. Supposedly, this is the subject of a police investigation, but more than a year has passed without a hint of any conclusion. Presumably, the affair has been buried.

Nadir, however, is not going to let sleeping dogs lie. Early in 1994, he exhibited his extraordinary resilience yet again by announcing from his northern Cyprus laager that he was going to challenge the government and the British legal system. This appeared not to be an idle threat. He had sufficient funds available to hire once more his old defence counsel, Anthony Scrivener, and another QC, David Pannick, to undertake a series of legal actions against more than twenty people in the British establishment, among them Sir Nicholas Lyell.

Nadir, then, had decided to take up where Mates had left off. It might be said that Nadir is wasting his time, that he can't roll back the past, that the British authorities have invested too much time and money to throw in the towel now. That is a moot point. There is a considerable backlog of embarrassment, incompetence and possibly illegal activity for Nadir and his advisers to wade through, much of which is likely to be laid at the door of the SFO. If that should turn out to be the case, the life of the Office will be quickly curtailed.

The SFO and the British government are badly disadvant-aged when it comes to handling the Nadir case. From Cyprus Nadir can play virtually any card he likes without any danger of being trumped. The British authorities have no choice but to adopt a passive role.

Nadir will continue to haunt them for as long as he cares to keep up his feud against British justice. He is uniquely placed to do so; he cannot be touched by the British authorities as long as Britain refuses to recognise the Republic of Northern Cyprus. He claims he is the victim of Greek plotting (there is no reason why he shouldn't be), a claim that makes him more sympathetic to the Turkisk Cypriot community who bear no love for their Greek neighbours in the south. He is something of a local hero, being the most successful Turkish Cypriot to have set foot outside the island. He has made a substantial contribution to the economy in the north of the island; it is said that by the late 1980s Nadir controlled 20 per cent of the economy there, which makes him a benefactor to be reckoned with. As long as he can remain friends with the ruling party in the north (he used to be its main private backer), there is a chance that he can sit pretty for a very long time, whether he finds his exile agreeable or not. He also has an excellent propaganda machine. It would seem, therefore, that the SFO is on a hiding to nothing and will remain so until the Nadir problem goes away. Rather lamely, they keep on saying that he should return and stand trial, as if that will magic him back.

The British authorities, of course, do have it in their power to smear Nadir *in absentia*. The joint administrators of PPI, Touche Ross, have alleged that £371 million has been spirited out of Polly Peck through banking routes that lead back to Northern Cyprus. They claim that much of this money (£98 million) was used by Nadir to buy shares in Polly Peck as part of his share support operation. In which case it has been a dreadful waste, as the money will never come back. They allege that £100 million was spent on buying newspapers and banks and that a further £38 million went 'walkabout' in providing cash and personal possessions for Nadir. If they are right, then they have found out a good deal more about the missing money than the SFO ever managed to do.

But that is probably about a third of a very large iceberg. What is not visible is some £200 million which was supposedly used to buy development land in the republic for building up the tourist industry. But no leases on the land have ever been granted and the property is in the possession of the republic's government. Nobody has the remotest idea where that money has gone, but the betting is that Nadir, a formidably shrewd businessman, not only knows but could be using it for other purposes. The government of Northern Cyprus could possibly be benefiting from it as well.

David Fawcus believes this could be the case. He does not think that Nadir has stolen the money. He remembers that in September 1990 Nadir told the PPI directors that he had made a lot of money available to the Turkish government. Almost 90 per cent of it was in banks over which Nadir had no control. There was well over £100 million in those banks at that time and by the following June the balance had risen substantially. The money would have gone from this country to offshore banks in Jersey and then to banks in Turkey. The Turkish banks would then have lent it to the government.

When PPI had its major crisis before its shares were suspended and the banks called in their loans, the government of the Northern Republic of Turkish Cyprus said that no money could be repatriated from the republic to London. It may well be, therefore, that Nadir had far less control over PPI's money once it was in Turkey or Northern Cyprus than people imagine. He was in one sense underwritten by Presidents Ozal of Turkey and Denktash of Northern Cyprus; they were his patrons. It seems perfectly reasonable they should have expected something in exchange; but something which had been taken very largely out of Nadir's hands. Levantine politics and business have subtleties not immediately apparent to Whitehall, to the people on Elm Street, or to highly paid accountants unused to detecting the *realpolitik* behind the figures.

There is another kind of *realpolitik* which may yet rebound on John Major's fragile government: the performance of the Attorney General, Sir Nicholas Lyell, throughout the Nadir affair, through the scandal of Mr Justice Tucker and the conspiracy, and during the row about privileged defence papers. Lyell never at any point demonstrated that he had a grip on events, or the remotest understanding of what was going on. Throughout the mounting problems of the SFO, which showed that the organisation was becoming increasingly shaky, he told Mates and anyone else who cared to listen that he was perfectly satisfied with the way things were going. In June 1993 he blithely told the Commons that privileged documents concerning Nadir's defence had not been circulated by the SFO; six months later, he had to admit to the Commons that he had misled the House. Two weeks later he defended the SFO over its dreadful bungle when Roger Levitt got off with 180 days' community service. Lyell must also have been aware of the cock-up over Nadir's escape and the Tucker scandal. Yet it seemed to him that the SFO was a smooth, well-oiled machine in no need of adjustment.

Lyell had little time for a troublemaker like Mates, who was constantly needling him and the SFO, and this was reflected in the increasing tetchiness of his replies to Mates.

'I think it was starting to dawn on him,' Mates said, 'that all wasn't well. Now my impression is, though I have no evidence for it, he felt that having let matters drift so far without doing anything, because he thought it would all go away, he was now left with no choice but to hold the line. Otherwise people would start to point the finger at him. But it wasn't just a question of the Attorney being fed up with me. Lots of people were fed up with the Attorney in government because they knew that something was wrong with the system, but they didn't know what. I do know that many people, including the Prime Minister, were not pleased with the Attorney's performance. But that just put him further into his trench.'

A typical example of that was Lyell's retraction in the Commons about the circulation and copying of Nadir's privileged defence papers. 'I regret,' Lyell said, 'that the fact that copies of privileged documents had been circulated was not acknowledged by the then case controller to Mr Nadir's solicitor, and that no attempt was made to retrieve them until December 1991, despite Vizards' [Nadir's solicitors] frequently expressed concern about the matter and the fact that the then case controller appears to have recognised, at least by January 1991, that copies of potentially privileged documents had been circulated.'

Lyell was simply brushing off a scandal as if it had nothing to do with him or the process of justice. One doubts if he even grasped the significance of what he was saying – namely that Mrs Lorna Harris, the case controller, had taken a whole year before she even attempted to retrieve the documents, knowing that they had been in circulation for twelve months. Did it ever cross Lyell's mind that this blunder might have affected the course of Nadir's trial, the case for the defence or the public's perception of the competence and fair-mindedness of the SFO? Did it occur to him that this was precisely the kind of thing that would persuade Nadir that he couldn't get a fair trial here and that he would be better off taking a plane to Northern Cyprus? And that it might very possibly persuade many people in Britain that Nadir had been given a raw deal and that what passed for British justice was a sham?

Fortunately for Lyell he sat on the very bench in the Commons where incompetence and deceit were everyday occurrences. It was Lyell, remember, who advised members of the cabinet to sign public interest immunity certificates over the Matrix Churchill affair. And his colleagues in cabinet were happy to sign them, knowing that they would be sending three innocent men to prison. With such standards prevailing in a tottering administration, Lyell probably gave absolutely no thought to the way the SFO was run or whether the people inside it were fit for the job. There was no reason why he should do so. If he believed in concealment over the Matrix Churchill business, he clearly didn't know the difference between black and white, right and wrong, or whether the SFO was up to the mark. By that stage he was probably in no moral or mental condition to judge anything.

With organisations like the SFO to oppose him and people like Lyell in charge of the system, Nadir was bound to do well from his bolt-hole. In the first place, he was able to build up Northern Cyprus as a power and business base, not simply by his presence there, but with his claim in January that in 1994 he would create another five thousand jobs, making ten thousand in all. No one will be able to dispute that and it looks good on his CV. He is also one of the few people in the area with the ability and skills to create a proper tourist industry, something Northern Cyprus badly needs.

Second, he has a propaganda machine capable of keeping

him in the news just often enough to be a nagging embarrassment to the British government, a constant reminder that here
is a man who seeks nothing more than a fair trial and who
might well be capable of taking the legal battle to British soil
in a series of high-profile actions.

Third, as long as he is around he will serve to remind the
SFO and others that he made fools of them. He can feed off
that for years. He can talk about his innumerable arrests and
how the SFO set out to smash his company. He can claim
that he was a victim of illegal collusion between the SFO, the
Inland Revenue and the Stock Exchange. He can argue that
once his defence papers had been seized, copied and stolen
he hadn't a cat in hell's chance of a fair trial. And he knows
he can do so without contradiction. He is well aware that
the SFO can do nothing about his allegations. He knows the
Revenue have a spot of bother with one of their top men on
corruption charges and, anyway, they are sick of allegations
of collusion. There won't be any resistance from that quarter.
He can go on for as long as he likes, creating the niggling
suspicion in the public's mind that he may after all be right.

As far as Nadir is concerned, the SFO and police did him an
enormous favour when they let him slip through their fingers.
He has a great deal to be thankful for, especially as there is
just a chance that he might come out of the whole business
smelling of roses.

He also has a good deal to thank Michael Mates for. It
isn't often that someone on major fraud charges can get the
backing of a minister who is concerned about the justice of the
system. Mates, one way or another, kept the issue alive for the
best part of two years, conferring on Nadir the publicity and
limelight he was seeking. It was a brilliant stroke when Mark
Rogerson told the MP of his concerns. It is a pity he has not
been taken more seriously, but then he has been confronting
a system of his own party's making and the first duty this
government has is to itself, not to anyone who might have
been a victim of a system which wasn't capable of delivering
the goods.

Some of Michael Mates's allegations in his long and sometimes bitter feud with the SFO and the Attorney General

were wide of the mark. Some – such as the allegation of MI6 involvement – cannot be checked. No doubt successive governments would have liked to find a solution to the problem of Northern Cyprus and the use of the security services could have been a covert means to that end. Mates thought there might be strong political pressure for Nadir to be convicted to achieve the desired solution. He was a big wheel in the economy there, so the argument went, and his conviction would almost certainly have led to its collapse. No one can say whether Mates was being fanciful. It is easy for the government to deny, and virtually impossible to prove. Nadir, on the other hand, was an important figure in Northern Cyprus and might just have presented an opportunity for some political or economic manipulation, not that any has come to light. This government's success rate is so bad anyway that anything along those lines would almost certainly have been bungled.

There were other issues, though, on which Mates was largely right and which would, in a society not dominated by a government so weak that it dare not countenance investigations into important institutions, normally require an inquiry. Lyell is in no position to order one; he has backed the SFO for so long that he is now a creature of the organisation he is supposed to be responsible for. An inquiry can come only from a new Attorney, once Lyell moves on or out.

There has been only one winner in the Nadir affair and that is Asil Nadir himself. He ought to send watches to all the members of the SFO in gratitude.

8

A BAD CASE OF DYSLEXIA

Many Asian businessmen in Britain have made money and prospered. Frequently, they are exhibited as examples of what thrift, hard work and determination can do in a cultural climate which at worst is opposed to ethnic minorities and at best patronising of their endeavours. That does not seem to have mattered: one family, the reclusive Hinduja brothers, are supposed to be worth at least £1.5 billion and there are others who run conglomerates with turnovers of £500 million or more. Their track record is exceptional, even if there have been one or two dramatic failures, notably Abdul Shamji, a chum of Margaret Thatcher and Norman Tebbit, whose empire collapsed like a pack of cards.

Nazmu Virani came up the hard way, not in Thatcher's Britain but in Idi Amin's Uganda, just as other Ugandan Asians did. Amin, a racial purist as well as a brutal, psychotic tyrant, expelled a large number of Asians from Uganda, doing his economy incalculable harm by deporting the very people who had the business skills to hold it together. Virani fled the regime in 1972, bringing with him his wife and eighteen-month-old baby but leaving behind a successful property business. In Britain he had to begin from scratch. The first deal was a supermarket in Dulwich. Over the next decade he and his two brothers built a portfolio of shops. These were quickly followed by the purchase of Belhaven brewery (he bought it, sold it and bought it back within four years) and what was to become his master company, Control Securities, a 'shell' with a Stock Exchange quotation which he was to turn into the twelfth largest property group in the country. Seven years after this acquisition, when the

SFO raided his house in Putney, Virani's personal wealth was thought to be some £60 million. By that time he had been voted Asian Businessman of the Year, was a generous supporter of charity and had a number of titled, wealthy friends. He had 'arrived'.

Virani's philosophy of property dealing was simple: he bought second-class property, what he sometimes called 'rubbish', from the big property men like Gerald Ronson of Heron and Tony Clegg of Mountleigh, and sold it on, generally to the Asian community. The deals were frequently done in the mosque – a ready-made, convenient bazaar for business transactions. Some of these deals, a retired Lloyds bank manager recalled in court, were done so rapidly that Virani often sold a property before the legal formalities had been completed on the purchase he was selling. But there was no element of criticism from the clearing bank manager, a cautious breed at the best of times; simply a factual report of how Virani often conducted business. Lloyds was an important provider of capital in those early days, when Virani was buying small guesthouses, or 'private hotels', and selling them on when he could see a profit. His calculation of return on investment, according to the Lloyds man, was always impeccable and the bank regarded him as a first-class client. Virani and the bank drifted apart only when the Asian found he could get loans on better terms elsewhere.

The rate at which Nazmu Virani expanded through Control Securities, and his family company Virani Group (UK) Ltd, meant that at one time he was using dozens of banks, among them the Bank of Credit and Commerce International, BCCI, a specialist in loans to Asian businessmen, which was later to become the most spectacular banking fraud in history. Virani used numerous banks to finance his deals and chose them not on the basis of whether he could defraud them but on the terms he could get. It was BCCI, though, which was to land him in prison; ironically, he had not swindled the bank out of a penny.

On 17 October 1991, the SFO raided his large, detached house in Chartfield Avenue in Putney. The road is broad, serene and well-heeled, more accustomed to the presence of Mercedes and BMWs than police cars. The time was 6.00 am, according to Virani, and the SFO was accompanied by a substantial contingent from the media. From that moment Control Securities, which was going through a very rough patch after the property bubble of the late 1980s eventually burst, began to atrophy. The market wrongly thought that it was Control which was in serious trouble, through something Virani had done with the company; it had no idea that it was Virani's relationship with BCCI that was the cause of the raid and the later fraud charges.

Once businessmen have been charged with fraud they enter a dreadful limbo which is filled, virtually to the exclusion of all else, with lawyers, accountants, thousands of documents and an interminable amount of personal homework dominating their waking hours. They eat, sleep and dream their case. They protest their innocence. They curse the SFO and challenge its assumptions. They abominate Section 2 interviews. In short, they become obsessed. The obsession becomes worse as time goes on. In fraud, the waiting appears to be endless. In Virani's case, from the moment the SFO arrived at his front door to his appearance at the main trial, two and a half years had gone by, every minute of which had been controlled by the SFO as it interviewed witnesses, gathered thousands of documents and held endless meetings at Elm House with staff and counsel. For men who have been charged it is a Kafkaesque world over which they have no control and which often destabilises them.

Virani was no exception. He regularly rose at five in the morning and pored over papers most of the day, an activity interspersed only by meetings with his lawyers or visits to his wife, who was in hospital from time to time. But while he was obsessed by his case and convinced of his innocence, Virani had the kind of resilience largely absent in other people charged with fraud. He is philosophical and fatalistic, a habit of mind and attitude he may have learned in the days under Idi Amin. Throughout his long ordeal, I never saw his face lined with worry or fatigue or the eyes clouded by doubt or fear. A short, well-padded man of forty-five, he lost no weight, took care of his appearance and outwardly hadn't a worry in the world.

These impressions were reinforced when I joined him one evening for dinner at his Putney house at the end of 1993. By that time he had been charged with fraud, his passport had been taken away and his businesses plucked from his hands by Control's board of directors who first suspended, then dismissed him. His private companies were wound up at the request of the Inland Revenue. The liquidator of BCCI had also slapped a Mareva order on him which had frozen all his assets. He had been allowed just £25,000 a year to live on, but in the drive there was a Mercedes and in the dining room there was an impressive sideboard loaded with bottles of fine malt whisky, champagne and liqueurs. It was a large, marbled, airy house on which a lot of money had been spent; the home of an entrepreneur who enjoyed his wealth and ran Control and other businesses with his brothers as a family concern. There was a strong sense of family about the Viranis; his wife joined us for dinner, a serious but sick woman, and his son served the drinks.

Virani grumbled much of the time about being a ruined man, yet there was no sign in Putney of enforced financial suffering. It was true that his substantial personal assets, amounting to millions, had been sequestrated by the liquidator, just as Control Securities had been taken away from him and restructured. That was what hurt most – the removal of his business, the empire he had built through twenty years of hard work. That he put down to the collapse of BCCI.

Virani's Control Securities had become one of the thousands of victims of the men who ran the Asian bank, many of whom had decamped to Pakistan, leaving behind BCCI's ruinous investments of billions of pounds in businesses which turned out to be useless. The money they used belonged to their hapless customers, most of whom were Asian. But BCCI, so it was said, was not simply a bank, it was a huge corporate entity supporting terrorism, drug laundering, corporate fraud and political bribery. When the Bank of England decided to close down BCCI's British operation on 5 July 1991, the closure came far too late to prevent inestimable damage to the bank's thousands of loyal Asian customers in this country.

For Virani the shutdown could not have been much worse. BCCI held 5.2 per cent of Control's shares, but among the company's shareholders were many ordinary Asians. The City had a look at the set-up and took fright. Three days after the BCCI closure, Control's share price dropped 8p to 12.5p. The tumble occurred not just because of the City's nervousness but because Asian shareholders who had lost money with BCCI wanted to realise their Control shares so they could get their hands on some desperately needed cash. A little later the shares rallied.

Three weeks later, at the beginning of August, Control brought out its annual results. There was a provision of £3.5 million against the loss of rental income from BCCI (Control was one of the bank's landlords) which was worth more than a million a year. The Virani family interests, represented by the Virani Group UK Ltd, had an exposure to BCCI of around £4 million. It was also said that Control had lost £3.8 million pounds' worth of deposits with the bank, but on the other hand it had a £2.5 million overdraft. In other words, the company was in deep water.

Nor were its financial prospects helped by the trading activities of a fraudulent young accountant called Mark Braley who was on full-time secondment to the SFO from the prestigious firm of Coopers & Lybrand. He was one of eleven accountants drafted in from Coopers to help the SFO investigation into BCCI. Braley, of course, had access to confidential documents relating to the failed bank. He had been working for the SFO for just two months when he decided to steal documents and sell them. Working with him was a freelance accountant, Bernard Lynch, four years his senior. Braley used the information to sell shares 'short' in Control (selling shares he didn't have and later buying them when they had dropped, the difference between the two prices being the profit). At his trial, Braley said that his immediate superior in the SFO 'made it clear to me that the objective in the job was to get charges against certain named individuals and that was the brief I had.' Braley went on to say, 'I would have done almost anything to achieve results.' It was admitted at Braley's trial that the leak of information caused the SFO to act against Virani when they did. Braley went to prison for three years.

Within an hour of the first raids on Virani and his brothers, the shares of Control were suspended on the Stock Exchange. There was no secrecy attached to any of these events. The media had been present when the police called at Virani's house; they had also been at the houses of his two brothers. There was no doubt that the media had been alerted. Indeed, one press release from the SFO said that search warrants 'are today being executed at' (the homes of the Viranis) before the police actually arrived. So much for the SFO's repeated claims that they never warned the media of impending raids and arrests.

It was no surprise, then, that the shares were suspended as soon as they were. Equally, it was no surprise that the SFO had not given any thought to the publicity arising from the raids and the damage it might do to the company. Any rational observer would have thought immediately that it was Control Securities, the publicly quoted company, that was in trouble; hence the Stock Exchange suspension. Not a bit of it, but then the SFO has never, unlike the DTI, paid any attention to the repercussions on City markets of its actions. Five days after the suspension, Virani's solicitors tried to extract from the SFO – and particularly Chris Dickson, the case controller – just how far Control Securities was a part of their investigation. A letter came back saying that Control was not under investigation and then made a brief reference to BCCI and Control's relations with the bank. Insofar as Control was concerned, then, it could be construed as a 'letter of comfort'. But it was much too late.

In fact there was no comfort to be had anywhere. Six weeks later, Chris Dickson agreed that if Virani were to be arrested, his lawyers would be told first. Between the end of January and early March 1992, Virani was interviewed twice by the SFO under Section 2. At the second interview, Virani's solicitors asked the SFO to confirm that their client was not under investigation. They asked because at the first Section 2, which took place over two days, the SFO had shown Virani documents, evidently signed by the Asian, which Virani said he did not recognise. This is the slippery slope to being a suspect. However, the SFO confirmed that Virani was not under investigation. It was also evident that the SFO touched only to a limited extent on Control Securities; the focus of its interest was BCCI.

Having been assured that Virani was not a suspect, Control's board decided to apply for a re-listing of the company's shares on the Stock Exchange. The shares had been in suspension for five months, from the moment the SFO had raided Control and the Virani houses. The company's management hadn't played much part in the running of the company since that time as their hands had been full dealing with SFO inquiries, and producing documents and any material the SFO demanded to see. But as time drifted by, it was evident that Control was marginal to the inquiry and it was time to get the company re-listed. Control had 17,000 shareholders, many of them Asians. It seemed only fair to everyone that it should be properly back in business.

Control's accountants, lawyers and brokers then went to work on a re-listing. Discussions were held with the Stock Exchange and the SFO, so that the people on Elm Street knew exactly what was happening. The circular to shareholders was agreed, which the SFO knew about, and it was planned to send it to all shareholders on 30 March 1992. As late as 27 March, Control's brokers had dealt with some last-minute queries from the Stock Exchange that had arisen after the market's authorities had held further discussions with the SFO. So everything was now set for mailing the circulars on March 30th.

Then, at 7.30 that morning, the SFO arrested Nazmu Virani. They also searched Control's offices again. The SFO had abruptly abrogated the gentlemen's agreement that, should they want to arrest him, he would come voluntarily to the police station at any hour they arranged. Virani's personal assistant, Michael McGuiness, was also arrested. Both men were taken to Bishopsgate police station where Virani was charged with one offence of conspiracy to defraud. The

SFO would not agree to bail, so Virani spent the night in prison.

The following day he appeared at the City magistrates' court, where the SFO objected to bail on the grounds that an unnamed informant had told them that Virani was planning to move between £50 million and £100 million of Control's money out of the country. It is an amount of money that very few companies have hanging around in loose change, least of all a company of Control's size in the property business, and in a recession. The SFO had not bothered, apparently, to check if the money existed in the alleged amount or, if it did, whether any attempt might be made to remove it. But that did not concern the magistrates. They refused bail and Virani spent another night in prison.

Virani's lawyers then decided to go to the high court to appeal against the magistrates' decision. Before Mr Justice Owen was able to hear the appeal, however, the SFO handed Virani's solicitors a fax on House of Commons notepaper, which apparently came from Sir David Steel, the former Liberal leader, together with a letter on the notepaper of Virani's solicitors, saying that Sir David would be attending the bail hearing on Virani's behalf. Virani's lawyers recognised the documents as fakes and challenged Chris Dickson, the case controller. Dickson later tried to laugh it off, saying that the whole thing was an April Fool's joke and that it would be 'churlish . . . not to be amused'. It was curious that the 'joke' should have been perpetrated on Sir David as he had written several times to the Attorney General questioning some of the SFO's actions in the Virani case. The coincidence looked deliberate and blatant.

Steel, not unnaturally, took up the matter with Sir Nicholas Lyell, the Attorney General, to whom the director of the SFO reports. Lyell is not notably robust in the conduct of his duties and, like the rest of the government, would absolve almost anybody of almost anything if there was a danger that it might reflect adversely on the administration. How other people might be affected, wounded or outraged is an irrelevance provided the government is kept out of trouble. He couldn't even summon up anything in the way of indignation or surprise about the incident when he replied to Steel.

He could – just about – recognise Steel's 'understandable annoyance about a letter purporting to be signed by you on House of Commons paper and indicating your intention to attend the first remand hearing [wrong, it was the second] and support an application for bail.' Lyell then limply trotted out what he had been told by the director of the SFO, who was anxious to protect his own back, but never at any moment did he express personal annoyance or dissatisfaction at what had occurred. Like some of his letters over SFO matters, he ended his epistle by saying that if Steel wanted to take the matter further he should talk to the police.

The affair of the April Fool correspondence immediately preceded the bail hearing in chambers before Mr Justice Owen, who had not been apprised of the Whitehall farce played out behind his back. Which was just as well; his lordship could have taken a very dim view of the matter. He did, however, refuse bail to Virani. He said he assumed the SFO were behaving responsibly over the unnamed informant and the removal of huge amounts of money from Britain. He thought that within a week the SFO would be able to substantiate their allegations – they had asked for Virani to be remanded for a month. Later that same day, after Mr Justice Owen's decision, Virani's lawyers discovered from the SFO that the allegation by the unnamed informant was nothing new at all, it had been hanging around for several months. In that case, Virani's advisers asked, why had the SFO arrested Virani out of the blue on 30 March, contrary to the gentlemen's agreement, and why had the SFO consistently said that Virani was not under investigation? Ah, the SFO replied, the evidence for the allegation only came to hand shortly before the arrest. The one had precipitated the other.

He spent another night in prison and then, on 3 April, a Mareva injunction was served on Virani and various Virani companies by the BCCI liquidators. A Mareva injunction freezes all the assets of a person or company so they cannot be touched or moved. This one was based on the unsubstantiated allegation that Virani was about to spirit £100 million out of the country.

Virani was held in prison for four more nights before being granted bail by the magistrates. The SFO was hardly in a position to oppose it by this time: it was still trying hard to stand up the allegation of the unnamed informant. It never did; it was not part of the case against Virani when he came to trial in 1994. The SFO had been led up the garden path by a mischief-maker.

Virani was granted bail on two sureties of £500,000 each and one of £250,000. Later that month he and his brothers were removed from the board of Control Securities. The new directors went a step further in distancing themselves from the Virani family when they cancelled Control's rental agreement for the company's headquarters, which were owned by Virani family interests, and moved elsewhere.

Apart from the charges laid against him by the SFO, Virani had other problems which had been exacerbated by the Mareva injunction. The court had allowed him £25,000 a year for all personal expenses, which included the running of his household, medical and education expenses and his legal fees, which by that time were enormous. His problems arose from outstanding tax liabilities, which he had been paying off at the rate of £30,000 a month (at that time the repayments amounted to more than £2 million). But the Inland Revenue wanted him to increase the repayments, something he couldn't do because of the Mareva injunction. He claims to this day that had the injunction been lifted he would have had quite enough income from his assets to pay off his tax liabilities. But the Inland Revenue had other ideas: they petitioned for the winding up of the Virani family companies. In effect, this meant they were unlikely to get anything like the amount they were owed.

Virani was charged with conspiring with Mohammed Haque, the BCCI manager who handled Control's accounts, and others 'to falsely account to the value of $4 million – or £2.3 million'. The SFO, in one of their earlier interrogations of Virani, asked him why he dealt with BCCI since the bank was run in such a corrupt and scandalous fashion. That was a piece of hindsight which beggared belief. At the time Virani was dealing with the bank it was a respected organisation in the Asian community. Its customers had no reason to doubt its probity. The first anyone knew officially about the corruption within BCCI was when the Bank of England closed it down – something, so a House of Commons select committee said, it should have done many months earlier. But by the time the Bank of England got round to tackling the problem, the Asian community in Britain had been swindled out of millions of pounds.

Haque, of course, soon after BCCI's closure, had taken refuge in Pakistan, with whom Britain has no extradition treaty, leaving Virani to face the music by himself. By April 1993 he was on legal aid, not the most auspicious beginning to a major fraud trial in which the accused ought to be represented not merely by a top counsel but one who is familiar with fraud; the two, as Roskill pointed out, do not necessarily go together. Fraud is quite different from rape, arson or murder; it is a culture of its own, demanding an understanding of balance sheets, complex movements of money and financial arrangements, and an insight into the minds which engage in this particular crime.

Virani was in luck when his solicitors managed to engage the services of Anthony Scrivener QC. Scrivener knows his way around fraud, having undertaken a number of high-profile cases in the Far East where the amounts involved are generally far larger than anything normally encountered in this country. He has an exceptionally quick mind and a huge appetite for work. He was ably supported by Tony Shaw as his junior who actually took silk during the course of the trial. Scrivener is known to have left-ish political leanings and does not make a point of turning down legal aid work on the grounds that it doesn't pay as well as wealthy private clients with large resources. Despite that, he still manages to scramble together a living of around £500,000 a year.

The case opened on January 17th, 1994, in court 21 in Chichester Rents in Chancery Lane. There are two courts here, neither of which bears any resemblance to a normal court of law. Court 21 is a large, rectangular room, probably measuring fifty feet by fifty, with low ceilings and neon lighting. Everyone except the judge and jury sits on one level: counsel, solicitors, the SFO and the accused. The public and the press share a small pen of some twenty seats in which there are a couple of tables for reporters to take notes. Next to them is the video projector operator whose job it is to project onto the video display units the documents as they are called for by counsel. Judge, jury, counsel and witnesses have VDUs, which are indispensable in complex fraud cases. Press and public are set to one side of the court and face the jury on the far side of the room. The space in between is occupied by counsel who operate, as it were, from the long tables set directly in front of the judge. Behind them and slightly to one side are heavy metal trolleys laden with documents (some 50,000 in the Virani case out of literally millions collected by the SFO), and behind these is another row of tables for instructing solicitors, advisers and the accused. Virani sat with his solicitor, Guy Harvey, a large, cheerful extrovert, and was quite impassive and emotionless throughout the court proceedings.

Prosecuting counsel for the SFO was Tony Hacking QC, as tall as Scrivener and like Scrivener scrupulously polite. Both men and their juniors chatted amiably to each other before and after each day's hearings. Indeed, this is a very significant aspect of the hearings in Chichester Rents. The trials tend to be long (Virani's took almost four months), the court is remarkably informal and after people have been thrown together for a few weeks most of them are on chatting terms. In the rooms adjacent to the courts, Scrivener and his solicitor drank tea and coffee and ate their sandwiches during the adjournments while discussing the progress of the case and reviewing evidence. Virani would walk about, offering people like myself an apple or a cup of tea. For the most part he seemed quite calm, but there were times when he lost his temper and turned the air blue with his language.

It's the informality of the proceedings and the environment that decriminalises fraud cases in Chichester Rents. One forgets quite quickly that a man is facing serious fraud charges and could well go to prison. Chris Dickson would often chat to me, refer to Nazmu as if he were an old friend and comment on the proceedings. Scrivener would sometimes offer an opinion on how things were going or tell hilarious stories about judges and their cases. It was not a trial so much as a low-key play.

Lady Maureen Thomas, one of Virani's sureties (for £250,000), attended the trial every day and was unofficial tea maker to the Virani group. Lady Thomas is prominent in charitable work and had got to know Virani through his work for charity. She was convinced of his innocence. Her husband, Sir Maldwyn Thomas, the prominent Liberal and himself a lawyer, had also taken a close interest in the case and turned up from time to time to see what the state of play was.

Throughout virtually the whole trial Virani managed to remain remarkably detached, although the charges, if proven, could land him in prison for up to ten years. There were four-teen counts in all, the most serious of which was conspiracy to defraud. The others related mainly to false accounting and furnishing false information.

The crux of the Crown's case rested on documents known as audit confirmation requests, or ACRs. ACRs told BCCI's accountants, Price Waterhouse, what BCCI loans were out-standing to various customers at any given time. Virani was supposed to confirm some of these with his signature, so that Price Waterhouse could draw up an accurate picture of BCCI's financial position. The prosecution said he signed these ACRs at Mohammed Haque's instigation knowing that they were false.

And why should Virani do that? Well, the documents were designed by Haque to boost the bank's profits and dress up its balance sheet. Banking is a curious business; loans count as assets, bank deposits as liabilities. A moment's reflection will show why. If a customer has a large deposit with a bank for, say, £100,000 he is entitled to withdraw it. It is therefore a liability in the sense that a bank at any moment might find itself short of £100,000. The same is true of all bank deposits. Loans, however, count as assets because these are what the bank is owed by its customers. If Haque could show that the value of BCCI loans was larger than it actually was, he would be increasing the bank's assets. That, in turn, would inflate the bank's balance sheet. The prosecution said that Virani signed these ACRs knowing that the companies did not owe BCCI anything like the amount written on them. In other words, he and Haque were partners in creative false accounting.

It was a difficult case to answer. Virani was a quick, intuitive businessman who knew exactly how many oranges made five. How could he possibly have signed documents knowing that they increased the companies' liabilities with BCCI when in fact the liabilities did not exist in the amounts stated on those documents? The defence would have to show that Virani did not know what he was signing. Before he went on trial, and when he was entertaining me to dinner, he told me that, in the course of a day, he signed literally dozens of documents which were put in front of him by his lieutenants. He did not have time to read any of them in detail. As he was a man in a hurry, I concluded, it was quite possible he worked like that. It was obvious to me he was also very impatient and that paperwork was probably the least of his interests. He was also quite contemptuous of the charge that a man of his wealth would bother to steal £675,000 (on this theft charge he was later acquitted).

So the defence would have to persuade the jury that here was a very successful businessman who didn't pay much attention to what he was signing. So much so, that he was capable of signing documents which apparently committed companies to debts with BCCI that did not exist. Was that really the action of an honest, highly successful businessman? It was a bit hard to swallow, to say the least. Not that Tony Scrivener seemed at all daunted by the prospect of putting that argument to the jury.

A main prop of his defence was that Virani suffered very badly from dyslexia. This was a new one on the prosecution, as Tony Hacking pointed out in his closing speech. But then the defence is not bound to disclose the details of its case, only the generality. There was also the question of handwriting. It was doubtful, Scrivener said, that all the signatures on the ACRs were Virani's. But the main argument rested on dyslexia and whether someone who suffered badly from it would be capable of signing ACRs in the way Virani did. The defence said he certainly would.

The jury were an assiduous, hardworking, dedicated twelve who took such copious notes that by the end of the trial most of them should have been suffering from repetitive strain injury. Sir Michael Hutchison, a pink-faced, unfailingly courteous high court judge with an eye for the female shorthand writers who sat on his right, often referred to the jury in appreciative tones, remarking on how closely they followed the case. Their foreman was a woman who seemed totally spellbound by the case and appeared to have no lapses of concentration in proceedings which inevitably had their longueurs. A fraud trial can be a desiccated business, even when large amounts of money have gone walkabout. But the judge was right: the jury was an alert, interested and evidently committed group of people, two of whom, so the story went, were bankers. One, a man, eventually dropped out of the case with severe back pain. The ideal number of jurymen as far as the defence is concerned is ten; it means they have to be unanimous on every count to bring in a guilty verdict. Now they were down to eleven. If another dropped out, the judge could still order the trial to go ahead, but it was much more likely that he would order a re-trial, something everybody dreaded.

Scrivener had to impress them with Virani's dyslexia. To do this he called a number of witnesses, two of whom were dyslexia experts and the others people who either worked with Virani or knew him through a business relationship. One of these was Mrs Matthews, a woman in her sixties who wore a black and gold two-piece suit and spoke in a strong, confident voice. Mrs Matthews had known Virani for sixteen or seventeen years in her role as an estate agent. She told the court that Virani had a wonderful ability to buy at the bottom of the market and sell at the top, and it was quite clear that she admired his entrepreneurial skills. These, she indicated, were unaffected by the fact that Virani was dyslexic. Mrs Matthews said she had lots of relatives who were dyslexic, and a characteristic they all shared was that they didn't like people watching them read or write. When reading they gave themselves away by either moving their lips or following the words with their finger. Sometimes they did both. In her experience, they wrote laboriously and with difficulty.

'I never saw Virani write a note in my life,' she said. 'In normal circumstances I would have expected him to write notes, but he didn't. He often handed letters to colleagues because he didn't want to be seen trying to read their contents.'

It was the kind of thing that Scrivener wanted to hear. Much of what Mrs Matthews said was confirmed by Derek Maynard, a PR consultant who worked for Virani from 1989–91. Maynard was a slight, dapper figure in his sixties who had previously worked for Shell. He joined Control at Virani's invitation to handle press releases and the chairman's annual speech. He told the court that Virani was a very slow reader because his reading ability was bad.

Scrivener: What was his comprehension like when it came to documents?

Maynard: Very slow indeed. His speeches had to be typed on cards and triple-spaced. He was incapable of learning the first line of a speech or the last line. He had to read everything from his cards.

Maynard went on to say that Virani preferred oral communication. He could absorb spoken information very quickly. He could sum up a situation rapidly and always wanted speedy results. The tenor of Maynard's remarks indicated that Virani could be very difficult to work for. Maynard had to redraft Virani's chairman's speech many times and said that Virani couldn't draft business letters, Maynard had to do it for him. Maynard also went through the morning's mail with Virani, often a pile of letters a yard high, a process which could take as long as four hours. In reply to Tony Hacking, Maynard said Mohammed Haque was a rather insignificant person and he did not think it possible that he could control Virani.

The picture that Maynard painted of Virani was of a man who was quick-witted and verbally agile but who had major problems dealing with written material. That was confirmed by one of Virani's first bank managers, Michael Murray of Lloyds Bank, who was managing a branch in Belgrave Road when Virani asked him for a loan of £100,000 to buy an hotel. Murray was a banker of the old school, retired now, softly-spoken, gentle, but someone of firm character. It was hard to see Virani making a fool of him.

'Once we had completed all the paperwork for a deal, the documents would be prepared for him to sign. He always signed in my presence and I noticed that he never read the documents.'

As far as Virani's probity in business was concerned, Murray recounted an incident when Virani had recommended an Asian acquaintance to Murray and the man did not pay the bank's £400 survey fee for the property he was thinking of buying.

'Virani paid the bill, although he did not have to,' Murray recalled.

These, then, were the recollections of people who had either done business with Virani or worked for him. They added up to inescapable conclusions: Virani did not take notes, had grave difficulty with reading and evidently did not read documents for his signature. But that would not be proof enough for the jury that Virani signed the ACRs given to him by Haque without knowing what they really meant.

Scrivener called Sir David Steel, who had extensive experience of working with Asians. He said they worked with each other on trust and took very little notice of documentation. He had known Virani for five years and trusted and admired him. He confirmed that Virani was a bad reader. Sir David then went on to give a total endorsement of Virani's good character. The inference here was that if a fellow Asian, Mohammed Haque, was giving Virani documents to sign, then in Virani's view they must be all right. On the other hand, the documents Virani was signing contained figures and Virani was a businessman who lived by numbers. Even Virani, it occurred to me as an outsider, would want to know more about those figures. Would severe dyslexia account for his lack of curiosity?

Scrivener was not content to rely on the observations of business acquaintances and employees. In technical matters, counsel frequently call expert witnesses. The first of these was Dr Chasty, a doctor of neural psychology who had been director of the Dyslexia Institute for fifteen years. His interest in dyslexia, he told Scrivener, went back thirty-four years. Chasty was a strong witness, delivering his evidence in a powerful voice, never hesitating for a word or phrase. He gave the impression of having considerable intellectual authority, which was exactly what Scrivener wanted.

Chasty told the court that Virani was very co-operative over the exhaustive series of tests he had given him, but was immensely sensitive about his problems and did not want them brought out in court. Dyslexia, the psychologist pointed out, restricts a person's competence in processing information. When it comes to reading (a key part of the case as far as Virani was concerned), a dyslexic would find that with long passages the memory can be so busy that he forgets the sense. Chasty said that Virani had major difficulties with his short-term memory. While this capacity varied from person to person, Virani's was much below average. That meant he would run out of memory very quickly when dealing with aural information. Chasty said that Virani had very marked visual problems and could take in only very small pieces of information. He took the example of an ACR, which the average person would process in chunks. Virani, on the other hand, would process it word by word or by segments of words. Virani would get there in the end, but it would take a lot longer and for his age and ability his recollection would be much less.

Chasty concluded that Virani was dyslexic, and that his difficulties were substantial enough to interfere with his understanding of the text in many of the documents he had to deal with. Of particular importance to Virani's case was Chasty's view that comprehension of ACRs would have been beyond Virani's capacity. In this context, the psychologist said that dyslexics did not want their disability to be discovered and would either sign a document immediately or deal with it later on. They would generally sign a document without reading it if they trusted the person who gave it to them. It might be thought at this stage that Virani's problems were so bad that he would be incapable of running a complex business. But when Chasty pointed out the irony that some Nobel Prize winners were dyslexic, the paradox of Virani's dyslexia became less confusing.

Tony Hacking, for the prosecution, took Chasty back to Derek Maynard's evidence. Maynard, who dealt with Virani's speeches and most of his mail, had told the court that Virani would not be embarrassed by taking time to read a document. Chasty replied that Virani knew Maynard well enough not to be embarrassed because Maynard was close to him.

Under cross-examination, Chasty became even more precise and didactic. Hacking put it to him that another psychologist, Dr Judith Haynes, did not agree with Chasty about Virani's non-comprehension of ACRs. Chasty replied that these documents had different levels of complexity, but that Virani would not notice the difference. This fitted in with Chasty's earlier evidence, but during the afternoon of April 6th, Chasty became less sure of himself. Hacking kept on asking him if Virani would recognise names of companies. Of course, Chasty replied. Hacking then took Chasty through various documents, selecting phrases and sentences, and asked Chasty if Virani would have been able to understand them. In every instance, Chasty said that Virani would have comprehended them.

The documents that Hacking referred to were not, of course, ACRs. Counsel was too smart for that; he knew that Chasty would immediately say that Virani would not have understood them. But to a jury, there would not be a world of difference between the two. It did not torpedo Chasty's evidence, but it did shed some doubt on it. That is one of the main functions of counsel; introduce doubt and you have the makings of a case. Hacking went a step further, introducing a wedge between the evidence of Drs Chasty and

Haynes. Dr Haynes, Hacking told Chasty, said that Virani could not do cursive or joined-up writing. Chasty, on the other hand, said he could. In fact, Chasty was right. Haynes had not tested Virani to see if he could do it.

These are details, but they begin to add up to a picture in the jury's mind. Chasty, under Scrivener's expert tutelage, had come over with authority and conviction. More important, the results of his tests were utterly convincing. Under cross-examination from Hacking, though, Chasty became much less sure of himself.

Dr Judith Haynes, in her fifties, with abundant brown hair and an intense, worried expression, was the antithesis of Chasty on the witness stand: nervous, hesitant and uncomfortable. She told the court that Virani had not developed a cursive script, in the sense that it was not his preferred way of writing, which she took to be block capitals. When shown an example of his cursive script, however, she had to change her tune, and agreed that it was perfectly legible.

On the other hand, she managed to be broadly supportive of Dr Chasty. She said that dyslexics had to work much harder because of their disability. They used a broad-brush approach, but put in a lot of detailed work in private. She maintained that if asked to sign a document a dyslexic would put it on one side for later consideration, but would sign immediately if he had to – which meant he would have no clear idea of what he was signing. Scrivener referred her to the evidence of Mrs Andrews, who had taken affidavits from Virani, and who described him as an incapable reader. Dr Haynes agreed with that view. In fact, Mrs Andrews had gone a good deal further than that: she said Virani had trouble reading the draft affidavits and took his pen, tracing the words and reading them out loud. Short passages had to be read out to him and then checked with him for comprehension. He reminded her, she said, of her seven-year-old daughter learning to read.

Chris Dickson, the case controller, was in court for this evidence, playing with paperclips while listening to the witnesses. He and the SFO had a lot riding on the case. It was vitally important that Virani should be found guilty and given a custodial sentence. It had been a long time since they'd had a conviction in a major trial and they badly needed Virani to restore their damaged credibility. Honours between prosecution and defence at this stage were roughly even, with the edge probably going to Scrivener. But there was not much in it. For the SFO's senior case controller and assistant director, his own reputation was very much at stake. His counsel, Tony Hacking, had been on the case from the very beginning and it was important for him, too, to get a conviction. Hacking had had a rough time defending Peter Clowes, who had of course gone to prison, and this was his first major case since.

The prosecution then produced Professor Brian Butterworth, of the department of psychology at University College, London, to rebut the defence's expert witnesses. Butterworth had been Professor of Cognitive Neuropsychology since 1991 and had also been a Cambridge Reader. As Scrivener had produced the dyslexia argument and his experts at the last moment, the SFO must have been running around in circles looking for the right expert to rubbish their evidence. Butterworth saw Virani for a consultation just two days before he gave evidence in court. Time had not been on his side.

Butterworth was small, squat, bespectacled and confident. He told the court he had spent ten years researching dyslexia in adults and had tested hundreds of subjects. He began well enough by attacking Chasty and Haynes for not using tests appropriate to adults. Chris Dickson's heart must have lifted when he heard that; it could not have done Tony Hacking any harm either.

Dr Chasty had gone abroad for urgent work, but Dr Haynes remained in court for Butterworth's evidence and she looked deeply unhappy about it. He tore into their findings with the relish of a man convinced of his academic superiority. Scrivener's experts had not carried out tests, he said, on Virani's phonological ability. It was a strange and serious omission in their tests. It was widely agreed, he went on, and agreed by Drs Chasty and Haynes, that phonological skills were a necessary pre-condition for learning to read an alphabetic language like English.

Hacking: May I interrupt you there. What is phonological ability and how do you test it?

Butterworth: OK. Phonological ability is an ability to be aware of the sound structure of your language; that is, you need to know that a word like pin contains separate sounds which we represent in English by P, I and N. If you cannot segment words into their component sounds it will be extremely difficult, if not impossible, for you to learn what sounds go with what letters. Therefore, it's important, if you wish to diagnose, try to diagnose a dyslexic condition, to see whether the subject can segment words into their component sounds. In addition, you need to know whether he can then use his knowledge of the letters to reconstruct sounds into complete words again.

Butterworth also told the court he wanted to be sure that his own tests would give a fair indication of Virani's cognitive (learning) skills. 'I can see no reason,' he concluded, 'why Virani shouldn't have understood and read the documents he saw.'

Professor Butterworth had an unfortunate manner. He seemed surprised that anyone should question his findings and looked puzzled when a hostile question was put to him. Nevertheless, Scrivener worked away at him until Butterworth began to get more and more uncomfortable. His natural fluency and articulateness suffered from Scrivener's sharpness. This was one of the very few times in the trial that Scrivener put any heat on a witness, preferring a soft, friendly approach. It is always a delicate judgement for an advocate when to become hostile towards a witness, because it can easily alienate a jury. Perhaps he had judged that Butterworth's arrogance would offset any downside effect his cross-examination might have had.

Scrivener was in no position to cross swords with him over the minutiae of psychological testing, but what he did remind Butterworth of was the evidence of Mrs Andrews and Mrs Matthews, and what they had said about Virani's dyslexia. Butterworth challenged Mrs Andrews's evidence about Virani reading like a seven-year-old when he 'clearly didn't'.

Scrivener nagged away at Butterworth as to why he had taken no notice of these witnesses; Mrs Matthews in particular, who never saw Virani take a note at complex business meetings when one would expect him to. Scrivener also pointed to the evidence of Derek Maynard who said he drafted letters for his boss because Virani was not up to it.

'I'd do the same,' retorted Butterworth, 'if I had professional advisers.'

It wasn't a bad, acid response, but Butterworth had not answered the question. He was the academic up against the people who'd had practical experience of Virani. Butterworth's danger to the defence was that he did not believe Virani was dyslexic, and in that opinion he was unshakeable. Scrivener tried to put him down by indicating that he had taken no account of the evidence of those who had dealt with Virani.

It would be intriguing to know just what effect the evidence of the expert witnesses had on Mr Justice Hutchison's diligent jury. On balance, I think Scrivener had put together a very persuasive defence which was not invalidated by Butterworth's forceful assertions to the contrary. The academics were lending intellectual credibility to the evidence of Maynard, Mrs Andrews, Mrs Matthews and the retired bank manager, Murray, all of whom had observed that there was something badly wrong with Virani's capacity to process information. I thought at the time that Scrivener managed to raise enough question marks over how Virani handled documents for the jury to give him the benefit of the doubt.

However, I had not sat through the whole of the case. I had not listened to Hacking's five-day opening speech in which he set out the case against Virani in considerable detail. Nor was I present on those occasions when Virani's friends complained that Mr Justice Hutchison had favoured the prosecution. This is an old complaint that stems from the criticism that judges do not have enough time to read themselves into major fraud trials. They have sufficient time to read the prosecution's case statement, which sets out clearly the Crown case, but they

don't have the time to read all the documents that could have
a bearing on the case, so they err on the side of caution
and favour the Crown. Scrivener complained to me that,
clever as Hutchison was, he had not had time to familiarise
himself sufficiently with the complexities of the case. Someone
also remarked to me that Hutchison could not possibly be
even-handed because he came from a white Kenyan family
and would be prejudiced against Asians.

What the jury could not know was that in the closing days
of the trial the SFO did something extraordinary, making
dramatic last-minute allegations which involved clearing the
court of the jury and imposing reporting restrictions on
the press. Two hard-faced men in blue suits (clearly police
from the SFO) listened to Tony Hacking as he outlined
some facts the SFO had discovered within the previous
twenty-four hours. According to Hacking, the SFO had
found out that Virani's brother, Zulfikar, had been trying to
borrow £800,000 from the Bank of Ireland. The assumption
was that he was trying to raise money to facilitate Virani's
escape from British justice. The SFO had in mind, of course,
Nadir's well-publicised escape to Northern Cyprus, and was
determined to stop an embarrassing recurrence. They were
now calling Virani's bail into question.

The SFO's action came like a bolt from the blue; there
had been no warning to the defence, no indication that
something was brewing. Neither Scrivener nor Guy Harvey
had an opportunity to take instructions from Virani. At this
point the judge asked Scrivener if he wanted an adjournment
to take instructions, but characteristically Scrivener declined.
He knew that Zulfikar had just arrived in court – something
he did quite often at the end of the day to see how things had
been going – and immediately put him on the witness stand.

It turned out that Zulfikar wanted to buy an hotel and
was trying to raise the wind from the Bank of Ireland. The
bank had alerted the SFO. The SFO had made no effort
to establish the facts of the situation. When Zulfikar took
the witness stand to be examined first by Hacking, then by
Scrivener, he named the property he was interested in and the
solicitor acting for him, and gave all the relevant details which

seemed perfectly satisfactory to Judge Hutchison. Scrivener had neatly avoided an adjournment and any likelihood of an allegation that the defence had 'got at' Zulfikar; he had also created the maximum impact on the judge and jury of Zulfikar's explanation.

Asked if he had consulted his elder brother Nazmu, who was something of an expert on hotels, about the proposed purchase, Zulfikar replied rather charmingly: 'No, he seems to have his hands pretty full at the moment.'

Scrivener kept the prosecution in the dark about whether Virani was going to take the witness stand or not. Dickson told me that it should make a fascinating confrontation between Virani and Hacking and seemed confident that Virani would take the stand. Scrivener played it right up until the last minute, then told the SFO Virani would not be giving evidence. It was a difficult decision to make. Virani could have been a brilliant witness or his own worst enemy. The problem was that he was a highly volatile person. His interrogation would have lasted for several days and his patience would almost certainly have broken – to the incalculable advantage of Hacking and his team.

Virani used to come up to me during adjournments and ask how I thought things were going. It was an impossible question to answer. On some days they appeared to be in his favour, on others against him. The good and bad days, of course, were determined by the witnesses and how they were handled by counsel. Scrivener told me that it's very important for counsel to appear to be on top of the case because juries are influenced by that. If counsel had a bad day, it was vital to counter-attack strongly the next day. Both Scrivener and Hacking had their low points but it was more obvious with Scrivener who has an ebullient, extrovert personality. Hacking, who is cast in the stoic mould, maintained the same unflappable front whether he was having a thin time or not.

Scrivener's team were dedicated to breaking the SFO case, but it was sometimes hard to know whether that determination arose from the case itself or an in-built dislike of the SFO as an institution. Scrivener never missed a chance to take a crack at the SFO, especially if he could paint it as being less than honest.

Towards the end of the trial, he decided to take up the question of witness immunity from prosecution, something the SFO offers when it suits it. The witness was Mr Karuthasami who worked in Haque's office, subordinate to him. By no stretch of the imagination was he easy to cross-examine in court because his English was imperfect and he was very nervous. What Scrivener was anxious to extract from Karuthasami at this stage was that he had been under pressure from the SFO to say that he had been present at the meeting when Haque had got Virani to sign the audit confirmation. (There had been an argument at an earlier stage in the trial about whether Virani's signature had been forged.) Scrivener produced an SFO note, from what is called unused material, of an interview with Karuthasami which said that he had been present at the meeting. Was that not correct? Scrivener asked.

K: That's not true.

S: Is that what you were saying at the time?

K: That is what has been recorded, sir.

S: Was that because you were under tremendous pressure?

K: Could be, sir.

Scrivener tried another tack.

S: Was it made clear to you if you did not co-operate you would be liable to be prosecuted?

K: Yes, sir.

S: And the co-operation they wanted was to get some answers against Mr Virani, was it not?

K: Yes, sir, they wanted to explain all the documents

and papers that have been bringing from bank and showing to me, what is all this.

S: What they were interested in was getting some answers against Mr Virani, is that right?

K: Yes, sir.

S: Were you ever told that you would not be prosecuted?

K: Yes, sir.

S: How long did it take?

K: Sorry, sir?

S: How long was it before they said you would not be prosecuted?

K: On the first, on the very first day after they met me and my solicitor, and then each time I keep asking them what is happening, all the time you are calling me and nothing. We want you to explain the paper and documents we have collected from your area, PID area, to explain what is happening.

At this point Mr Justice Hutchison tried to get matters clarified. He asked Karuthasami when he was told he would not be prosecuted.

K: On the very first day from my solicitors, they told me they had a discussion with my solicitor outside, and then my solicitor told me you have to co-operate with them. You have to explain everything, and all papers and they will not be prosecuting you.

This was an extraordinarily opaque cross-examination, but by the end of it Scrivener had managed to extract the following information: that there was no SFO guarantee that Karuthasami would not be prosecuted and that Karuthasami felt that if he had not co-operated with the SFO he would have been prosecuted or, as Karuthasami put it, 'If they don't get Mr Haque, they will get me.'

With that much established, Scrivener then turned to Chris Dickson and asked him if Karuthasami had ever been given a letter telling him he wouldn't be prosecuted. Dickson replied, 'I am saying that he's been told he wouldn't be prosecuted but he hasn't had a letter.'

He changed that very quickly, however. Referring to a letter written by Dickson to Virani's solicitor, Scrivener asked whether the letter was correct when it said that Karuthasami had not been told in terms that he would not be prosecuted. Dickson said: 'I'm not aware of telling him in terms that he would not be prosecuted. I think it must have been clear to him that he would not be prosecuted.' That was quite contrary to his earlier answer.

Dickson then dug himself in deeper, when Mr Justice Hutchison put it to him that he had said on two occasions that Karuthasami was being interviewed as a witness. Dickson agreed with that, but then the judge asked if we were to equate that with being told that he would not be prosecuted.

Dickson: Yes, my lord, yes.

Hutchison: But many people are told they are being interviewed as witnesses, are they not, to make it clear they are being interviewed in that capacity and not as a potential defendant; but that does not confer immunity from prosecution?

Dickson: It does not confer immunity from prosecution, no.

Hutchison: Nor does it necessarily implant in their minds that they have immunity from prosecution, does it?

Dickson: No, not necessarily, but I believe that it did in this case.

That was quite unfounded, of course, as Scrivener pointed out to Dickson. It was not a cross-examination to inspire confidence in either Dickson or the organisation which he served. It took one back to the early days of the case when Virani was told he was being interviewed as a witness but ended up in the dock. One wondered whether this would poison the jury's minds against the SFO – that if it could behave like this in one instance, there was no reason to suppose it was not standard conduct.

There were also complaints from the defence about access to documents. Abu Dhabi revealed documents to the SFO on a letter of request which went through the Foreign Office. When the defence applied for the same courtesy, it never got a response. Members of the SFO, accountants and lawyers, so the story went, were made honorary members of the Grand Cayman police so they could gain access to BCCI documents. There were also important documents which took days to get. Documents in the SFO's possession were released one at a time under the eye of a policeman. If the defence wanted a copy, the policeman would then go to an SFO lawyer for permission. But the process took an inordinate length of time – in some instances, up to one a day for a single document.

The SFO have a standard response to complaints of this kind: ignorance. This is because it either uses deliberate delaying tactics in the hope that the defence will be deprived of important evidence (some documents were only released by the SFO on the day Hacking finished his opening speech) or it genuinely does not know what is going on. If the SFO is capable of circulating privileged documents for photocopying, as it did in the Nadir affair, then it could be considered capable of anything. One has the impression that there are people at the SFO who are convinced that the dice are loaded against them in a prosecution and that cutting corners to rectify the balance is fair play. In the investigations leading up to the trial of Michael Ward in the European Leisure case, the SFO showed that their competence and understanding of the law as far as unused material, including tapes, was concerned was well below the standard expected of a senior prosecuting authority.

Towards the end of Virani's trial, he had become little more than a bystander. Depressed and cheerful by turns, there was

simply nothing he could do to influence events. All was in the
hands of his solicitor and Scrivener. Virani by now was simply
an incidental to the proceedings, anxious to get the wretched
business over. Forlorn would have been the best adjective to
describe him.

However, he still tried to keep up appearances by taking
an interest in the outside world. He would frequently inquire,
'What's in the papers?' I recalled that a witness, probably
Maynard, had said Virani wanted daily digests of the papers
when he was running Control. Why? Because his dyslexia
couldn't cope with the news in bulk. That was confirmed to
me by Lady Thomas; he often asked her the same question.

During an adjournment I asked him what happened if
he was found guilty. It would, I suggested, mean that he
would never be able to raise money to return to the property
business.

Not a bit of it. He shrugged his shoulders. 'Money is
not a problem,' he said. 'The most important thing in this
business is know-how, who to buy from, who to sell to. I
will start again.'

Fraud trials do not give counsel a chance to display their
theatrical and debating skills. The material is dry as dust.
The defendants do not have their hands covered in blood.
Poisons do not lurk in potting sheds. There is an absence of
high human drama.

Scrivener wanted the charge of conspiracy to defraud
dropped. This is a most unsatisfactory indictment, a catch-all
provision which says that if two or more people conspire
together to commit an illegal act, they are guilty even if
they did not commit it. The judge would not agree and
gave a ruling that even the jury felt they had to question
in the judge's summing up.

Hacking had a good bite at the case in his closing speech.
Scrivener took half the time, being careful to emphasise not
once but several times that if the jury had the slightest doubt
on any of the indictments, they were bound to return a
verdict of not guilty.

Scrivener conceded to me that Mr Justice Hutchison was
altogether too nice for his taste. 'He's got the jury on his side

by being very nice and considerate to them all the time. They
will like that. He has also been very fair to counsel. There has
been no opportunity to have a row with him. If you can do
that with a judge who's being really unreasonable, then you
can get the jury over to your side. There's been no chance of
that in this case.'

There were a number of technical points, though, in the
judge's summing-up which were questioned by the jury. These
involved Mr Justice Hutchison and counsel in several hours
of discussion to iron out mutually agreed corrections to the
summing-up. At that point, Judge Hutchison's critics said
that his mastery of the case had not been as good as his
early performance had indicated.

The judge told the jury that he wanted unanimous verdicts
on all fourteen counts. After a day and a half it was clear
there was not a chance of all eleven jurors agreeing, so the
judge ordered majority verdicts (that is, ten in agreement).

After five days they trooped back. One of the jurors, a
woman, was in tears. They had found Virani guilty on seven
of the charges of false accounting: five of these were majority
verdicts and two unanimous. They could not decide on four
of the charges, and on three, including the two most important
counts, conspiracy to defraud and theft, they found Virani not
guilty. By no stretch of the imagination could the result have
been called a walkover for the SFO. Indeed, there had clearly
been some hard-fought battles in the jury room. Scrivener told
the judge that in more than thirty years at the bar he had
never seen a juror in tears before. Later, at the Old Bailey,
the judge sent Virani down for two and a half years. The
grapevine said that had Scrivener not made such an eloquent
plea in mitigation, Virani could well have received double that
sentence.

Virani was imprisoned in Brixton. It is normal for fraudsters
to be transferred to an open prison after a few days. Seven
weeks later, he was still in Brixton, gaining some comfort in
the prison hospital because his heart was giving him trouble,
and being given light duties in the prison mess. At the time of
writing his case was due for appeal at the end of 1994 and there
seemed little doubt that it would be sympathetically heard.

Most people who practise fraud do it for gain. Virani had gained nothing in money terms. He had been found guilty of false accounting, in other words of signing documents which were not true. I wonder, if he came to read the judgement, whether he traced the words with his pen and formed them with his lips.

9

BLUE ARROW

Apart from the Nadir case, the worst failure by the SFO was the investigation and prosecution of County NatWest Bank for its role in the takeover of a company called Manpower by a much smaller British business, Blue Arrow. It was the most expensive fraud case in British legal history, £40 million, and it achieved precisely nothing except ten acquittals. It was also the most complex of cases, involving manipulation of the markets by County NatWest and other subsidiaries of the giant NatWest banking group.

The case was initiated by the first director of the SFO, John Wood, but he left shortly after it began, leaving it in the hands of Barbara Mills, who pursued it with her customary zeal. The inspiration for investigation and prosecution had come from two inspectors appointed by the DTI, Michael Crystal QC and a top accountant, David Spence, whose report on the conduct of the takeover was extremely critical. The prosecution turned out to be a huge and very expensive mistake; it should never have been tackled by the SFO.

It concerned the more recondite sections of the Companies Act, which were bound to test judge and jury to the limits of their physical and intellectual endurance, and it was unique in that no one stole anything or profited by so much as a shilling. The argument was all about market practice, not cars, personal jets, yachts or villas in the South of France. In that sense, one might have been forgiven for wondering what all the fuss was about. Yet it was sufficient to force Lord Boardman from the chair of NatWest's boardroom before retirement date, and two of the bank's most senior executives also had to leave. And that was well before the trial.

The Blue Arrow story is something of a City fairy tale, written by City folk; at its centre is a man they identified as one of their 'darlings'; in other words, a high flyer. City folk had no idea when they spotted the tall, attractive, prematurely balding figure of Tony Berry that they were looking at someone who was indirectly going to give many of them much more trouble than he was worth, in the process bringing his own colourful career at that stage to an abrupt end.

Tony Berry was an accountant who had worked for twelve years with Brengreen Holdings, a contract cleaning company which had been started by the right-wing vulgarian, David Evans, later Tory MP for Welwyn Hatfield. By the time he was forty, Berry was an executive director. But he was ambitious. In June 1982 he acquired a controlling interest in a small company called Blue Arrow Group Services Limited, whose business was staff recruitment and travel operations. Berry became chairman and chief executive.

He speedily worked wonders with his acquisition. Sixteen months after taking over he had more than doubled the company's turnover to £10 million from its 1981 figure. Ten months after that, Blue Arrow became a public limited company. And later in the same month, July 1984, just two years after the change in ownership, the company secured a quotation on the Unlisted Securities Market, the USM.

After that the company's growth was phenomenal. Berry acquired Brook Street Bureau, which provided secretarial, accounting, legal, industrial and office personnel through more than a hundred outlets in the UK and overseas. Brook Street cost Berry £19 million and made him the biggest employment services group in the country with a turnover of £80 million. This was quickly followed by the acquisition of Hoggett Bowers, which had a high profile in the executive search and selection business, and a public relations company, Trevor Bass Associates. The 'synergy' of the last two was a little doubtful, but Berry did not let that deter him. In July 1986, four years after he had taken over Blue Arrow, the company got a full listing on the Stock Exchange with a market capitalisation of £87 million.

Berry's progress now was unstoppable. He gobbled up

four more companies in the employment field in the United States for $57 million in the year he got his Stock Exchange quotation. He financed that by a one-for-three rights issue in the same year, which raised £30 million. The market was so impressed by him that 95 per cent of the issue was taken up by the shareholders. Remarkably, the results for the year at the end of October 1986 (which included only a small contribution from his American acquisitions) showed an increased turnover to £97 million compared with £34 million in the previous year. Profits before tax more than quadrupled to £9 million. Seven months later Berry bought four more executive search and selection businesses in the States. It was little wonder that he became the City's darling. Another Lord Hanson was in the making.

Then, in September 1987, Berry made the 'quantum leap'. He had been in his new business just over five-and-a-half years when he decided to take over the world's largest temporary employment agency, Manpower. It was American of course, and three times the size in turnover terms of Blue Arrow. It had 1,300 offices in more than thirty countries. It was also generating annual turnover (sales) of $1.2 billion and pre-tax profits of $60 million. A grouper was about to swallow a shark.

The money involved was equally silly. It was simply the biggest rights issue that had ever been seen in the British market. It was £844 million. Every shareholder would get five shares, for which he had to pay 166p each, for every three Blue Arrow he held. That was how the purchase price for Manpower was going to be financed. Smaller companies have often taken over bigger ones but it was the scale of the financing for Blue Arrow which was breathtaking.

County NatWest, the merchant bank which advised Blue Arrow, was the merchant banking arm of the NatWest Bank group. The group at that time had assets employed of £98.6 billion. County NatWest was by no means in the front rank of merchant banks. It was not a Warburg, Lazards or Barings. If the rights issue for Blue Arrow worked well, it would be a feather in County NatWest's cap and a useful marketing tool for getting new customers onto its client list. Blue Arrow, then, should have been a crucial addition to the bank's prestige. In the event, the rights issue turned out to be a nightmare, costing the group millions of pounds and leading to trial at the Old Bailey.

Lord Boardman was chairman of the group when the trouble blew up. He had been in the top job for four years but he had already spent several years as a main board director. He was a Tory meritocrat at a time when the party did not have much time for people who were state educated or did not have good family connections. He was a grey man, a solicitor by profession, who had made a point of doing the right things. He had served in the Northants Yeomanry, ending up as commanding officer. That gave him a Territorial Decoration, which showed he was keen. He became an MP in 1967 and subsequently enhanced his political career as Minister for Industry and later Chief Secretary to the Treasury. The directorships, too, came in effortlessly, among them NatWest.

The number of chairmen of clearing banks who have been professional bankers can be counted on the fingers of one hand. Boardman was an establishment figurehead, with good connections in the Tory party. He was also president of the Association of British Chambers of Commerce, a solid if uninspired organisation which runs a poor third to the CBI and Institute of Directors. But by no stretch of the imagination was he a banker, which meant in a vast organisation like NatWest that his chances of knowing what was going on in the lower reaches of the bank were remote. Boardman had a chairman's committee composed of three deputy chairmen (one of them a former chairman of IBM), the group chief executive (the most important man in the bank, and a professional), two deputy group chief executives (NatWest career men), and the general managers of the NatWest Bank. 'The main function of this committee,' according to the DTI inspectors who were to look into the Blue Arrow affair, 'was to consider and evaluate matters of current significance to the NWB group and to take urgent decisions. Issues of importance were reported to the board.' The board at that time had no fewer than twenty-two non-executive directors.

The bank had a top-heavy superstructure which invited the danger of capsize.

There were other committees, of course. Apart from Boardman's, there was the County NatWest chairman's committee under Charles Villiers, who was to resign over Blue Arrow. Among its members there was a sprinkling from the main board of the group together with executive directors from other NatWest subsidiaries.

The remit of Villiers's committee was to sanction exposures (money which could be at risk) of more than £10 million. It had another duty: to tell the Bank of England on an informal basis of any exposures which exceeded 25 per cent of capital. The Blue Arrow exposure fell comfortably into that category.

One other committee in which the DTI inspectors took an interest was the management committee of the NatWest Investment Bank, of which County NatWest was a subsidiary. Many of the names on this committee were the same as those on the chairman's committee of County NatWest, plus executives from other divisions.

But the people directly responsible for handling the Blue Arrow rights issue were two executive directors of County NatWest, Nicholas Wells and David Reed. Many others were involved as well, but Reed and Wells were two of the big players.

The purpose of any share issue, rights or otherwise, is to be a success. If all the shares on offer are taken up by investors, then it merits a three-star rating. Sometimes a really hot share will be over-subscribed – in other words, there aren't sufficient shares available to satisfy demand – in which case the share will go to a premium over its issue price. Had that happened with Blue Arrow, there would never have been a whisper of trouble.

What a company wants to avoid is a débâcle in the market place, when a major part of an issue isn't taken up by investors and it is left with the underwriters, the people who charge a hefty premium for taking up the balance of unsold shares. The market knows immediately whether an issue has been a success or not; word spreads remarkably quickly. If it's a failure, the shares in the after-market are marked down below their issue price and the company suffers.

Tony Berry had already looked at Manpower as a possible takeover target but had come to the conclusion that Blue Arrow was too small for the job. Then he revised his ideas. If he didn't launch a bid for Manpower now, it might grow out of his reach altogether. He discussed this idea with Nicholas Wells of County NatWest. A strategy was then formed with Blue Arrow's American advisers, Dillon, Read. This was for Blue Arrow to buy Manpower shares ahead of the bid. The thinking behind this was perfectly sound. A takeover bid for any company is a very expensive exercise: merchant banks, brokers, lawyers, accountants and underwriters have to be paid. In addition, the bid may not succeed – another bidder might step in with a higher offer. But by then a lot of unavoidable costs will have been incurred. If that should happen to Blue Arrow it would have a war chest of Manpower shares in the bank which would automatically increase in value because of the higher bid. This would help to defray the costs of Blue Arrow's own bid. Such was the thinking.

But the strategy got out of hand. Dillon, Read went into the market and started buying Manpower shares. The first tranche was bought on 14 July 1987, for $2.7 million. Dillon, Read reported the purchase to Wells and Berry on the same day. Twenty-four hours later Dillon, Read plunged in again with a purchase costing $4.8 million. London gave no instructions to stop buying, apparently, so Dillon, Read were back two days later with another purchase, this time costing a mere $365,000.

Two things happened as a result of this buying spree. Blue Arrow didn't have the ready cash to pay for it, so Wells arranged for County NatWest to make the company a loan of $9 million. The second effect was much more serious. Blue Arrow had broken the Stock Exchange's rule known as a Class 2 announcement. This lays down that when a company buys shares in another company representing between 5 and 15 per cent of the value of the buyer's consolidated net assets, then it is obliged to notify the market. The Manpower purchases represented around 11 per cent of Blue Arrow's consolidated net assets.

Blue Arrow and County NatWest now had a problem. If they declared the purchases, the market would know they were after Manpower. Once that information was out, Manpower's shares would rise in price, making the bid – if Blue Arrow went ahead with it – much more expensive or, quite possibly, putting it completely out of reach. There were a number of options available, all equally disagreeable. The first was to ask the Stock Exchange for a waiver of the Class 2 announcement rule (there had never been a waiver before). The second (at Wells's suggestion, never taken up) was to put the shares into another company, perhaps jointly owned by County NatWest and Blue Arrow, or by County NatWest itself. The third option was to sell the excess shares, but legal advice said that would not remedy the breach of the Class 2 requirement and could give rise anyway to allegations of price manipulation because the offer was known to be imminent. The fourth option was to tell no one.

Phillips & Drew, Blue Arrow's brokers, despatched a letter to the Stock Exchange testing the water about a waiver. It was a subtle letter because it did not admit to breaking the Class 2 requirement. The crucial words were: '*In these exceptional circumstances, I am writing to request a waiver from the obligation to disclose Blue Arrow's investment in the target company until 4th August, in the event that further share purchases are made in the target company*' [original italics].

The DTI inspectors didn't like the letter at all, nor did they appreciate the conduct of everyone involved. Nicholas Wells came in for censure – he had been irresponsible towards the obligation of disclosure. With the collaboration of the other people involved – Stainforth, Fraser and Alcock, all from Phillips & Drew – Wells was able 'to succeed in his objective which was to avoid any premature announcement likely to prejudice the offer being made'.

They all decided on the fourth option, which was to tell no one.

It was to be the first of several decisions in which County

NatWest and its associates were to be economical with the truth. Meanwhile, County had yet another problem: what to do with its financial exposure if the rights issue was not fully subscribed. County NatWest had underwritten the issue, but was anxious to hive off some of this exposure to sub-underwriters. In the event, they had to lean on their friends for every penny they could raise. Altogether there were 504,354,212 shares to be issued, of which Phillips & Drew arranged sub-underwriting for almost 326 million, County NatWest Investment Management came in for just over 25 million, and MIM for a little over 24 million shares. That left County NatWest with 129 million shares (25.6 per cent of the total) at a horrendous cost of £214.2 million. County NatWest never produced a particularly convincing reason as to why they couldn't get more sub-underwriting.

But the press gave the sub-underwriting exercise a good write-up, even suggesting that the issue had been fully sub-underwritten. No one contradicted the reports. The announcement of the offer, though, triggered a sharp fall in Blue Arrow shares by 32p to 184p. Shortly after that, County NatWest bought 750,000 Blue Arrow at 180p to ensure, according to Wells, that 'the share price did not fall unduly'. The next day, August 5th, 1987, the bank bought 2.5 million. But the support operation did not work; a few days later Blue Arrow fell below the rights issue price of 166p.

While Phillips & Drew were frantically busy organising presentations to investing institutions to tell them what a first-class investment the rights issue was, Nicholas Wells at County NatWest was trying to protect the bank's back. If the issue was not fully subscribed, County would be landed with a sackful of shares. Worse, if the sackful represented 5 per cent or more of the total issued capital, County would have to disclose that to the market. The disclosure could have a damaging effect on the price of the shares because the market would realise there was an 'overhang' of Blue Arrow which investors didn't want.

Wells tried to deal with this threat by, first, approaching Dillon, Read to see if they would take some of County's shares, but they refused; second, he tried out Phillips &

Drew, who thought about a deal but nothing came of it. There was an assumption by the advisers working for Blue Arrow that there would be a 70–80 per cent take-up of the shares, but they received a rude shock when they met on the evening of 28 September; the offer had closed at three that afternoon and the registrars had been preparing a preliminary assessment of the take-up. By 6.30 the bad news had come in: the take-up was 35 per cent, later rising to 38.04 per cent.

The whole of the Blue Arrow camp was sunk in gloom. One view was that the 'rump' of unsold shares was far too big to place with investors the next day and that the shares would have to be taken up by the underwriters. If that happened, though, the share price would probably fall. It would also be a big financial knock for County NatWest.

Phillips & Drew thought they could probably place 180 million of the rump the next day, but that would leave a 'gap' of 132 million shares, or 26 per cent, representing £219 million. Wells and Reed of County decided they would try to save the issue and not leave it with the underwriters, but if that was to be done County would have to increase its exposure and so would the others acting for Blue Arrow.

By now, there were more problems than solutions. One of the major obstacles to be overcome was Phillips & Drew's belief that on a 38 per cent take-up they wouldn't have a hope of placing the rump with the institutions the next day; 50 per cent would look far better. County had found some more money so the bank asked Phillips & Drew if they would buy 10 million Blue Arrow in the rights issue rather than doing so in the placing the next day. Gibbs of Phillips & Drew wondered if that was legal, but apparently Wells of County told him it was all right. Phillips & Drew decided to go ahead. Wells then tried to tap Dillon, Read for the same amount. They were worried about the legal propriety of doing so but gained the impression from Wells that it would be 'perfectly all right'. The inspectors upheld Wells when he denied he had told Dillon, Read that this specific proposal had been cleared by lawyers. Anyway, Dillon, Read came on board for 10 million shares which were 'added in' on the evening of September 28th. These shares came from County

NatWest. Together with the acceptances by the registrars (38.04 per cent), the add-ins (10.83 per cent) brought the total to just under 50 per cent (48.87).

It was not 50 per cent, but in the circumstances beggars could not be choosers. On the morning of 29 September, Phillips & Drew salesmen hit the telephones with instructions to place 180 million shares. The DTI inspectors said that 'by any standards it was an exceptionally large placing'. County NatWest managed to place 44 million shares with its clients, among them Beazer and Pleasurama. By 10 o'clock that morning it was virtually all over; just 10 million shares needed to be placed. It was not much in the sum of things, but there was one snag: under the terms of the offer *all* the shares had to be placed, otherwise they would all have to be taken up by the underwriters. Faced with that hideous alternative, Phillips & Drew and County had little option but to take another 5 million shares each.

It had worked, but at what a cost. County had ended up with 91.5 million of the shares, or 18.2 per cent of the whole rights issue; its affiliates had bought another 2 per cent; Phillips & Drew was in for 34 million shares, 6.8 per cent of the issue; and Dillon, Read signed up for 10 million shares, or 2 per cent.

But the saga still had a long way to go. On the day the add-in shares were allocated to the overall total, County NatWest issued a press release saying that acceptances represented 48.9 per cent of the rights issue. The DTI inspectors took strong exception to this part of the statement. It was not, they maintained, the whole truth. They put it to Wells, who had authorised the release, that it was misleading. Wells said it was factual. But, said the inspectors, the issue had only been subscribed, first, as to 35 per cent, then to a figure of 38 per cent. So why hadn't Wells said that? The banker replied that County and other parties had taken up 10 per cent of the rights issue on the evening of the 28th and he felt there was no need for the market to know that because it would have made the placing very much more difficult.

The inspectors came down on Wells like a ton of bricks, saying that his explanation was quite unacceptable and amounted to a deliberate decision to mislead the market. Nor were they any kinder about the assertion that 'all of the remaining new ordinary shares . . . have been sold in the market'. The inspectors contested that. They said the use of the words 'sold in the market' disguised the fact that a very substantial number of shares had been retained by County NatWest and Phillips & Drew – far too many to fall 'within normal practice'.

They went on to say that Messrs Reed and Wells, of County NatWest, and Gibbs and Stainforth, of Phillips & Drew, were responsible for misleading the market. 'We regard their conduct as falling well below that to be expected from responsible executives of CNW and Phillips & Drew.'

This was the second big rap over the knuckles for three of the men, and the third for Nicholas Wells. As people involved in the affair were to find out, it didn't pay to earn the opprobrium of the inspectors.

For Wells, there was a bit more to come, especially for the way he avoided the rules affecting disclosure of shareholdings. The day after the Blue Arrow rights issue closed, County NatWest found itself in the unenviable position of holding almost 95 million Blue Arrow shares, or 13.4 per cent of the enlarged share capital of Blue Arrow after absorbing Manpower. This was well above the 5 per cent level which the rules laid down had to be disclosed to the market. County NatWest had to split this holding three ways so that no single holding amounted to 5 per cent. It left 4.9 per cent with CAD (the Corporate Advisory Division of NatWest Bank); another tranche of 4.43 per cent was 'acquired', according to the inspectors, by County NatWest Securities, the market-making arm of NatWest Bank; while the final tranche of 3.9 per cent was expected to be held by Phillips & Drew.

But it was the County NatWest Securities' holding that was going to be the trickiest part of the equation. Market makers had exemption from disclosing the number of shares they held in any company as long as the holding was for the purpose of the market maker's business. But no statutory limit was

placed on the size of the holding, which made the exemption
pretty arbitrary. The Stock Exchange, however, made its own
rule which said that any market maker holding 5 per cent
or more of a company's shares would have to declare it to
the Exchange within five days of the holding having been
acquired.

No market maker worth his salt is going to have large
amounts of capital tied up in shares he can't trade profitably.
That was the County NatWest Securities view anyway. Furthermore, by taking just under 5 per cent County NatWest
Securities would find themselves stuck with a bill for more
than £58 million – a figure, one of the firm's senior executives
said, which was more than the total amount of capital they
used for running a book of 1200 stocks. Small wonder they
were unhappy about the deal.

A substantial part of that weight was lifted from their
shoulders when Wells of CNW said that County NatWest
Securities would only be responsible for the 3.3 million
shares he had 'added in' for County NatWest Securities on
the evening of 28 September. The remaining 31.3 million
shares down to County NatWest Securities would be funded
by County NatWest Bank. County NatWest Securities now
had three separate amounts of Blue Arrow shares: there were
those it had on its trading book; there were the 3.3 million
that had been added in – these now went to the 'back book';
and there were the 31.3 million shares, which CNW were
guarantors for if anything went wrong – these went to the
'back back book'.

The DTI inspectors liked none of this. They did not believe
County NatWest Securities could reasonably expect to trade
31.3 million Blue Arrow shares – 3 to 5 million, yes, but
nothing like the number the market makers had been landed
with. It was true, they said, that the size of the holding did
not take it outside the exemption of 5 per cent (at which
they had to declare), but no one could be expected to
believe that 31 million shares was a normal holding for
its market-making activities. The object of the exercise, the
inspectors concluded, was to avoid disclosure. Once again,
Nicholas Wells came in for censure: 'We regard his conduct

as falling well below that to be expected from a responsible executive of CNW.'

The County NatWest bank group, in a written submission to the inspectors, said the use of the market maker's exemption to support the Blue Arrow rights issue was unacceptable. It agreed with the inspectors that the arrangements between County NatWest and County NatWest Securities were not an appropriate use of the exemption. But the group submitted that the 31.3 million shares did fall within the exemption, whereas the inspectors had decided for a variety of reasons that this was not the case.

There was one other big player in the scramble to make the Blue Arrow rights issue a success. This was the Union Bank of Switzerland, the biggest of all the Swiss banks and the parent of Phillips & Drew, the brokers to the Blue Arrow issue. Phillips & Drew had been asked by Nicholas Wells to take a large block of Blue Arrow stock from CNW in return for a no-loss indemnity. The deal included a 30 per cent share in any profits from the sale of the shares and reimbursement of interest charges. Phillips & Drew were being asked to take 4.5 per cent of Blue Arrow for more than £46 million. As there was no downside risk and as all the costs were being picked up by County NatWest, and there was the added attraction of a profit, it looked too good not to consider. Nicholas Wells also told Phillips & Drew that he had been advised that the arrangement was legal.

Phillips & Drew decided to ask its parent company, UBS, if it would take up the shares. The answer was yes, but the bank placed particular emphasis on the legality of the deal. The lawyers said there was no problem about disclosure to the market, it was not legally necessary. There was an exchange of letters between those acting for the various parties, including letters of indemnity. But one crucial phrase, used by Allan & Overy, solicitors to Phillips & Drew, caught the eye of the DTI inspectors. It was in the solicitor's letter to the London branch of the Union Bank of Switzerland: 'We have also commented that, irrespective of the legal issues, any publicity given to this arrangement would be adverse to UBS and Phillips & Drew since the arrangement consists of an endeavour to avoid a legal obligation to notify an interest in shares.'

The inspectors thought the law was unsatisfactory in this respect, as it was open to abuse, and suggested the Companies Act 1985 might be amended to prevent further abuse.

While the directors of the NatWest group's subsidiaries were up to their necks trying to save the rights issue, the senior executive directors of the main bank were to find themselves not only in trouble but out of their depth. Before they met Messrs Reed and Wells, there had been a formal UK Business Committee meeting at the headquarters of NatWest in Lothbury, a building which lends new meaning to the phrase, the marbled halls of banking. The ground floor is a huge, whispering, mahogany and marble temple to Mammon. It is not a place for jokes or the commonplaces of social intercourse. The building is about money. And that was what the top dogs were most interested in. The bank's money and where things went next.

Upstairs the Business Committee, chaired by Sir Edwin Nixon and supported by Lord Harrowby, Sir Philip Wilkinson and Messrs C. Green, T. Green, Plastow, Cohen, Casey, Reed and Rimell, were listening to an exposition by Cohen about how desirable the Blue Arrow rights issue was. But first, Sir Edwin pointed out that the bank's audit committee had wondered if the Corporate Advisory Department, which had been advising Blue Arrow on its successful acquisition of Manpower, thought this was an appropriate risk for the group to be taking.

Mr Cohen, the chief executive of County NatWest, then replied in extraordinarily bullish terms, saying that he was totally confident about the transaction which many believed would be seen as one of the corporate highlights of 1987 within the City. 'The transaction,' he said, 'has already raised the stature of County NatWest with a number of major corporate groups.'

Apparently, the overriding impression given by Mr Cohen to the committee was that the rights issue had been a success. It is a known fact that clearing banks do not have the brightest of people in their top echelons, to which they always add businessmen whose knowledge of banking is limited to their own bank accounts and what they can borrow from banks to finance their acquisitions. Clearing banks have a huge client base which gives them their income. Merchant banks, on the other hand, live by their wits and their reputation for bringing home the bacon. Mr Cohen's words were taken at face value; there was a very good chance that no one else around the table could grasp the mechanics of rights issues, placings or underwriting.

Shortly afterwards, Messrs Reed and Wells of County NatWest went to see the Greens (Messrs T. and C., both directors and deputy chief executives of NatWest Bank) and Mr Plastow, an executive director of NatWest Bank. At this meeting some of the bad news began to trickle upwards to the bank's top echelons. Wells said the issue had not gone as well as expected and that they had gone for a placement rather than falling back on the underwriters. But that had involved County NatWest in a considerable exposure to support their client, Blue Arrow. Wells emphasised the importance of confidentiality about the arrangements CNW had entered into to avoid disclosure, and T. Green said they queried the holding with the market makers (by his own admission, Green knew very little about how market makers worked). The three directors were reassured that there was a clear exemption as far as NatWest was concerned. They were also told that the merger would be successful and that there would be a strong market in Blue Arrow shares.

Apart from these reassurances, and the indemnity arrangements for Phillips & Drew, which worried Green, he felt a good deal more comfortable when he was told that County NatWest had taken legal advice, that the Bank of England was in the picture and that Blue Arrow knew about the shareholdings.

'The fact,' he said, 'that the Bank of England was being kept informed showed that Mr Reed and Mr Wells were not hiding anything from the regulators . . . Considering the assurances that we were given regarding legal advice, the knowledge of Blue Arrow and the Bank of England, there was no reason for me to do other than accept what was said by Mr Reed and Mr Wells.'

While the other two executive directors were broadly in agreement with Mr T. Green about what had been said at the meeting, there was some confusion about who said what to whom concerning the market maker's exemption and the legal advice that went with it. The inspectors concluded that Messrs Reed and Wells did not tell the three executive directors they had obtained legal advice telling them they could rely on the market maker's exemption. The inspectors also said that no request to see such legal advice was made by any of the three executive directors.

They also noted that Mr T. Green placed a lot of emphasis on the Bank of England being kept in the picture, but in fact the Bank were not approached until the day after the meeting with the three directors. When asked by the inspectors if he had inquired how and when Messrs Reed and Wells informed the Bank of England, Mr T. Green said he had not. Asked why, he replied, ingenuously to say the least, that he took their word they had advised the Bank of England. One wonders if they do that kind of thing so readily with their hard-pressed clients.

The inspectors were far from enamoured with the conduct of the three executive directors. They should have appreciated that elsewhere in the NatWest Bank group there could well be other Blue Arrow holdings. 'Enquiries would have revealed that this was in fact the case. The consequence was that NWB did not perform its relevant statutory duties . . . we regard the conduct of Messrs C. Green, T. Green and Plastow as falling below that to be expected from responsible senior executives of NWB.'

NatWest was getting a pretty bad write-up, but worse was to follow. The next day, September 30th, Clark and Wells of County NatWest shot round to the Bank of England for a meeting with officials from the banking supervision division, among them Messrs Carse and Merriman.

Wells laid his cards on the table, saying that County NatWest had an equity exposure in Blue Arrow of £150 million, one third of which had been acquired by the exercise of rights and the rest in the placing. He believed that he told the meeting that only 38 per cent of the shares had been taken up, but no one else present remembered the figure being mentioned. That, apparently, was of no concern to the Bank of England; it was the level of exposure that worried them.

Carse told Wells that the Bank did not approve of banks being long-term investors in companies and would like to see CNW 'out' of Blue Arrow by the end of the year. Wells then told the Bank about the distribution of Blue Arrow shares so that there was no necessity for disclosure. That alarmed the Bank officials. They wanted to know about the legality of what County NatWest had done. Wells assured them he had taken 'double, even treble' legal advice. The DTI inspectors accepted that was what Wells told the Bank, but added that it was 'quite untrue', as Mr Wells knew. Once again Nicholas Wells had his knuckles rapped by the inspectors.

Thereafter it was downhill all the way. There was a small patch of blue when County NatWest invoiced Blue Arrow for its fees and commission. The bill is worth looking at:

General financial advice	£4,000,000
Joint Dealer manager fee on the offer for Manpower	£1,621,000.53
Underwriting commission of ⅛% on working capital facility of US$300 million	£231,481.48
Underwriting commission on rights issue net of sub-underwriting commission	£6,606,975.74
	£12,460,440.75

But that was a spit in the ocean compared with NatWest's overall losses, which were compounded by the stock market crash ('Black Monday') of October 19th, 1987. County NatWest held almost 95 million Blue Arrow shares. Each time the shares dropped a penny, CNW lost a million. It was like watching the bathwater pouring down the plughole.

Ten days after the crash, Charles Villiers, chairman of County NatWest, went to see Mr T. Green and told him that at a price of 98 pence CNW had lost £46 million before taking into account the fees of the Corporate Advisory Division of the NatWest Investment Bank; a cool £13 million. Villiers was wondering how he should respond to media questions if he should be asked how the group had been affected by the dreadful state of the markets. But he did not get much of an answer.

County NatWest was then hit by another problem which it had either forgotten about or, in the flurry of the rights issue, had ignored. This was the 1.2 million shares which had been taken up by Handelsbank (86 per cent owned by NatWest). Charles Villiers only learned of this holding on 18 November 1987, and immediately fired off questions wanting to know how the holding affected CNW's disclosure obligations. When Handelsbank took the shares from Nicholas Wells, Wells had imagined they were for clients and staff. Subsequently, Handelsbank sold some 200,000 to clients and staff but its holding still gave the bank a disclosable interest over a period of seven weeks. The gap was later bridged by transferring one million shares from County NatWest to County NatWest Securities. In this particular transaction, Mr Reed, an executive director of County NatWest, caught it in the neck from the inspectors, who did not think he behaved responsibly.

The inspectors also found it regrettable that County NatWest didn't heed the advice from the Bank of England on 24 November 1987 that CNW should discuss their disclosure requirements with the Stock Exchange. And they said there was no justification for delaying for seventeen days an announcement to the Stock Exchange that they had bought and sold Blue Arrow shares (the requirement was that a deal of that kind should be reported within five days).

However, something else was creeping up on NatWest which was to lead to another massive loss. By the end of

November 1987, Lord Boardman and the top brass of the banking group had been told that the net loss on the books of NatWest Investment Bank was £39.3 million, and that was after profits of £33.4 million which had been made from a 'hedging' operation on the Footsie index and the fees for servicing Blue Arrow in the rights issue.

Unpleasant as that news may have been, there was still the unresolved problem of the deal County NatWest had done with the Union Bank of Switzerland. UBS had taken 28.2 million Blue Arrow shares at 166.25p which, together with interest charges, amounted to a thumping £47.78 million. UBS had been very happy about the deal at the time because CNW had guaranteed to indemnify them against any loss and give them 30 per cent of any profits should the shares rise above the issue price. This arrangement had to be unwound by the end of December 1987, when the agreement was to be formally terminated.

Now that the top echelons of the NatWest group had become involved in the Blue Arrow affair, Lord Boardman, the bank's chairman, told the DTI inspectors that he couldn't understand how County NatWest could have a profit and loss sharing arrangement with UBS without having an interest in the shares. Boardman's concern was that if County NatWest was shown to have an interest then the total of Blue Arrow shares the bank now had was way over the disclosure level.

This nightmare was circumvented by the negotiations which followed with UBS. Part of that agreement was that UBS retained its Blue Arrow shares, so that they came nowhere near County NatWest. But on the other issue, the indemnities to UBS in the event of a loss on the shares, the Swiss bank had NatWest on the ropes. During the period of the negotiations, which was only a fortnight or so, Blue Arrow shares fluctuated between 83p and 90p. But UBS's Mr Studer, a member of the bank's executive board, proved to be a tough nut to crack. He drove the price of the shares UBS were holding down to 63p. The lower the price, of course, the bigger the indemnity County NatWest would have to pay out. County were in no position to call any shots at all; the agreement with UBS must have been drawn up very loosely for County to have been so badly wrong-footed. County was forced to write out a cheque to UBS for just over £30 million. Between three and six months later, UBS sold its total Blue Arrow holding for prices varying between 105p and 118p, giving it a total net profit of more than £11 million.

On the same day – 17 December – that UBS pocketed its cheque, NatWest issued two press statements. The first simply said that NatWest Bank was injecting £80 million into County NatWest, and the second referred to County NatWest's holding in Blue Arrow, described as 9.5 per cent, or 67.6 million shares.

The inspectors quibbled with the figures in the press releases. That was not surprising. The County NatWest holding of 9.5 per cent gave the impression that that was the total of Blue Arrow shares held by the NatWest banking group. It was not. Over 8 million more shares were being held by the group as part of Blue Arrow's issued share capital.

The inspectors also examined the internal disclosure rules operated by the NatWest banking group as a whole. It looked at the way they worked in each subsidiary and came to the conclusion that the 'obligation to disclose can be postponed through inefficiency. We regard this as unacceptable as it is clearly open to abuse.'

Late in February 1988 – after Charles Villiers, the chief executive of NatWest Investment Bank and chairman of County NatWest, and Jonathan Cohen, deputy chief executive of NWIB and chief executive of County NatWest, had resigned – the NatWest Bank decided to conduct its own investigation into what had happened. Sir Philip Wilkinson was appointed to head the enquiry; it had apparently been forgotten that he was one of the three deputy chairmen who had seen the two deputy chief executives when the Blue Arrow mess began to emerge. Notwithstanding that, Wilkinson's interim report – which had been designed to identify areas which would be subject to scrutiny should an outside investigation be called for – was pretty damning. Its main findings were that the legal advice so frequently referred to did not seem to have been confirmed in writing and that, as far as disclosable shareholdings were concerned, CNW had not only been in breach of the Companies Act since 29 September, but the spirit of the law had been totally disregarded as well.

DTI inspectors are generally cautious with language, but reading between the lines there can be no mistake about the situation at County NatWest and County NatWest Securities. Michael Crystal QC and the accountant, David Spence, concluded: 'The events referred to in this report give rise to concern. The market was misled. Provisions of the Companies Act 1985 were not complied with. There was no justification for what happened . . . In its written submission, the NWB group informed us that all possible steps were being taken to ensure that all investment banking activities within the NWB group would be carried out to high standards of integrity and propriety. The matters referred to in this report disclose a highly unsatisfactory state of affairs. It is therefore important that all necessary steps are taken by the NWB group to fulfil its objective.'

Whether what happened at County NatWest justified the enormous fraud prosecution that followed was another matter. As the inspectors pointed out, the market had been misled and parts of the Companies Act had not been complied with. Executives had told less than the truth. There had also been incompetence and inefficiency. But no one had stolen anything. No one personally benefited from what happened; indeed, there were a number of voluntary resignations well over a year before the DTI inspectors appeared on the scene. What seems to have been the situation was that the bank's executives had been totally seduced by the high-profile rights issue they had landed and were determined to make it work. Success would have put a second-rank merchant bank up with the stars in marketing terms and the cutting of corners was a risk worth taking. The media would have viewed County NatWest in a new light and the kudos for the executives involved would have been substantial and marketable. Financial greed may not have come into it, because nothing was stolen, but greed for success and the limelight must have been an important factor in the highly competitive environment of the City. Conversely, none of these bright young City bankers wanted to be associated with a disaster.

Nor could the overall losses that NatWest suffered as a result of the affair – £65.1 million – be put down to anything other than bad judgement and the market going against the bank at a crucial moment. There was no calculated conspiracy to deprive the bank of money; the only conspiracy involved was to make the rights issue a success at all costs. If there was ever a case for the market regulators to consider sanctions, then County NatWest and Blue Arrow could have been the biggest challenge to their effectiveness. If the regulators had survived that test with credit, it's unlikely that other cases would have fallen automatically into the hands of the SFO.

But at Elm House, the wheels were already in motion. Four months after the inspectors reported in July 1989, the familiar pattern of dawn raids and arrests was to be seen in the media. In the first half of November 1989, there were arrests in London and the Home Counties and ten senior executives and a solicitor were taken to Bishopsgate police station where they were charged with fraudulent conspiracy.

Many of those charged had already been the subject of comment by the DTI inspectors: Charles Villiers, former chairman of County NatWest; Jonathan Cohen, the bank's former chief executive; Timothy Brown, director of Phillips & Drew; Nicholas Wells and David Reed, both former directors of NatWest's Corporate Advisory Division; Elizabeth Brimelow, compliance director of County NatWest; Stephen Clark, executive director of County NatWest; Alan Keat, former legal adviser to County NatWest on the Blue Arrow bid; Martin Gibbs, former head of corporate finance at UBS Phillips & Drew; Paul Smallwood, director UK equity sales, Phillips & Drew; and Christopher Stainforth, the former transaction team leader in the corporate finance division of Phillips & Drew. There were three corporate defendants as well: NatWest Investment Bank, County NatWest and UBS Phillips & Drew. These three, together with eight other defendants, were charged with conspiring 'together and with other persons fraudulently to induce persons to enter into agreements for acquiring or subscribing for securities, namely shares in Blue Arrow plc'. That carried a maximum jail sentence of seven years.

The second charge, for which the maximum sentence was ten years, was that all the defendants 'conspired together and with other persons to defraud such persons who had or might have had an interest in dealing in shares in Blue Arrow plc, or National Westminster Bank plc, or in dealing on the *Financial Times* Stock Exchange 100 Share Index'.

It is easy to see what the charges were driving at, because they were the legal extrapolation of what the DTI inspectors had said in their report. The market performance of Blue Arrow shares, for example, might have been very different if County NatWest had disclosed its full shareholding to the authorities. Indeed, one of the reasons why County NatWest executives had been so anxious to avoid disclosure was that they wanted the rights issue to be a success and the price of the shares to hold up. The big institutions might have been a good deal less keen on taking up the issue if they had known the true state of play.

Technically, the jury was being asked to digest a lot of financial detail in respect of charges which involved no one putting their hands in the till. Most juries understand theft, especially when the prosecution makes a proper job of presenting its case. The difficulty here, as far as the jury was concerned, was that stealing was not involved. The prosecution based its evidence very largely on the transcripts of the DTI inspectors' investigation, which were voluminous, and which the defence tried to cut down to manageable proportions. A third of the case was actually spent in legal argument. However, ninety-two prosecution witnesses were still called.

Judge Stuart McKinnon, a charming man by all accounts, had been a high court judge for only two years and had never had a criminal practice when he was a barrister. He was further disadvantaged by the fact that he was allowed a meagre ten days to read himself into a case which was immensely complex even for those counsel who had had time to get to grips with the 5,000 pages of transcripts of evidence taken at the DTI inquiry by Michael Crystal. One senior counsel complained to anyone who would listen that this was unfair on the judge, unfair on the defendants, unfair on the whole system. It was exactly the kind of thing that Lord Roskill had wanted rectified. Furthermore, McKinnon was not equipped for what was to be an arduous and difficult case. He was not the right horse for this particular course, but it looked as if he was the only runner available, bearing in mind the shortage of high court judges – a shortage which the Treasury is too mean to rectify. The upshot was that when someone like McKinnon – new to this particular game and faced with a formidable array of counsel – deserved all the time he needed, he was probably given sufficient only to read the prosecution's case statement.

Nicholas Purnell QC had been instructed by the SFO to lead for the prosecution. Purnell is something of a prodigy at the bar. Even the most detached observers regard him as a brilliant advocate, never at a loss, never thrown and capable of arguing for half a day on a point he has never thought about before, and doing it well. A very persuasive advocate, apparently, but arrogant with it. His opening speech for the prosecution lasted for some five days, during which he spoke without a note. He also has a habit of cross-examining witnesses for hours on end without reference to notes having, as it were, a total mastery not only of his brief but of every single witness statement in the case. These virtuoso performances, however, can be marred when he cannot remember what he said several days or months earlier.

He has another failing, one counsel told me: he is never wrong, so that once the case is laid before the court it is set in concrete. There are no compromises, no changes in the indictment. The result, of course, is that he will only do deals which involve no climb-down on his part. It might have paid him to do a deal in the Blue Arrow case. He started off jauntily enough by telling the judge that the case would last no more than three or four months. Instead it lasted twelve, as most people told him it would.

One of the big stumbling blocks to engineering a shorter trial was that one of those charged was an eminent solicitor, Alan Keat, a partner in Travers Smith Braithwaite, who were legal advisers to County NatWest. It *might* just have been possible to persuade the other defendants, the City operators, to offer a plea of guilty to making reckless statements, thereby encouraging people to invest. That would have been an admission involving no dishonesty. On that basis the judge would no doubt have been able to indicate that if the plea was acceptable to the prosecution, there would be no custodial sentences. The SFO could also have claimed a modest victory.

But that was never going to be acceptable to the Crown unless all the defendants, including Keat, were to plead, and there was never any possibility of Keat doing that. He had always maintained his complete innocence of any wrongdoing and the case against him was dismissed when the judge ruled there was insufficient evidence against him at the end of the prosecution case.

Keat should never have been charged. If the Crown had accepted this, dropped the case against him – as they had been urged to do – and accepted pleas from the others (though there is no certainty that the others would have offered pleas), the case would have been over in a few days. As it was, it went the distance. Forty million pounds' worth of distance, as it happened, double the cost of the Guinness trials. And everyone got off. From arrests to acquittals, the wretched affair took nearly three years, and from the share issue, five.

The SFO's director, George Staple, argued that the case was beyond his office's scope (at the time of Keat's arrest, John Wood was in charge of the SFO; it had been Mrs Mills's decision to prosecute). Scope there certainly was. There was no shortage of defendants, nor of counsel, nor of money for the defence; NatWest's defence costs alone were £13 million.

But that is not the measure of whether a case is worth bringing. That should depend on how solid the prosecution is, and what the purpose of the prosecution is; it could be no more than to show the public they are going about their business with due diligence, calming public fears that the SFO is not actively prosecuting fraudsters. One sometimes thinks that the only purpose of an SFO prosecution is to show that the Office is doing something. Public life is full of busybodies anxious to please their political masters; the SFO is quite good at creating that impression.

Finally, and most importantly, we should ask whether the Blue Arrow case was tried in the right arena. Juries, as one eminent senior counsel told me (he has prosecuted and defended many fraudsters in his time), understand only one thing when it comes to fraud: an act of dishonesty; the theft of other people's money for their own use. The Companies Act, disclosure, bending the dealing rules, market rigging, share ramping and the rest of it is so much pie-in-the-sky to them. They understand the real pie when it's in some crook's back pocket.

The Blue Arrow case had a profound effect on Mr Justice McKinnon. He said it was more than the jury or the defendants should have had to bear. There must, he said, be some other way. It was his bad luck that so early in his career as a high court judge he should have been landed with such a complex case. But that was not his fault, it was the fault of the administration which, even today, simply hasn't the manpower to appoint judges with the requisite skills to try every big fraud case.

There is a final, ironic postscript to the Blue Arrow case. Tony Berry, the man whose whole object in his business life was to create a large empire of labour, employment and cleaning services agencies through the takeover of Manpower in the United States, and whose ambitions were ultimately responsible for this huge and wasteful case at the Old Bailey, was also tainted. In an earlier report, the DTI had branded him as someone whose conduct was clearly not acceptable '. . . for someone in a position of authority in a public company'. Consequent upon that, the DTI tried to get him disqualified as a company director, one of the most damaging sanctions that can happen to an ambitious businessman. But late in 1994, when the case was heard, the department failed in its application.

However, Berry lost his empire well before that. Mitchell Fromstein, the chief executive officer of Manpower in the States, whose company had been seized from him by Berry in the takeover, took it back. The wheel had turned full circle.

10

COUNTING THE COST

A prominent solicitor who specialises in fraud cases told me that in order to defend yourself in a major fraud case 'you either have to be very rich or very poor'. The economics of the cost of defence are as basic as that; there are no halfway houses, no special cases. The legal aid system, which is used by most people who are charged with fraud, lays down that the defendant must spend all his capital down to his last £3,000. The only asset he is allowed to keep is the roof over his head. If he has a second house, that is a capital asset which the court takes into account. His wife's assets are taken into the computation as well.

In addition, he will be asked to make a contribution from his income, assuming that he is still in employment for much, or part, of the time he needs legal aid. In practice, once society knows that a man has been charged with fraud, he will almost certainly lose his job. If he works for himself as an entrepreneur, the chances are that his suppliers will no longer supply him, his bank will get extremely tough if he has an overdraft or loan facility, and anyone else who has a financial relationship with him will want to distance themselves from the defendant. In other words, most financial life-support systems will be withdrawn from him. He is on his own.

'People who are regarded as successful businessmen,' one northern solicitor told me, 'are often financially destroyed just by the investigation itself, even before they are charged, because their business simply evaporates in front of their eyes. So you find that in the majority of fraud cases the defendant either contributes nothing towards the costs of his case or very little.'

There is, though, an important gap between those early interviews in an investigation and the time when a suspect is charged. In the intervening period, the suspect may have to undergo Section 2 interviews, when the presence of a solicitor should be mandatory to protect his interests. Section 2s are covered by the rules governing police station legal aid. The suspect gets legal aid automatically, and this is not means tested. The difficulty arises during the period between when a suspect is first interviewed to the time he is charged. Solicitors maintain that there is a good deal of important work to be done during that period, but if the suspect doesn't have means of his own then the solicitor does not get paid.

'In those circumstances – and if we think it is going to be a major case – then we take a view of it and say we'll take those costs on the chin. We can't claim costs retrospectively because the suspect hasn't yet been charged. Costs can only be claimed once the suspect has been charged.'

It sounds as if the solicitor at this stage is not getting much of a deal. But one should never feel sorry for lawyers. Good solicitors are paid for their expertise in certain fields. Once that expertise has been acquired, fewer man-hours are required on a case because much of the work is routine and quickly accomplished. If a firm has a particular reputation for dealing with major fraud cases, then the volume of the work in that field will grow. Volume leads to regular income and that pays the wages and profits.

Of course, all solicitors dealing with fraud prefer to deal with rich men with bottomless pockets. Rich men want the best, expect to pay a fortune and are resigned to huge costs, often resentfully. That is all very well, but sometimes they face costs that are incalculable. While the SFO likes to think it can polish off cases, from investigation to the end of trial, in two years, that is never the situation in a major, complex fraud; Elm House will leave no document unturned, no witness unquestioned, no avenue unexplored. It is prosecution by saturation and, as one top fraud solicitor told me, it means that the SFO can define the playing field, and choose its dimensions. The bigger the trial, the bigger the field, and while a rich man prepares himself for estimated legal bills in excess of a million pounds he may be landed with a good deal more than that because the case drags on interminably as the SFO continues to ferret for information.

Should the rich man be acquitted, he faces another problem: recovering his costs. He will have gone to a top solicitor and will have employed the best counsel available; the bigger the case, the more legal firepower he will need. Their rates and fees for a private client are likely to be very different from those acceptable to the Legal Aid Board when it is paying for someone who has no money. Consequently, his bills will be 'taxed' by the taxing master at what he considers to be a 'reasonable' rate of remuneration. 'Reasonable' in this context is likely to be well below the final figures on the bills. So the well-heeled defendant, even if acquitted, can expect to be out of pocket, sometimes by substantial amounts.

(All bills submitted by solicitors and counsel for legal aid work, on the other hand, are 'taxed' by the taxing or determining officer. Taxing is a bad word. The correct phrase should be 'rigorously checked' to see that the State is not being overcharged for legal aid work. All lawyers complain that bills are taxed downwards. If a serious dispute over fees arises, then the matter can be taken to the taxing master, who is an official of the Lord Chancellor's department. Many legal aid bills are left unpaid by the government for as long as a year, one reason being that the money very often is not available to pay out.)

There is a school of thought which says that there is no reason why a rich man should be treated inequitably, or lose money, if he has been acquitted. The public perception is that if he has the wealth to pay for an expensive trial, then he should be made to stump up, that there is no reason why the taxpayer should be liable. This notion is based very largely on emotion; the feeling that a man is not charged with serious fraud without good reason, and even if he is acquitted 'there is no smoke without fire'.

This makes the dangerous assumption that if a man cannot be punished in one way, there is no reason why he should not be punished in another. No one has ever argued that the wealthy should not be liable for every penny of their costs if found guilty. But there is no good reason why they should be caught for costs if acquitted. A more equitable way of handling the problem, some solicitors argue, would be to put the rich man on legal aid from the beginning of proceedings. If acquitted, he does not pay a penny and if guilty he collects the whole bill.

Most people charged with fraud, though, resort to the legal aid system either in whole or in part, depending on their means. A man who does not have to make any contributions from his own pocket will get a solicitor to advise him, a junior counsel (not a QC in the early stages) to look after his case up to transfer proceedings to the crown court, when a leading counsel will appear on the scene, the services of accountants, experts in the more arcane aspects of law if his counsel cannot handle them, and other expert advice if the solicitor can make a reasonable case to the Legal Aid Board for hiring them. Once a legal aid certificate is granted on the production of accounts to show there is an entitlement to aid, defence solicitors have to be careful not to buy in services without discussing them with the legal aid people first. Prior authority is the phrase that is key to the way the solicitor operates. Accountants, for example, vary enormously in skill, prestige and cost. In a small fraud case, it would be impossible to justify to the Legal Aid Board the use of a top firm of accountants. In a complex fraud of national importance a solicitor is much more likely to be able to make a case for using a prestigious firm, though the firm is likely to be paid on a stage-by-stage basis. It is important for the defence that the accountants should have credibility in front of a jury.

Solicitors claim that their bills are watched with a keen eye by the central taxing unit. Even though hourly rates are agreed in advance, there is a complicated formula of 'uplift' by which the hourly rate can be increased by up to 130 per cent, depending on the complexity of the work involved. Most solicitors say that when they accept serious fraud cases on legal aid they are often moving into unknown territory because they do not know how much work is regarded by the court as being reasonable; nor will they know what percentage of uplift the court will regard as fair. On the whole, though, most solicitors seem to regard legal aid for major fraud as reasonably satisfactory, if cumbersome.

Senior counsel don't abhor it either. It is difficult to imagine Britain's top criminal barrister, George Carman QC, tackling a fraud case on legal aid; he is a star and earns in excess of £500,000 a year. He doesn't, as they say, need the money. The rest – and there are some pretty good ones in the criminal field – seem quite happy to take the taxpayer's money in major fraud cases. For one thing, their inordinate length is gratifyingly helpful to maintaining cash flow; and, second, the brief fee for preparing the case is likely to be pretty substantial because of the fraud's sheer complexity. Six hundred hours spent on a brief at £250 per hour is £150,000 to begin with. Add to that the cost of court appearances for, say, six months, at a daily rate of £400 per day over twenty-four weeks, and the silk will pocket another £48,000, taking his earnings for that case to just about £200,000 for nine months' work. If the case is very high-profile, he might be able to squeeze another £100 per day court appearance money out of the system, which would add £12,000 to his earnings – assuming he chose to be in court every day of the case. Of course, had he been working for a rich man he would probably have received £350,000 – or £100,000 more – for doing the same job. But, as we know, by far the major proportion of fraud cases are on legal aid.

There is little doubt that the SFO, with its remit to tackle serious and complex fraud, has served the lawyers extraordinarily well. By lawyers' standards – especially at the top end of the scale – they do not make a fortune from legal aid; on the other hand, it is a comfortable living. Nor do those who are charged with serious fraud do too badly out of it. The fees for counsel are shrewdly pitched by the court at a level which enables them to get the services of the best counsel. That is a good deal more than can be said for other crimes, such as murder, rape or arson.

While someone charged with fraud can be reasonably sure he will be defended by a counsel of quality, he has no guarantee that if he is acquitted he will be able to return to his old way of life. For example, it is pretty well axiomatic that any merchant banker who has been through that process is unlikely to be re-employed in the City. There have been marginal cases of bankers being fired from their jobs *pour encourager les autres* because they were on the fringes of a major fraud but never charged; a number of these have found their way back into City boardrooms and senior jobs after a decent lapse of time. But appearance in court on charges of major fraud, even though proven innocent in the end, is tantamount to career suicide, especially for a City man.

There have been one or two rare exceptions. Charles Villiers, at one time chairman of County NatWest, joined the board of Abbey National as managing director of corporate development in January 1989. Ten months later he was charged, along with ten others, in the Blue Arrow case. Sir Campbell Adamson, at that time chairman of Abbey National, held an emergency meeting of his board which decided to keep Villiers on as a director. The decision was vindicated when Villiers and the rest of the defendants were found not guilty. Villiers has held the same job on the Abbey National board ever since. Many of his County NatWest colleagues, though, fared less well, finding themselves jobs well out of mainstream City business. Purists will argue that while Villiers is a main board director of a well-known bank, he is no longer part of the merchant banking fraternity. That's true. Nevertheless, he did not suffer the humiliation of being sacked from the board of Abbey National; other merchant bankers have suddenly found themselves cast on the scrapheap once they have been charged with fraud.

While merchant banks appear to be quite callous in the way they treat their directors and employees once the chips are down, they do not in fact call the shots. The Bank of England does. The Bank is very good at being wise after the event, but it doesn't pay to argue with its advice. If Threadneedle Street suggests that a merchant bank director should be sacked, for whatever reason, then he will be sacked if the merchant bank wants to stay in business.

A central City figure in the Guinness case, though he was

COUNTING THE COST 223

not a banker, was David Mayhew, a valued partner of the brokers Cazenove, variously described as 'blue-blooded', brokers to the Queen, the aristocracy and so on, against whom all charges were eventually dropped. Cazenove at that time were held up as a prime example of corporate loyalty: throughout the period Mayhew was being investigated by the SFO and right up to the time the charges against him were dropped, Mayhew continued to work at Cazenove. This demonstration of loyalty had nothing to do with the fact that most people at Cazenove are Etonians or Wykhamists and are therefore expected to stand by each other (another public school myth that doesn't hold water). The reason was much more prosaic: Cazenove was and is a partnership, therefore all its partners faced unlimited liability if it came to the crunch. If Mayhew had gone to trial and been found guilty, and if there had been subsequent actions against Cazenove running into millions of pounds, all the partners would have been liable for the money. Sacking Mayhew before the trial began would not have made the slightest difference to that liability. What looked like a league of gentlemen standing by an old chum was in fact an action informed only by pragmatism.

Senior executives of major companies who have been found guilty of major fraud in recent years have been few and far between. Ernest Saunders of Guinness is now fighting his case in the European Court of Human Justice but he has never been re-employed, except for occasional consultancy, in a senior corporate job. Gerald Ronson, who was also found guilty in the Guinness trial, had his own substantial private company to return to and is a very rich man. Thomas Ward's legal practice in America was unaffected by his appearance in the Guinness trial (he was found innocent) and he gives the appearance of enjoying a flourishing career.

It is the City men, by and large – the bankers, the brokers, the dealers, the fixers – who find themselves in trouble once the dust has settled. Very often they have no money and no prospect of a reasonable job. They have been tarnished, rightly or wrongly, by the image of fraud and the stigma, apparently, cannot be washed away by a verdict of not guilty.

Lord Spens has taken the Guinness affair particularly badly. Even though found innocent, he has been indelibly marked psychologically by the experience. A substantial room in his large house in Kent is devoted entirely to numerous arch-lever files filled with Guinness documentation, and a large table is covered with neat little piles of memoranda, Hansard extracts and other references to the affair. He devotes much of his time to attacking the system that set up the SFO, and when he is not doing that in the press or the Lords, he sits at home brooding on what he considers to be the grave personal injustice inflicted on him. Nothing will shift him from that belief. He is convinced that he was a marked man from the beginning of the Guinness investigation, that the government was calling for heads and that he was high on the hit list; in other words, the Guinness prosecutions were a show trial, orchestrated by the government, to show the City it meant business.

For a man who was found innocent, this obsession strikes one as being self-destructive. He is suing the Bank of England for the loss of his job at Ansbacher on the grounds that it was the Bank who told Ansbacher to fire him the moment the Guinness affair hit the headlines; it was either Spens's head or face the removal of their banking licence. He is unlikely to win; the Bank is the linchpin of the City establishment, virtually unassailable. It is just possible that a discreet pay-off to Spens might be engineered to avoid an embarrassing public row.

But Spens has no future in the City; the Bank will never forgive him his writ, for one thing. Apart from no future, Spens has also been left with very little money. He will recoup some of his legal expenses, perhaps £300,000 if he is lucky. That might give him an annual income of £25,000 before tax; nothing for a man who before his arrest lived high on the hog, with a taste for the best brandy and Churchillian-sized cigars. Meanwhile, he is sustained by a loyal and loving wife, Barbara, who goes out to work to supplement their meagre income and who is immensely supportive of his campaign against the fraud system in this country and the SFO in particular. But he now sits in Kent nursing his grievances, frozen in a time-warp called Guinness. It seems a singularly sterile form of existence.

If he has weathered the affair, he has been left a bitter and resentful man. He has been helpful to me and I have chased a number of hares on his behalf. He may very well be right: the intelligence services may be behind much of what the SFO and the judiciary do; perhaps judges do act on the instructions of the government or its agencies. Stranger things have happened. But if the judiciary is at the mercy of the government in some aspects of its work, then there is no hope for democracy in this country. And if judges have been instructed to persecute fraudsters by whatever means, then they have made a singular hash of it. Their track record, as case after case has failed, shows that the judiciary has little appetite for being manipulated by government.

But when a man gets his teeth into a cause, he can make a career of it. That is what has happened to Spens. He is obsessed by the notion of dark forces at work whose object is to enhance the government's profile as a law enforcer in the field of major fraud at more or less any cost. The row over public interest immunity certificates doesn't help, of course. Once a government gives the impression that it will cover up anything to remain in power, then it can reasonably be assumed that it will do whatever it likes to stay there. The trouble is that it adds fuel to Spens's resentment and makes him even more paranoid and suspicious about the world he lives in.

Spens was found not guilty on the back of Roger Seelig's trial, commonly known as Guinness 2. Seelig was the star corporate banker at Morgan Grenfell, generally in the limelight when Morgan were involved in big merger and acquisition deals and rarely out of the City pages. He has considerable charm, but would probably be murder in the heat of a big takeover battle. By his own admission he loved every minute of the wheeler-dealer days of the eighties.

'One was surrounded by intellectually gifted people who loved the challenge of a big deal. It was enormously stimulating, exciting and exhausting. But one could work very long hours because the adrenalin was constantly recharging one's batteries. I have to confess I miss it.'

Seelig made a lot of money in the City. He bought a fine Palladian house in Gloucestershire (Prince Charles is a near neighbour), but quickly realised he would lose the house and every million he had if he went on paying for expensive lawyers. He called a halt when his costs rose to a million pounds and decided to undertake his own defence.

It was a risky thing to do, but he had little to lose. If he won, he would keep his money. If he lost, he would still hang on to his assets although he would have to spend a year or two in prison before he could enjoy them; much better than paying every penny he had in legal fees and ending up in Ford open prison.

But he had something else in his favour. Fraud charges are well-known wreckers of marriages and family life. He had no family pressures. He was under forty-five when the investigation began, unmarried and without children. He could play his own game without domestic pressures. He could still afford two homes. He could manage the bills. Above all, he could concentrate his formidable energy and determination on marshalling everything he had on defending himself.

'I enjoyed the intellectual challenge enormously. But it was physically and mentally very exhausting. After a day in court I would go home and type out all the next day's questions for cross-examination of witnesses, then type in all the alternatives if the answers started to go one way rather than another. That was a process that generally lasted until two in the morning and then one was up again at five.'

In the end, Mr Justice Henry decided that Seelig's health was being affected. Seelig had been in court for the best part of six months and Judge Henry decided that the strain was becoming too much for him. He ordered Seelig to be examined by psychiatrists, who confirmed the judge's impression.

'I actually pleaded with him in chambers – I remember being in tears – to let me go on, but he wasn't prepared to do so.'

It was not the acquittal Seelig wanted, but it saved him from

Ford open prison or crippling fines. It did not, however, save any future he may have had in the City. A man of his ability and charm, though, did not lose the capacity to go on earning large private fees advising many of his old clients at Morgan Grenfell.

'None of them stopped talking to me as a result of the Guinness case. Of course they all have their own advisers, but they sometimes want an outside view and that's where I can be helpful from time to time. Curiously, people in my own profession sometimes recommend me to new clients, which I find particularly encouraging.'

Seelig is in the fortunate position of being able to maintain a handsome lifestyle both in London and the country, but he could not do that if his ability wasn't recognised in the market place. When he was at the top of his form at Morgan Grenfell, he had one of the highest profiles in the City – an advantage he had over bankers who ended up in court in other cases but who came from second- and third-tier merchant banks. They were never likely to command any presence in an independent private consultancy market.

In that sense, Seelig is unique. He is unique, too, in that he does not appear to harbour any bitterness against the authorities. He finds that counter-productive. Mentally strong and agile, he wants to get on with life and it is quite obvious where he would prefer that life to be – back at a first-rate merchant bank working in corporate finance.

But that is where the City's opaque moral ethos comes into play. The reality is that the Bank of England plays an important part in steering firms into deciding who remains in the City after a major scandal, and who gets out. The Bank has been to blame for negligence in banking supervision in the past – namely, BCCI and the secondary banking crisis of 1974 in which it authorised licensed deposit takers who had no right to be in the market at all – but that has never affected its status as an arbiter of competence or morality. The Bank has one supreme sanction: it can take away a bank's banking licence, which effectively means that the victim has to close its doors the next day. This strengthens its 'advisory' role enormously. No one will quarrel with the Bank, not on matters of conduct, supervision or personnel. It is more than their balance sheets or shareholdings are worth. No merchant bank, however powerful, would remotely think of inviting Seelig or Spens or even the County NatWest bankers, who were all found innocent in the Blue Arrow trial, to join its board without first feeling the temperature of the water in Threadneedle Street. Most would not even bother to try.

In a number of instances, the careers and earnings of men of first-rate ability have been irreparably damaged by being associated with major fraud. In the case of merchant bankers, who are controlled by the Bank of England, there is no arbitration or tribunal system whereby a banker can ask to have his case reviewed after an agreed number of years. There is no established route for finding his way back into the community in which he has probably spent all his working life. It is bad enough for a man to spend the best part of four or five years out of work, subject to the immense psychological strain which a major fraud investigation imposes on him, without having the additional burden of knowing that even if he is found innocent he will never be employed in the City again. That seems grossly inequitable. A proper, formal system for applying for re-admittance, before a panel fully acquainted with the facts of his case and his record in the City before his trial, would at least give him the opportunity to state his arguments for returning to his old career.

Another man who is suffering the same kind of fate as merchant bankers, but not for the same reasons, is Andrew Kent, who was a senior employee with the brokers T.C. Coombs. Like some of his partners, Kent comes from the fast-living, fast-track world of Alan Bond which helped to give the firm a particular niche in the Australian market. The firm also helped to pioneer new markets, such as Thailand and the Philippines.

Kent at the present time has a number of writs out against various people, the details of which are too complex to describe here. But they followed an SFO prosecution against Kent and his partner, Paddy Mahon, which failed dramatically in late August 1993. Both men were charged with conspiracy to defraud the Securities Association, the

Authorisation Tribunal and the Appeals Tribunal or, as Judge Clark put it more succinctly: '. . . those two conspirators . . . conspired to acquire and maintain authorisation [to act as a broker and dealer] under the Financial Services Act 1986 by unlawful means. Put briefly and colloquially, by telling lies is what it really comes to.'

The judge found there was no evidence of conspiracy and directed the jury to return verdicts of not guilty on each count for each of the defendants.

'Having said that,' Judge Clark went on, 'there are two observations I would like to make. First of all, my decision represents no criticism of the Serious Fraud Office. Any prosecutor can only act and take action on the material which is supplied to him in the shape of witnesses and documents. He can investigate that and, on the face of it, if it appears valid he makes his decision.'

But all the SFO's decisions to prosecute have been valid in the eyes of Elm House. What the judge failed to comment on was the prosecutors' lack of judgement in deciding to proceed, a common delinquency at the SFO where the urge to nail supposed criminals appears to take precedence over a balanced view of a case.

Judge Clark then made another point, which had relevance to two other major fraud trials, Guinness and County NatWest/Blue Arrow. 'The second thing I would like to say is purely a personal view. I cannot help thinking that this sort of inquiry in a case where there has been no financial loss to any individual would be far better left to the regulatory jurisdiction of the appropriate bodies rather than a full-blown criminal trial which takes up the time of the jury. The regulatory bodies have powers to conduct proper inquiries and they have sanctions which they can impose which in this sort of situation I would have thought would have been far more appropriate than a criminal trial. But that, as I say, is only a personal view of the matter.'

When I put it to Kent that his experience of the regulatory authorities had scarcely been uplifting, and that in an ironic way he probably did better at the hands of the SFO, he could not agree.

'My experience of the appeals tribunal of the Securities Association was excellent. I found them totally fair and objective. If we'd gone before the regulatory authorities at the beginning, I don't think we'd have ever had all the subsequent hassle.'

The hassle was considerable. T.C. Coombs and Kent were raided by the SFO late in November 1990, and Kent did not walk out of court an innocent man until August 1993, almost three years after the investigation began. Many of his papers had still not been returned by March 1994, and his financial assets were showing all the signs of a prolonged, time-consuming assault by the SFO. After a time he was compelled to resort to legal aid and the total bill for his defence was in the region of £900,000. He has one remaining valuable asset: his large house in Chelsea Square, which is worth more than £2 million. He has been using this as collateral for his borrowing.

When I spoke to him early in 1994, Kent was not gainfully employed but that was not a worry to him. He is bolstered by a huge philosophical reserve, in which resentment against the system that put him in court plays a tiny part. That keeps him sane. He also has a network of contacts, particularly in Australia and the Far East, which would be the envy of a conventional banker or broker in the City. He has never been purely a broker: he is a deal-maker by instinct and that embraces everything from the most arcane financial instruments to company restructuring. He will find a niche before too long because he is an immensely determined, intelligent jungle fighter who does not know the meaning of surrender.

'I take the view that one's survival after the SFO is entirely down to one's personal chemistry. Some people are permanently broken by the experience, others are strong enough and flexible enough to pull through and rebuild their careers. But make no mistake – once you've been through the SFO mill, it's an experience that will probably stay with you for the rest of your life, however tough and resilient you are.'

11

THE FUTURE FOR FRAUD

When the economy begins to grow again, serious and complex fraud will take another leap forward. Even George Staple, the present director of the SFO, realises that. There is always more money around in a growing economy and consequently more people available to take it from. That is why fraud did so well in Thatcher's day.

But even if the economy does not grow, serious fraud will certainly rise to £7 billion a year, representing an increasing threat to the stability of personal investments, savings and pensions. To quote Roskill: 'If the government cherishes the vision of an "equity-owning democracy", then it also faces an inescapable duty to ensure that financial markets are honestly managed, and that transgressors in these markets are swiftly and effectively discovered, convicted and punished.'

It is easy to become confused by this emotive prose. In the financial markets, 'transgressors' encompasses more than fraudsters who steal from their victims; it embraces those who transgress the rules and the law but who are not guilty of plain old-fashioned theft. The Blue Arrow affair was a good example of that, and much of Guinness was 'technical'; and they are two of the most expensive fraud trials ever held in this country. One of them failed totally, the other succeeded only in part.

This says something about the system: logic says that fraud has a two-tier structure – technical and theft – yet the system throws them into the same pot where they are dealt with in the same way. That has not been at all helpful to the successful or speedy prosecution of fraud and it is certainly not what Roskill had in mind. The adage 'horses for courses' holds as good for fraud as it does for people. Blue Arrow was a case for the regulators, not the crown court. Barlow Clowes was a case for the crown court, not the regulators. The former, while it broke the law, was technical; the latter was a case of naked, unabashed theft.

It stands to reason, then, that the SFO should not deal with market abuse because juries are not equipped to understand it. They are not interested in technical infringements, even if these break the law. The SFO should concentrate on those cases where actual theft is apparent; where juries have a good chance of comprehending the issues and where their interest can be kept alive throughout the trial.

That leaves a very substantial part of the field to the self-regulatory organisations, those who govern various sectors of the market and who are responsible to the Securities and Investments Board. At one time these SROs were run by people who should not have been there, deadbeats from the financial services industry or civil servants who had dropped out. That is beginning to change as more people with market experience join them. But they still need more quality and the best quality can only be bought. The regulators also need a high degree of personal authority – of the kind Lord Shawcross had when he was chairman of the Takeover Panel. Transgressors who appeared before him never forgot the experience and determined not to appear again.

The regulators still have a long way to go. When the Maxwell scandal blew up, it was clear that IMRO, the SRO responsible for pension funds, was not up to the mark, and it was lucky not to have its recognition withdrawn. Since then, Andrew Large at the SIB has instituted a programme of reform which has now been put in place. He acted within a month of taking the chair at the SIB and the remedial work he ordered was across the board: a new chairman and chief executive were appointed and there were substantial changes to policies, rules, procedures, monitoring and resources.

Large was a successful banker before becoming a professional regulator. He has the earnestness of a dedicated school prefect, but is tough-minded and very bright. In the short time he has been at the SIB he has breathed new life into a regulatory system which the Financial Services Act of 1986 did absolutely nothing to simplify. Large was quick to recognise that not all City offences should find their way into the criminal courts. Early in 1994 he said that the SIB had reached broad agreement in principle with the Serious Fraud Office about the sort of cases which might in future be better dealt with by the civil regulators, and those which must be regarded as cases for the criminal courts. The self-regulatory organisations now have very substantial powers: unlimited fines, expulsion from the market, the authority to suspend membership and therefore a firm's business, and so on. The powers vary from body to body, depending on the type of business they are regulating, but they are perfectly adequate for dealing with market abuse.

That does not mean, of course, that market abuse and related offences will not occur. Routinely all SROs are required to inspect their members' procedures to ensure that they are conforming to the rules and practices laid down by their SROs. Anything may happen between one inspection and another, but the SIB and the SROs now have a market intelligence system which can detect misconduct far more quickly than criminal investigators can; an early warning system that includes transactions, and auditors' reports on client money handling; besides which the regulators are very close to day-to-day market activity and rumour. In addition to that, there is the Financial Fraud Information Network, set up by the Bank of England after the BCCI débâcle, and the important contribution made by the SIB to the Shared Intelligence Service. In other words regulation, in the hands of people like Large, is beginning to get a much sharper cutting edge which will make the civil regulatory process complementary to the criminal one.

It would be foolish to imagine, however, that self-regulation is an end in itself. It is not. All the SROs at the top level are stacked with people who are financial industry insiders and who are abundantly liberal to their old colleagues in the insurance industry when it comes to rapping their knuckles over the mis-selling of pensions to those people who opted out of occupational pension schemes. The industry needs far more public interest representatives who are not flannelled by the smooth talk of the old hands who have corporate interests at heart and not those of the public. One day, of course, self-regulation will be seen for what it is worth: a wretchedly poor cousin of statutory regulation, such as the Securities and Exchange Commission in the United States, which has real bite. Even so, it is quite possible to use what we are stuck with rather more effectively.

A more sensible distribution therefore of what cases go into which arena might take a good deal of pressure off the SFO. Both George Staple and Andrew Large are in favour of plea bargaining. This is a system which has never been formalised in this country, but which, in the United States, is an institution without which the criminal justice system would cease to function. Prosecutors are allowed to address the judge on the question of sentence and to make specific recommendations on what the sentence should be in a particular case. It is therefore possible for the parties to agree that the defendant will plead guilty and that the prosecutor will recommend a certain sentence. The general practice is for the judge to ask the defendant a series of questions to ensure that his plea is voluntary, informed and genuine.

The difficulty for the SFO about plea bargaining is a philosophical one. Even SFO lawyers, and certainly the police who work at Elm House, frequently believe that sentences are not heavy enough. The SFO had certainly expected Roger Levitt to get seven years, because they thought that was what he deserved. The question arises, therefore – what does the SFO want? Does it want plea bargaining and a sentence to fit the crime at the same time? If it does, which would of course be ideal, it won't be able to have its cake and eat it because the two are incompatible. All plea bargaining rests on a reduced sentence for pleading guilty and the court getting on with the next case. Would the SFO have settled for a reduced sentence for Peter Clowes in return for a plea of guilty? If it had, there would have been public outrage.

The SFO would undoubtedly get through its cases more expeditiously, at less cost and with a better-looking score sheet, if it opted for plea bargaining. That would be to accept substantially reduced sentences even in cases where the size of the fraud and the consequential suffering for investors run into many millions. It would probably make fraud even more worthwhile than it is at present, especially if the fraudster ensured that he had a nest egg to come out to, and it would certainly stir up public resentment.

The last and most notable plea bargain was the Roger Levitt case where the judge, Mr Justice Laws, indicated to Levitt's counsel that he would not give a custodial sentence. It was the last thing the SFO wanted, but too much water had passed under the bridge at the preparatory hearing for the matter to be rectified. Probably the only justification for plea bargaining is that the public has the satisfaction of a guilty plea, instead of the danger of a guilty defendant being acquitted. It also saves a great deal of money. On the other hand, the public is also throwing away the chance of seeing a major fraudster getting his 'just deserts'. If the punishment is to fit the crime, and if fraud is to be seen as not being worth the candle, then plea bargaining is a dangerous road to travel.

It would, however, definitely help to improve the SFO's poor record. There are a number of reasons for that record: indifferent directors, a lack of professionalism, tackling the wrong cases and poor morale. In the end an organisation is, quite simply, only as good as the people who lead it. It is no good saying that because the SFO is a civil service institution its structure and competence are set in stone. A good, strong director would soon change that. Not all civil service organisations are the Rolls Royce machines they would have us believe: some creak with inefficiencies, self-interest and lack of direction. That is what the SFO is suffering from.

Nor does it seem capable of coming to terms with the cultural clash inside the organisation. The police perform invaluable work, but they tend to be sidelined in importance by the civil servants who take the decisions. One senior policeman remembers a crucial case meeting where the views of the police were ignored. A senior policeman told the assembled civil servants: 'You have been given the advice today of policemen who collectively have had eighty-six years' experience of fraud, but you've chosen to ignore everything they've said.' Nor does it help the SFO's work when one or two case controllers are capable of treating the police as second-class citizens subject to orders and not friendly direction.

It has also been a victim of its own publicity. High-profile arrests, huge cases, big-name defendants – these have all given the impression that the SFO was going to take on the world and win. It simply was not capable of living up to that. That does not mean, of course, that there will be an official government inquiry into its competence, integrity and objectives. There is an inquiry already looking into what should be done about the investigation and prosecution of fraud in this country, mainly in organisational terms. One would not be surprised if it recommended a new structure, possibly the merger of the SFO and the Fraud Investigation Group of the CPS. A piece of marketing like that would take the pressure off the SFO and help people to forget its regrettable ineptitudes. It would also be an opportunity to put in place a structure which was not dominated by civil servants and in which the police had a bigger say. If it did, then the betting would be very strong that the SFO would be subsumed into it and quietly forgotten.

INDEX